Pedagogized Muslimness

Waxmann Verlag GmbH
Steinfurter Straße 555, 48159 Münster
info@waxmann.com

Religious Diversity and Education in Europe

edited by
Cok Bakker, Hans-Günter Heimbrock,
Robert Jackson, Geir Skeie, Wolfram Weisse

Volume 27

Globalisation and plurality are influencing all areas of education, including religious education. The inter-cultural and multi-religious situation in Europe demands a re-evaluation of the existing educational systems in particular countries as well as new thinking at the broader European level. This well established peer reviewed book series is committed to the investigation and reflection on the changing role of religion and education in Europe. Contributions will evaluate the situation, reflect on fundamental issues and develop perspectives for better policy making and pedagogy, especially in relation to practice in the classroom.

The publishing policy of the series is to focus on the importance of strengthening pluralist democracies through stimulating the development of active citizenship and fostering greater mutual understanding through intercultural education. It pays special attention to the educational challenges of religious diversity and conflicting value systems in schools and in society in general.

Religious Diversity and Education in Europe was originally produced by two European research groups:
ENRECA: The European Network for Religious Education in Europe through Contextual Approaches
REDCo: Religion in Education. A contribution to Dialogue or a factor of Conflict in transforming societies of European Countries

Although books will continue to be published by these two research groups, manuscripts can be submitted by scholars engaged in empirical and theoretical research on aspects of religion and education, especially in relation to intercultural issues. Book proposals relating to research on individual European countries or on wider European themes or European research projects are welcome. All manuscripts submitted are peer reviewed by two specialist reviewers.

The series is aimed at teachers, researchers and policy makers. The series is committed to involving practitioners in the research process and includes books by teachers and teacher educators who are engaged in research as well as academics from various relevant fields, professional researchers and PhD students. It is open to authors committed to these issues, and it includes English and German speaking monographs as well as edited collections of papers.
Book proposals should be directed to one of the editors or to the publisher.

Mette Buchardt

Pedagogized Muslimness

Religion and Culture as Identity Politics
in the Classroom

Waxmann 2014
Münster • New York

Bibliographic information published by die Deutsche Nationalbibliothek
Die Deutsche Nationalbibliothek lists this publication in the
Deutsche Nationalbibliografie; detailed bibliographic data
are available in the internet at http://dnb.d-nb.de.

Religious Diversity and Education in Europe, Vol. 27

ISSN 1862-9547
Print-ISBN   978-3-8309-3143-0
E-Book-ISBN 978-3-8309-8143-5

© Waxmann Verlag GmbH, 2014

www.waxmann.com
info@waxmann.com

Cover Design: Pleßmann Design, Ascheberg
Printed on age-resistant paper, acid-free as per ISO 9706

Printed in Germany

All rights reserved. No part of this publication may be reproduced, stored in
a retrieval system or transmitted in any form or by any means, electronic,
electrostatic, magnetic tape, mechanical, photocopying, recording or
otherwise without permission in writing from the copyright holder.

Contents

Acknowledgements 8

PART 1
STUDYING THE CURRICULUM
OF 'RELIGION' AS SOCIAL PRACTICE 9

1. Prologue: The desire for knowledge of 'the Muslim pupil':
   a problematization of a problematization 9

   1.1 Gülsen in the mosque and the church.
       The knowledge desire of the researcher 11
   1.2 September 12: Monoculturalism, multiculturalism, and anti-racism
       in education? 14
   1.3 The main questions, the object, the data 16
   1.4 From dissertation to book – from Danish into English: Studies of Danish
       schooling in an international context 17
   1.5 The structure of the book 19

2. The approach to curriculum, knowledge, and the classroom 21

   2.1 The understanding of curriculum in relation to research on education 21
   2.2 Recontextualizing, pedagogizing, and the pedagogic device 23
       Model I 25
   2.3 Forms of curricular knowledge conceptualized sociologically and
       social-epistemologically 26
   2.4 Top-down or micro-politics? Locating curriculum through
       the concept of recontextualizing 28
   2.5 Recontextualizing knowledge about 'religion,' 'culture,' and 'identity'–
       an initial localization as a framework for asking questions in the classroom .. 30
   2.6 The emergence of 'the immigrant pupil' 32
   2.7 Research on religion in schools and its impact on this study 34
   2.8 'Religion'/'culture' as knowledge and identity politics 36

3. Conceptual architecture: recontextualizing and the pedagogic field
   of practice studied as discursive regularity and social economy 38

   3.1 Operationalizing the Bernsteinian understanding of field
       and discourse 38
       Model II 39
   3.2 Pedagogic discourse and discursive regularity 40
   3.3 The grammar of the classroom: language as social practice 42
   3.4 Classroom as social space: positioning and dispositions of the agents 44
   3.5 Forms of capital: The economy of the symbolic –
       the symbolism of economy 45
   3.6 Conceptualizing the classroom: social classification and knowledge 47

4. Two classrooms in the socioeconomic landscape. Constructing
   the empirical material 48

   4.1 Constructing the data – constructing the classroom 48
   4.2 The official text of the classroom 55

	4.3	The detailed focal points in analyzing classroom conversation 58
	4.4	Practices of the turn-taking system 63
	4.5	The socioeconomic backgrounds of the pupils: teacher, pupil, and parent descriptions and information 64
	4.6	Between and across the analysis of dispositions, positions, and positioning and the analysis of knowledge- and subject production 65

PART 2
DIFFERENTIATED 'MUSLIM' CLASS STRUCTURE 68

5. The teacher articulation of the official classroom text 69

    5.1   A differentiated ideal of respect... 69
    5.2   'The Muslim pupil' as a structuring figure 71
    5.3   Separate and stable, yet flexibly changeable 72

6. Muslimness as differentiated school capital 74

    6.1   Culture as religion, religion as culture in the teacher's characterizations 75
    6.2   To be or not to be legitimate, to be or not to be 'subject matter-relevant' 84
    6.3   Those in whom one can invest expectations 87
    6.4   Summing up: the socioeconomic landscape 92

7. Production of 'the Muslim subjects' 95

    7.1   Situating the text sample: educational module and lesson 96
    7.2   Ritual as the structuring theme – Sulayman as the content 99
    7.3   Intimacy and distance 102
    7.4   Modality at work 103
    7.5   Summing up: the Muslim subjects 106

8. Intimization and flexibilization of acknowledged 'Muslimness' 108

    8.1   Social classification: recognition of dispositions and position 108
    8.2   Pupils in the game of knowledge and experience 110
    8.3   Categories of knowledge, production of subjects 110

PART 3
SUBJECTIVITY WITHIN THE PERIMETER OF 'MUSLIM TRADITION': MUSLIM AS 'LOW CLASS' 112

9. The school and the teachers' articulation of curriculum 113

    9.1   The educational module and the teacher speech about curriculum 114
    9.2   Muslims and Christians: experience knowledge and factual knowledge 116

10. 'Christianity' as 'universal human conditions' versus the predictable 'Muslim tradition' 119

    10.1   The universal human funeral: organization of 'Christianity' and 'funeral' 120
    10.2   The 'Muslim' tradition: organizing 'Islam' and 'funeral' 127
    10.3   Producing subjects, generating pupil experience 136
    10.4   Summing up: constructing the objects Christianity and Islam 139

11. The hierarchy of problematization: teachers' interest and teachers' concern 143

    11.1   The empirical material 143
    11.2   Gülsen and Amalie: "A kind of girl that … lacks some social filters" and "The most social and diplomatic child" 146
    11.3   The girl group hierarchy: the academics' daughter, a girl who thinks she's clever, and one who's out of proportion 151
    11.4   Those that bring bad influences from other institutions and those that bring it from home 154
    11.5   The categorization practices of the teachers in descriptions of pupils 158
    11.6   Summing up: pupil disposition and -positioning, teacher recognition and the opposite 162

12.   Assembling knowledge production and social classification 165

    12.1   Speech about types of pupils and forms of knowledge 166
    12.2   Remaining an under-achiever; winning a space, but not legitimacy 167
    12.3   Knowledge and speakers in an agent-, practice-, and capital perspective......168

PART 4
RELIGION AND CULTURE AS KNOWLEDGE AND SOCIAL CLASSIFICATION 172

13.   Pedagogizing religion. Concluding remarks 172

    13.1   Religion as race and class 172
    13.2   Religion as 'experience knowledge' 174
    13.3   The differentiated Muslim class structure at the B-school: the Muslim subjects 175
    13.4   Subjectivity within the perimeter of 'Muslim tradition.' The Muslim underclass at the C-schools highly differentiated class structure 177
    13.5   Recapitulation: production of knowledge and production of social classification as interlinked 178
    13.6   The school's production and classification of knowledge and bodies. 'Muslimness' and 'universal Danish Christianity' pedagogized 179

References 181

    Legislation and other documents 191

Appendix A: The B-school, selected text sample. Original Danish version.......... 193

Appendix B: The C-school, selected text samples, original Danish version 195

    Text sample 1 (TRT1-6) 195
    Text sample 2 (TRT1-6) 196
    Text sample 3 197

Acknowledgements

This book is based on my PhD dissertation *Identitetspolitik i klasserummet. 'Religion' og 'kultur' som viden og social klassifikation. Studier i et praktiseret skolefag* [Identity politics in the classroom. 'Religion' and 'culture' as knowledge and social classification. Studies in a school subject on practice level] which I defended at the University of Copenhagen in October 2008. It also draws on my later research in the field of history and sociology of education and curriculum. The last chapter (Chapter 13) is an elaborated version of an article which has previously been published in the *British Journal of Religious Education*.[1]

I am most grateful to the editors of the Waxmann book series *Religious Diversity and Education in Europe* Prof. Cok Bakker, Prof. Hans-Günter Heimbrock, Prof. Robert Jackson, Prof. Wolfram Weisse and Prof. Geir Skeie for their interest in and support of publishing an elaborated English language version of the work, as well as for their useful comments. A special thanks goes to Geir Skeie who was also one of my opponents in the public defense of the dissertation. Also my warm thanks to my editor at Waxmann, Beate Plugge.

The process of changing the originally Danish language research based on Danish language data material would not have been possible without the professional help and assistance of Liv Rolf Mertz (Mertz Lingo, Berlin), Nina Trige Andersen (LynxText, Copenhagen) and Magdalena Rodríguez (London). Last but not least thanks to Liv Fabrin (Aarhus University, Copenhagen) for comments and critique during the writing process as for our cooperation throughout the years.

Note: All names of informants and places that appear in the empirical material analyzed in this book have been altered to ensure anonymity.

---

[1] "When Muslimness is pedagogized. 'Religion' and 'culture' as knowledge and social classification," *British Journal of Religious Education* 32 (3):259-273.

PART 1
STUDYING THE CURRICULUM OF 'RELIGION' AS SOCIAL PRACTICE

1. Prologue: The desire for knowledge of 'the Muslim pupil': a problematization of a problematization

> All major scholars recognize the existence of a distinct Islamic civilization […]
> Samuel P. Huntington (1998[1996]:45)

Europe has a thing with its Muslim population. Denmark especially has a thing with its Muslim population. This became common knowledge worldwide when the so-called cartoon crisis became a global spectacle in early 2006. In a Danish context, however, the daily paper *Morgenavisen Jyllands-Posten*'s publication in 2005 of a number of caricatures of the Prophet Mohammad – which became the point of departure of the crisis – should not be regarded as an isolated incident. Rather, it was a culmination of a decade-old preoccupation with 'Muslims' in Denmark/Europe, in which interest in and the problematization of 'Muslim children' has been and remains a central element.

Since the 1970s there has been an increasing focus on migrants – labeled 'immigrants' in public debate – in Denmark, as well as in other European countries in various forms (e.g. Modood & Werbner 1997, Hussain et al. 1997, Hervik 2004, 2011, Hvenegård-Lassen 2002). This has also been the case with regard to the children of migrants.

In the case of Denmark, a remarkable pattern in public debate as well as in the professional field of education has been that 'culture' has become an increasingly central category of analysis and description through which the pupils identified with a migrant history are perceived (Buchardt 2011a, b, 2013c, Buchardt & Fabrin 2010). This category of culture is – across social fields – often intertwined with the category of religion, especially 'Islam' and what I will call 'Muslimness' (Buchardt 2010. See also e.g. Hervik 2002, Nielsen 2011, Sheikh & Crone 2011). Other European countries have seen a similar pattern as has North America (Nielsen 2004, Razack 2008, Fetzer & Soper 2005, Mamdani 2005, Fekete 2004, Hervik 2004, Qureshi & Sells 2003). Not least since the moral panics engendered by the cartoons in 2006 has the case of Denmark been subjected to particular attention (e.g. Klausen 2009, Nielsen 2011).

This book explores what becomes of the categories *religion* and *culture* when they appear in the educational field; it is about how school as an institution can be understood as a place producing meanings ascribed to religion and culture and as such, as a scene not for religious practice in a literal sense but for social and epistemological practice related to religion, when 'religion' as a socially practiced concept is filled out with and understood as 'culture.'

As its core, this book presents a curriculum-sociological and social epistemological study of 'religion' in the classroom, originally defended as a PhD dissertation in 2008. More specifically, it is a study inspired by Bernstein, Foucault, and Bourdieu that examines various forms of identity politics connected to 'religion' and 'culture' as these concepts unfold in the classroom in relation to knowledge production and social classification. The empirical material of the project is based on observations of two delimited educational modules on the primary school subject *Kristendomskundskab* (literal translation: Knowledge about/of Christianity) at two different schools located in the same Copenhagen neighborhood, conducted between 2003 and 2005. Both educational modules deal with several religions, particularly Christianity and Islam.

This core analysis is framed and put into perspective by means of my research on the history of curriculum in Denmark since the 1970s about the emergence of the children of migrants as a particular object for schooling and how this group of pupils became increasingly seen in context of what was framed as their relatedness to religio-cultural categories, or what I call their 'Muslimness' (Buchardt 2011a, 2013c).

In the analysis in this book, the category Muslim – as is also the case with the category Danish, which often appears as its counterpart and as such is also its epistemological twin – is viewed as a locus for knowledge production and the production of social difference. The main analytical questions are therefore: What knowledge of religion is produced in relation to these categories? What spaces for subjects are produced? Which ways to be a pupil become accessible to whom? And in what ways do 'Muslimness' and 'Danishness' – which is frequently used to represent 'Christianness' in the contexts I study – emerge in the social economy of the classroom? This means that in a broader sense, the classroom is studied as a micro-political arena for relations and politics concerning what in the Danish public debate is also phrased as the relations or contradictions between, for example, 'ethnic minorities and the majority' or between 'immigrants and Danes.'

The main argument in this book is that 'religion'/'culture' can be understood partly as forms of knowledge, partly as subject-producing technologies coloring and shaping bodies, and as such as identity-producing knowledge clusters. These knowledge clusters are, in turn, colored by the social economy attached to the pupils' bodies, making it a productive and potent part of social classification. Categories such as Muslim and Danish/Christian are in others words to be understood in themselves as processes of social classification and distribution. Hence the book suggests that 'religion' can be understood as a class-producing practice when religion is transformed and produced in the pedagogic field of practice, but – and this is an equally important point – in what I call a pedagogized form. When categories such as religion and culture appear in the field of education they are reshaped and woven together in what the Bernstein-inspired Swedish curriculum sociologist Stefan Selander calls *the pedagogic loom* (Den pedagogiske väven, cf. 1984). On the one hand, the book points to how religion and culture can be seen as part of what sociologists of education have conceptualized as the reproductive function of schooling with not least Bourdieu & Passeron (2000) as a landmark in this respect, and thus how the practiced curricular content of schooling can be seen as inseparable from the function of the school institution in relation to the division of labor in society. On the other hand, it underscores what Bernstein calls the specific grammar of schooling and as such how broader social categories are translated into the features of schooling and in this process attain new school-specific forms. The main theme of the book thus centers on the social production of knowledge: How school produces knowledge about religion and culture, and how teachers and pupils, the daily agents of education at classroom level, form part of this knowledge production as it occurs in two educational modules of the school subject *Kristendomskundskab*.

1.1 Gülsen in the mosque and the church. The knowledge desire of the researcher

To make knowledge production the core of a study about religion and culture in the school, or more specifically to explore how categories such as Muslimness and Danishness can be understood as knowledge clusters, draws theoretically on conceptualizations from the work of Michel Foucault, more specifically on the understanding of knowledge as regime and knowledge production as a form of confession which produces identities (Foucault 1997, 1998, 2000b).

Such an interrelation between knowledge production and confession can be found in the data material from the classroom research which is the center of this book, namely in an excerpt from an interview conducted with a pupil during one of the field observations. In this interview fragment, I become not only an interviewer and field researcher, but also the transmitting speaker of *a particular type of knowledge desire*, despite the fact that my errand is quite the opposite, namely to analyze exactly such forms of knowledge desire, and certainly not to exercise it myself.

The 10-year-old pupil, whom I am about to interview in this excerpt, has Turkish-born Kurdish parents and is herself born in Denmark. In other words, the pupil cannot be strictly defined as 'ethnic minority' as some scholars describe the category: She can hardly be characterized as a "foreigner, residing in Denmark and fled or emigrated from other parts of the world than the Nordic countries, EU and North America" (Moldenhawer 2001:15). But even though Gülsen – as I will call her in this book – was indeed born in Denmark, she is exactly 'ethnic minority' as this category is practiced in research, in statistics, in the media, as well as in public and parliamentary debates. She belongs to the part of the Danish population which, for instance, in the statistics from the Municipality of Copenhagen, is categorized as "immigrants and their descendants" (Municipality of Copenhagen 2004a, b). She is also what in Denmark is often labeled as 'Muslim,' a categorization which especially since the fall of the Berlin Wall, and hence the disappearance of the specter of communism from the Eastern European states, has become increasingly prominent in the Danish context.

In Gülsen's case, her Muslimness is based on her putative history of migration – in her case, not even her own migration history, but the history of her parents – namely one of connection to a nation-state and a geographical territory which is perceived as related to the religion 'Islam.'

Such a conception – what I would call a characteristically post-Cold War logic – can also be found in Samuel Huntington's *The Clash of Civilizations and the Remaking of the World Order*, where it is unfolded as a notion of various distinct civilizations struggling against each other. The naming of the civilizations is of particular interest in this context: on the one hand, a so-called Western and a Latin American civilization; on the other hand, a so-called Islamic and a Hindu civilization. What is at stake for Huntington is thus the designation of geopolitical formations for which the category religion is put at the forefront in the naming of some, while not for others. Hence, 'religion' becomes a geopolitical category as well as a geopolitical distinction. A map in *The Clash of Civilizations* shows the world according to Huntington as divided into these civilizations, and Turkey, the state in which Gülsen's Kurdish parents are born, belongs to the Islamic civilization, along with, for instance, the Arab peninsula, Pakistan, and North Africa (Huntington 1998:27-28). Huntington is not alone in the enterprise of mixing religion with geopolitics. At the schools where I conducted field observations, the pattern is that teachers identify pupils with a migration history related to these countries as "Muslims" and as "Muslim pupils." This is also the case with Gülsen.

Gülsen is a pupil who is difficult not to notice, at least for me. She is what during my childhood was called a *boygirl* – a literal translation of the Danish expression *drengepige*, a term close to but not quite as charged as the English expression tomboy or, as one of her teachers expresses it, "a sports girl." This term is used to describe another pupil, though, as deviant ways of doing gender is not the characteristic of Gülsen that attracts the teachers' attention, as will be unfolded in the analysis. Expressed in the idiom of 1990s gender theory, one could nevertheless say that Gülsen has female signs on her body, while wearing clothing which connotes 'boy.' With a progressive daily-life terminology, one might say that she is breaking the stereotypes of what a 'girl' is, especially what a 'Muslim girl' is. She plays soccer with the boys, she does not wear a headscarf, etc. As a figure, in other words, Gülsen appeals to the cultural tastes and, as such, the intellectual interests characterizing big parts of the Nordic left intellectual middle class (to which this researcher, whether I like it or not, helplessly belongs). The way her deviancy appears is, so to speak, culturally legitimate and intellectually appealing: an object of sensitive interest in the social constructionist and queer-theoretically informed part of university life, of which I am culturally a part, despite being academically and scientifically distant from such theoretical approaches. In addition, Gülsen seems to be easy for me to interview: She appears as observant, interested in the interview situation and in the lectures about religion, about which I am interviewing her. In short, the fragment shows a highly engaged, positive, and interested interviewer – me – who becomes so enthusiastic about the smooth interview situation that she forgets her carefully prepared interview script which certainly does *not* contain specific and distinct questions about 'Islam' to specifically and distinct 'Muslim pupils.' But as we shall see, the interview takes a quite different turn than my self-produced manual prescribes, a detour caused by the voice of the interviewer, the voice that in this context becomes mine.

The topic of the interview conversation in the fragment in question is Gülsen's speech about two school excursions that have been part of the observed lectures: one, a trip to the local Evangelical Lutheran parish church, and the second to a local mosque. Earlier in the interview, Gülsen has spoken highly of the lectures about which I am asking her: She has learned a lot of "exciting" stuff about Christianity as well as about Islam. About the latter she says that

> [...] I'm also Muslims myself [...] and I got to know things from a Muslims because I kne- didn't know that much about Muslim.[2]

After a committed description of the church visit, in which, for instance, she tells me about how the pupils, upon her request, were allowed by the pastor to touch the baptismal font, my knowledge desire seems to carry me away:

> MB: How did you like being in the mosque?
> G: I think it's... actually I don't know but... they are actually okay... so is the church...

In her answer Gülsen is describing the mosque and the church on equal footing, both are "okay," and no specific interest in the mosque is expressed, be it a positive or a negative one, but this does not seem to stop my knowledge desire for something distinctly Muslim:

> MB: Yes ... did you come to know something that you didn't already know?
> G: Yes ... I came to know that Muslims- because my mother doesn't wear a headscarf... so I got that ... that Muslim women they ta- they should wear scarf- no not should but the man becomes jealous because somebody ... they walk around in the streets and then some man can look at them ... that's why ... so they become jealous
> MB : yes ...

---

2 The words Muslim and Islam are the same in Danish as in English, but many Copenhagen area school children, regardless of relation to migration history, use the wording 'en muslimer': a Muslims (singular plural, so to speak) about a person, and 'Muslim' about Islam.

G: so I came to know that
MB: Yes ... what do you think of it?
G: I think ... I think it's okay.

When I read the utterances above, what strikes me is the voice of an interviewer who perceives Gülsen and the way she positions herself with regard to 'the headscarf' – and to what has been said in the mosque about its use – as a specifically interesting and problematic object; a field of knowledge, which is to say, a field for knowledge production as well as for the grafting of knowledge, which implies a desire that – in this case – requires Gülsen to *reflect upon* herself and *contribute* to this knowledge *with* herself. Gülsen's school visit to the mosque is seemingly more interesting to me than it is to her. My interviewing voice is pushing her, in effect, forcing her to voice specific opinions about a religious context with which she identifies on the one hand, but on the other hand from which she distances herself by means of comparison – a method that relates to the school content in the lectures we are discussing in which the two religions in question have been compared. In other words, we can interpret her effort to produce distance through comparison as a result of the curricular instruction that she seems to embrace, whereas I on the other hand am headed in exactly the opposite direction.

In this excerpt, I have entered into an overexposed field of knowledge, and have begun to *co-produce* it instead of exploring or interrogating it. In Foucault's words, it could be called a field of *problematizations* where objects are made to appear as a result of being subject to *moral solicitude* and *ethical concern* (see Foucault 1992:10-37).[3] In our exchange, I seem to demand that Gülsen adopt a personal stance, a special form of reflexivity, namely that she speak of herself as a Muslim subject in a way that satisfies my knowledge desire.

The interview excerpt draws my attention to the fact that the place which throughout the analysis in this book is occupied by teachers – who have allowed me to observe them, and thus made it possible for me to produce the empirical data needed for my PhD dissertation and subsequently this book – that place I could just as well have occupied myself.

1.2 September 12: Monoculturalism, multiculturalism, and anti-racism in education?

My dissertation project was not my first scholarly work in the field of education. Nor was it my first work dealing with educational phenomena related to religion in schools, or more precisely religion as an object of education and instruction and pupils as subjects to this instruction. On September 11, 2001, I was in the midst of conducting field observations at a school in the Copenhagen area. This was part of

---

3 'Moral solicitude' and 'ethical concern' refers to *Préoccupation morale* and *souci éthique* in the original French, used in an overlapping and complementary meaning, e.g. Foucault 1984:16.

an action research project where a group of teachers had set out to develop an approach to the teaching of religion that did not take Christianity as its point of departure, but rather sought to represent religions, not least Islam and Christianity, on equal terms (Buchardt 2006a). Besides subverting the Danish state version of religious education, where the name *Kristendomskundskab* indicated for teachers a qualitative stance in favor of Christianity, the broader intent was to develop a religious education which could contribute to disbanding the distinction between 'us' and 'the others': a mission statement that can be characterized as partly multiculturalist and partly deconstructionist. Such pedagogic intentions, being alternatives to so-called monoculturalist approaches, are conceptually unfolded and elaborated upon within the traditions for as well school practice and educational research experiments which in an English-speaking context are known, variously, as Multicultural Education, Critical Multicultural Education or Anti-Racist Education (Banks 1986, Parekh 1986, Sefa Dei & Calliste 2000, Kampmann 2006, Buchardt & Fabrin 2012).

When I returned to the school on September 12, all hell had broken loose. 'The Palestinian kids' came to school after having partied all night long, or at least that was what some teachers said, and some of the teachers in the action research group declared that a boundary really needed to be drawn now, since "we do not tolerate such behavior in our democracy" (Buchardt 2007:18). It was not clear whether "such behavior" referred to the attack on the World Trade Center or partying through the night. What was clear, however, was the distinction between 'the Danish children, coming to school and being sad' and then a category of 'others,' the latter including more than the Palestinian children who had allegedly been partying.

I never found out which – if any – of the children had actually celebrated. Neither, I suspect, did any of the teachers in the action research group. At any rate, the question slipped out of the discussions during the weeks that followed. The pictures of dancing Palestinian women, which had been broadcast worldwide on the evening of September 11, were found to have been from a different occasion, or so the rumor went, and at the school the outcry about this replaced the outcry about the alleged Palestinian celebrations.

The question nevertheless remains how to understand the fact that multicultural ambitions can change overnight into categorizations, culturalizations, and racializations that group the son of an exiled Iranian left intellectual and the grandchild of a Kurdish farm worker into the same category as the Saudi rich kid and right radical Islamist, Osama bin Laden? Are such phenomena radically different from each other, and is it then solely because of an extraordinary and monumental event that they get conjoined in such a way that they become interchangeable? Or are multiculturalism and monoculturalism (and even Islamophobia) rather to be understood as two sides of the same coin? Can such ideological conceptions and prescriptive didactic traditions as 'multiculturalism' and 'monoculturalism' appropriately describe and explain school practice?

This book is epistemologically based on the premise that *intentionally loaded* educational conceptualizations and research approaches, such as the prescriptive didactic traditions, cannot in and of themselves provide an understanding of educational practice, nor of how categories such as Muslim – as well as Christian/Danish/Western, a categorical assembly of elements that are often used interchangeably, as synonymous with each other, and as the counterpart/s of 'Muslim' – are produced in school. With this study, I seek to outline another type of research approach, for which the main problem or question to be answered is not what should be done in school practice, but rather: What is actually going on in school? And how can we understand what takes place? More specifically: *How do categories such as religion and culture operate in school, and how are they connected to agents and to the production of their identities?* A second and related premise for this work is the assumption that religion in an institutional form is not only to be found in what is traditionally understood as religious institutions, but also in other institutional systems such as the school. The book focuses on how religion is designated and ascribed meaning in and in relation to the school subject *Kristendomskundskab*. Other school subjects could have been empirically prioritized since 'religion' operates in many curricular subject areas and in other types of school practice. It is relevant, however, to conduct a field study focusing specifically on teaching in *Kristendomskundskab*, inasmuch as this subject and its context provide a rather potent example not least of how 'Islam' is ascribed a type of meaning that mirrors the meaning ascribed to 'Christianity,' as well as how both categories are filled out by and connected to other knowledge categories.

1.3 The main questions, the object, the data

This book is a study of the identity politics connected to religion and culture as this plays out in the classroom in relation to knowledge production and social classification. Categories such as Muslim and Danish are thus disrupted and unsettled in a study of the classroom as space for knowledge production and the production of social difference. As such, the classroom emerges as a micro-political arena for the production of social relations of 'minorities' and 'the majority.'

The research questions guiding this study are:

- What space do pupils who participate in primary and lower secondary school (*Folkeskolen*) religious education have for articulating identity? The question is examined for pupils associated with minority as well as majority status (in relation to migration history and categories such as 'nationality,' 'ethnicity,' 'culture' and 'religion').
- How are connections between specific 'religions'/'cultures' (and related phenomena attached to these categories) and the bodies of pupils, parents, and teachers established in the classroom?

- How does the production of spaces for subjects/subjectivities and patterns of recognition in relation to institutionally generated spaces (for instance, 'pupil,' 'teacher' and 'school parents') form part of the production and transformation of knowledge about 'religion' and 'culture' in the classroom?
- How does knowledge production relate to the production and social classification of agents? How do the speech and practices of the classroom incorporate and elicit what these agents bring with them into the space of the school?

To answer these questions I have produced a set of data from two different, selected schools (*folkeskoler*) in Copenhagen (see Chapter 4), in which I have observed educational modules on *Kristendomskundskab*. The empirical material consists of: official documents from the schools articulating the curriculum and pedagogic approach; interviews with teachers before, during, and after the educational module observed; sound recordings of classroom speech, systematic registrations focusing on turn-taking; interviews with the pupils; and, at one of the two schools, questionnaires aimed at collecting socioeconomic data from the parents.

1.4 From dissertation to book – from Danish into English: Studies of Danish schooling in an international context

In the process of revising the original Danish version of what is a much more extensive PhD dissertation, primarily comprehensible in a Nordic context, into a shorter English-language book, some notable choices and changes have been made.

Most importantly I have downplayed the quite extensive and detailed observations of turn-taking practices in the observed school classrooms and only included the most central findings. The full body of these data and a more preliminary analysis of the data are to be found in the original dissertation (Buchardt 2008:174-193, 255-282, 360-363, 368-379).

Since my doctoral defense, relevant new research has been published and is now included in the book along with perspectives from my own later and more expansive classroom studies of school subjects in the humanities (Buchardt & Fabrin 2010, 2012).

As mentioned I will also draw a more explicit relation to my historiographical research into how pupils with a migration history have been perceived in the Danish curriculum history since the 1970s, and thus my research in the genealogy of 'the Muslim pupil' (Buchardt 2011a, Buchardt 2013c). Thus, on the one hand, this book includes part of my curriculum-historical work on culture as a pedagogic category in a Nordic welfare state context during the 20th century. On the other hand, this historiographical research is conducted in relation to my classroom field studies regarding the meanings ascribed to and practices around 'culture' and 'cultural difference,' especially the study presented in this book on pedagogized forms of Muslimness and Christianness in Danish state school classrooms.

An additional mediating process has been reworking the study from Danish into English, including making a Danish institutional context intelligible outside Denmark and the other Nordic countries. Particularly difficult and/or important issues and features specific to the Danish context will be commented upon as they appear in the book, and the historical and structural context of the relation between schooling, religion, and pupils with a migrant history will be unfolded as a framing of the field study (Chapter 2). There are, however, a few specific features that need to be explained from the outset.

Comprehensive education in Denmark as it developed throughout the 20th century is – broadly speaking – based on a common school for the primary and lower secondary levels, called *Folkeskolen* (People's School). This schooling system, within which the classroom studies in this book were conducted, consists of a one-year so-called pre-school class (*børnehaveklasse*, or Grade 0, mandatory since 2009) followed by 9 to 10 years of schooling. A total of ten years of primary and lower secondary education is mandatory. This does not necessarily have to take place in the state school, but can be attended either in so-called free schools (including, but not exclusively, religious schools), in private schools, or in the home, as long as the education complies with the goals formulated in the state school curriculum.

The school subject *Kristendomskundskab*, in which the empirical observations of instruction in this book have taken place, forms part of the *Folkeskole* curriculum within the so-called school subject area of Humanities. The school subject is taught in all grades except the year during which the Confirmation ceremony and the preparation for this take place in the Evangelical Lutheran People's Church (either during the 7th or 8th grade, depending on the local parish). *The Act of the Folkeskole* grants the right to be exempted from instruction in this school subject.[4] The official translation of *Kristendomskundskab* is *Christian Studies*,[5] but the wording 'kundskab' (similar to 'kunskap' in the Swedish school subject), directly translates as 'knowledge,' often leading to the translation 'Knowledge about Christianity/ Knowledge of Christianity,' though the meaning of the word *kundskab* is closer to the German 'Kunde.'

The school subject has frequently spurred discussions revolving around whether it is and should be oriented towards so-called objective and academic knowledge about religion, or if it should be, or in effect is, teaching to the Christian faith. As in the religious education subjects in the neighboring Nordic countries, world religions form part of the curriculum in *Kristendomskundskab*, but Evangelical Lutheran Christianity retains the most prominent place, namely as the so-called

---

4 *Act on the Folkeskole of 1993 (The Danish Primary and Lower Secondary School)* (Copenhagen, Danish Ministry of Education) 1994, § 6, stk. 2. The exemption paragraph remains unchanged up until today, e.g. *Folkeskoleloven 2010-2011. Sammenstilling, bemærkninger og gennemførelsesbestemmelser m.v.*

5 http://eng.uvm.dk/Education/Primary-and-Lower-Secondary-Education/The-Folkeskole/Subjects-and-Curriculum. Retrieved August 15, 2013.

main area of knowledge (for a general overview, see Buchardt 2014; for the history of the school subject, Bugge 1979, 1994). This is a visible example of the institutional ties that remain in effect between the Evangelical Lutheran People's Church and the state of Denmark: According to the Constitution (*Grundloven*), "[t]he Evangelical Lutheran Church shall be the Established Church of Denmark, and as such shall be supported by the State."[6]

A central part of the professional as well as academic vocabulary concerning the content of education, not least in the *Folkeskole*, is the word *faglig*, close to the German word *Fach*. It has no exact equivalent in English, but carries a variety of meanings such as 'vocational,' 'professional,' 'subject-related' and 'school-proper content.' In its inflection as *faglighed* it could, depending on the context, be translated as 'school subject-relatedness,' 'proficiency'/'school-related proficiency,' 'school skills,' or 'vocational skills.' These words will be used respectively to convey as precisely as possible the original meaning, and when necessary the original Danish word will subsequently be placed in brackets. Though the study is tied to the specific context of classrooms within the *Folkeskole* in the nation-state of Denmark, it does nonetheless address school life – as well as daily life in other social institutions and fields – more broadly.

Likewise, this work provides insights into how the Nordic model of comprehensive schooling – in the (post-)welfare state – plays out in daily life and with what effects. More generally, the findings of the study also contribute to a deeper understanding of how knowledge is produced in school, as well as the ways in which school operates as an arena for the production and distribution of social difference and classification, and how religion, especially Muslimness as a social category, can be understood in this context.

1.5 The structure of the book

This book is comprised of four parts. In addition to this introductory chapter, Part 1 consists of three chapters explaining and situating the theoretical and methodological approaches of the study, including the selection of the schools and classrooms and the production of data. Part 2 presents the analysis from the first school, which I call the B-school.

Following an introduction to the school, the educational module observed, the teacher and the teacher's articulation of the curriculum, the analysis is unfolded in two chapters, each focusing respectively on one of the two main analytical tracks that structure the study: an analysis of social classification based on an understanding of the classroom as a social space, inspired by Bourdieu, followed by an analysis of the classroom as a micropolitical arena in light of Foucault's

---

6 *The Constitutional Act of Denmark*, Article 4, Copenhagen: The Folketing 2013, http://www.thedanishparliament.dk/Publications/The_Constitutional_Act_of_Denmark.aspx. Retrieved April 16, 2014.

conceptualization of discursive regularity. The findings are then synthesized in a concluding chapter.

Part 3 presents the analysis from what I call the C-school, and follows the same structure as part 2, except that the order of the analytical tracks is reversed. Finally, Part 4 is the concluding chapter that sums up and discusses the analytical findings from the two different school settings, the scope of the analysis, and the relation between my findings and other research.

2. The approach to curriculum, knowledge, and the classroom

In this chapter, I will introduce my theoretical approach to curriculum in relation to the concept of knowledge and explain the primary framing concepts that inform this particular study of curriculum on a classroom level. I will furthermore place the study in the landscape of research on religion in schools, as well as situate the study in a historical perspective.

2.1 The understanding of curriculum in relation to research on education

The empirical point of departure for this book and the main research project behind it is instructional practice in a specific school subject in specific institutional settings. Focus is on the speech in and about what I call the official text of the classroom (Chapter 4), meaning teacher speech and pupil speech as it unfolds in the organized settings labeled instruction, be that in plenary sessions with the entire school class or in group sessions. This speech is broken down through an analytical focus on knowledge production and the social structure encompassing the agents, respectively, including in particular how the social histories of the pupils are recognized or not recognized, interpreted, and thus *produced* in the classroom. As a whole, these processes are conceptualized as the practiced curriculum of the classroom. This means that even though this is a curriculum study, the main focus is not on the written curriculum (based on various political decisions), but rather on the practiced curriculum understood as political and embedded in the broader social field that extends outside the classroom.

This understanding of curriculum situates the research presented here within curriculum sociology and history, especially the theoretical approaches developed from and in relation to the work of Basil Bernstein, particularly the concept of recontextualizing, as well as conceptualizations of curriculum developed in the work of Ulf P. Lundgren and Ivor Goodson.

This implies that the study can be characterized as explanatory research within the wider field of educational studies: That is to say, the type of knowledge that I aim to produce here seeks to describe and explain educational and pedagogic phenomena, in this case the practiced curriculum, as micropolitics (a conceptualization to which I will return later in this chapter) and as embedded in what can be conceptualized with Bourdieu as social space (Chapter 3). As such the study differs from so-called normative research which – based for instance on philosophical categories, certain norms, values, or ideologies – seeks to develop appropriate criteria for what might be considered 'good instruction.' Likewise, this work differs from prescriptive research which, on the basis of empirical verification, purports to identify certain educational practices as the most effective (Grue-Sørensen 1965:11ff., Lundgren 1981:22-23, cf. Buchardt 2004). Within the landscape of what Hofstetter and Schneuwly call *the educational sciences* three main scholarly traditions are especially concerned with the content of education: the primarily

Continental tradition of *didactics*; *curriculum theory*, mainly developed in the Anglo-Saxon context; and research which according to Goodson understands curriculum as a social construction (and thus close to not only sociology of education, but also sociology of knowledge), namely what I will call *critical curriculum studies* (Goodson 1992:66, Hofstetter & Schneuwly 2002, Englund 1990, Pinar et al. 1995, Westbury 2000, Hopmann & Riquarts 2000, Schnack 1999, 2001, 2004). The latter include the curriculum sociology and history inspired by e.g. Bernstein, central to my study (Goodson 1988, 1990, 1992, 1995, Lundgren 1981).

As I see the landscape, another important approach to critical curriculum studies is social epistemological curriculum history inspired by e.g. Foucault upon which I also draw and to which I will return later in this chapter (Popkewitz 2001, 2007, Popkewitz & Brennan 1998, Baker 2001, 2009a). Generally speaking, one could say that – whereas the didactic research tradition is featured in the normative research type, and curriculum theory traditions are foregrounded by the prescriptive research type – critical curriculum studies can be mainly characterized as *descriptive-explanatory*. Inscribing my work in the latter approach, however, does not imply that I consider this study to be above normativity in a scientific or philosophical sense. Elaborating upon the words of Lundgren, every attempt to explain social phenomena has normative implications and consequences (Lundgren 1981:23). The point is to explicate where this piece of research places priority with regard to purpose and perspectives, and thus the conditions for how it constructs its object of study.

When I seek to construct my object of study without ideals about good instructional practice and without any ambition of prescribing a best or better practice, it is not because I find such an enterprise irrelevant; rather it is because I want to produce a different type of knowledge, namely, a knowledge about what is produced by and through instructional practice as a social space and political arena. In other words, I want to render visible what takes place in schooling viewed as a socio-political practice with social consequences. My research interest is therefore not to determine whether what goes on in the classroom curriculum is 'right' and relevant in terms of effectiveness or *Bildung*, but rather to discern the patterns of what is actually produced. In turn, the criteria of relevance and legitimacy – be they criteria for what is relevant and legitimate knowledge or for how to be a relevant and legitimate pupil – as these criteria are practiced in instruction, form a central concern of my research.

In this chapter, I will show how the concept of recontextualizing (further elaborated in Chapter 3) as the overarching curriculum-sociological frame makes it possible to study curriculum at the classroom level in relation to other social fields and institutional levels.

I consider recontextualizing to be a key concept in Bernstein's theoretical framework that grasps the interplay between the political and practical levels that make up the educational system. Furthermore, recontextualizing is a concept that makes it possible to understand educational practice as a central element in social production. In short, the concept implies that educational content is viewed as so-called pedagogized forms of the knowledge, identities, and social structures from other social fields, for instance the intellectual field, the bureaucratic field, the media field, etc. Curricular forms of knowledge and identities are thus seen as social categories. Consequently, questions concerning the social transformation of categories of knowledge, when moved into the field of state schooling, become a central field of research (see also Buchardt 2013a, b).

Importantly, the detailed and complex universe of subconcepts and concept pairs – which fills out and is connected to the overarching concept of recontextualization and which makes it possible to grasp the processes of recontextualizing – includes conceptualizations of the *field* of practice as well as of *discourse*. The concept recontextualization is thus opened up for deeper studies of what, with Foucault, I call discursive regularity in relation to knowledge production. I combine this approach with a Bourdieu-inspired in-depth analysis of the classroom as social space through the concept of capitals.

In Chapter 3, I will elaborate upon the conceptual architecture that I build up in relation to these two combined analytical features with the concept of recontextualizing as the frame. Likewise in Chapter 4, I will discuss the methodological consequences of this theoretical framework for the data production and my concrete analytical strategies.

But before turning to such operational theoretical and methodological choices, it will be necessary to deal with my approach to curriculum and what consequences this has for the understanding of the classroom and the knowledge production that takes place there. I will explore this question at the conceptual level (and also with regard to how this relates to other disciplinary approaches to understanding the content of schooling), as well as with regard to how to understand the curriculum-historical frame of the classrooms that I study. By extension, I will also clarify which understandings of 'school subject' and 'religion' I build upon.

2.2 Recontextualizing, pedagogizing, and the pedagogic device

The concept of recontextualizing is first and foremost used here to locate knowledge of 'religion' and 'culture,' especially with regard to the school subject *Kristendomskundskab* and the handling of children with a migration history in the *Folkeskole*, respectively, in processes operating between the field of education or the pedagogic field, on the one hand, and the intellectual field and other social fields, such as the parliamentary political field, the ministerial bureaucracy, and the media, on the other hand. In Bernstein's optic, the pedagogic field is a new context for discourse, emergent from other contexts. In *Pedagogising Knowledge: Studies in Recontextualising*, the rise of the notion of 'competence' is explored in this light: "What is at issue is how a concept which arose in the intellectual field, and whose authors had little or no initial connection with education, came to play such a central role in the theory and practice of education" (Bernstein 2000c:44). This is not explained as an issue of transfer, nor is it presented as a top-down model explaining the relation between such fields and forms of knowledge as seepage. Instead, the question posed concerns: "[...] how recontextualised 'competence' constructed a specific pedagogic practice [...]" (Bernstein 2000c:44). In my study, the approach is basically the same: Namely, how does knowledge about 'religion' and 'culture' with special regard to 'Muslimness' and 'Danishness'/'Christianness' come to be pedagogized in school?

A central implication is that when discourse moves and is transmitted from one field to another (for instance, from an academic discipline to a school subject), it is transformed by this new context. As a context, pedagogic practice is to be understood as relatively autonomous (e.g. Bernstein 1990:172ff.). Consequently, ministerial formulations of curriculum are not to be viewed as equal to their academic sources of inspiration, just as classroom practice around a school subject cannot be understood as simply a transfer of the ministerial orders and guidelines for the subject. Pedagogic practice can be understood neither as practiced academic knowledge or practiced theory nor as simply a realization of political decisions and bureaucratically designed prescriptions. The concept of recontextualizing also captures the fact that knowledge is not necessary originally produced in the context in which it is relocated, and thus recontextualized and transformed. Summing up, this means for instance that academic or political discourse is not simply reproduced in its original shape when reappearing in pedagogic practice, e.g. in a school subject. Such forms of knowledge from, for example, the intellectual and the political fields are transformed by the pedagogic field's own device – the pedagogic device (Bernstein 2000b, 1990:180ff., Maton 2000, Singh 2002).

In the case of the notion of 'competence' which entered the pedagogic field after having been generated in other contexts, e.g. linguistics (Bernstein 2000c:42), this process has in fact changed the meaning of the concept. Moreover, this process has also changed the field it has entered through the field-specific mechanisms of selection which dislocate as well as relocate and transform knowledge and social structure into a new field-specific order. Such mechanisms – the selection principles – Bernstein characterizes as pedagogic discourse: "*Pedagogic discourse is a principle for appropriating other discourses and bringing them into a special relation with each other for the purposes of their selective transmission and acquisition*" (Bernstein 1990:183-184. Bernstein's italics).

This can be analyzed through a series of rules for pedagogic discourse which are operationalized as an interplay between respectively regulative and instructional discourses, connected to the specific form of communication in the field, namely, instructional practice (e.g. the classroom). This is further concretized respectively in the concepts of *framing* which seeks to capture the regulative part of instructional practice, the *how* of instruction, and as such is connected to *control* of the classroom, and the concept of *classification* which seeks to capture the division of *power* (the question of *who*) and the borders instituted in relation to *knowledge* (the question of *what*) (Bernstein 1990, Chouliaraki 2001, Moldenhawer 2007a, b). Framing as well as classification can be either weak or strong.

This study deploys the principle of pedagogical discourse and the subconcepts of framing and classification. The concept of framing denotes the forms of control in the practiced classroom curriculum, such as the use of the turn-taking system, or the use of group work versus explicit teacher-controlled plenary sessions. The concept of classification denotes relations between agents and their identities and relations between forms of knowledge, and furthermore, relations between these two types of relations. Thus, opening up the classroom and the data collected there for a detailed Foucault-inspired analysis of relations between production of knowledge and subjects, while also allowing for a Bourdieu-inspired analysis of how the agents' social histories are interpreted in the classroom text, it becomes possible to discern how knowledge and social structures around 'religion' and 'culture' are recontextualized and thus pedagogized in the practiced curriculum of the classroom.

At this opening stage, this process can be pictured as below. The use of arrows in the model (pointing downward) is not to be interpreted as though discourse and structure is transmitted in a top-down manner. What the conceptual model seeks to grasp are transmissions and transformations of knowledge and social structure in social contexts related to the educational system:

Model I

Fields of production
The intellectual field (e.g. the Academic disciplines Comparative Religion, Academic Theology)
The media field (e.g. public debate about 'religion,' 'culture' and 'immigrants')
The political field (e.g. educational politics directed towards 'children of immigrants,' curricular politics regarding religion – the school subject Kristendomskundskab)

Official recontextualizing field
(e.g. acts and ministerial orders and guidelines, commission reports etc.)

Pedagogic recontextualizing field:
The pedagogic device
↓
Rules for pedagogic discourse
(regulative discourse) (instructional discourse)
↓ ↓
The pedagogic field of practice
↓ ↓
Framing   Classification (strong/weak)

25

2.3 Forms of curricular knowledge conceptualized sociologically and social-epistemologically

Curriculum sociology can be described as a sociology of education that is specifically concerned with the content of education, in the tradition of the so-called 'new sociology of education' which is characterized by a special interest in formulating the relation between knowledge production, systems of thought and mentalities, and the reproductive function of schooling (e.g. Young 1971, Bernstein 1971, Bourdieu 1971, Bourdieu & Passeron 2000). Ivor F. Goodson, a UK-Canadian historian and sociologist of curriculum, simultaneously expresses the challenge and articulates the framework for such a sociology: "Sociologists of Education who are interested in the school curriculum have long faced a paradox. The curriculum is avowedly and manifestly a social construction. Why, then, is this central social construct treated as a timeless given in so many studies of schooling?" (Goodson 1992:66).

Goodson inscribes his approach to the study of school knowledge in relation to the early work of Bernstein, where the concepts of framing and classification are used to understand the relations between a subject matter and its content. Moreover, in line with Michael Apple, for instance, Goodson turns to look at how social interests are asserted through forms of knowledge 'within' and 'inside' school subjects (Goodson 1992:66-67, 75, Apple 1979). Drawing on the so-called *Conceptions of "mentalities,"* Goodson seeks to conceptualize the relation between the differentiation of knowledge/consciousness and the division of labor, namely that forms of labor can be understood as mirrored in forms of knowledge and consciousness. This is concretized through the conceptual distinction between *decontextualized knowledge* and *contextualized knowledge* which bears resemblances to Bernstein's early distinction and analytical inquiry into how the boundaries around what is legitimate school knowledge are drawn between "everyday community knowledge" and "educational knowledge," and thus taught and transmitted in the pedagogical realm (Bernstein 1971:53, cf. 52-54). Bernstein's interest mainly concerns how different social experiences are realized in education, and in this sense recalls his strongly criticized work from the 1960s concerning a socio-linguistic approach to social learning and the distinction between the elaborated and restricted codes of respectively middle-class and working-class pupils (e.g. Bernstein 2009. See also Lindblad & Sahlström 2002:260).

Goodson's conceptual distinction rather addresses how differentiation moved from differentiation between different school types into internal differentiation 'inside' curriculum, and thus becomes "separate types of schooling 'under one roof'" (Goodson 1992:72). An example of this is the transformation of the British school system during the 20th century from the so-called tripartite school system (with 'grammar schools,' 'technical schools,' and 'secondary modern schools' directed toward manual labor) into a comprehensive school model. Institutional differentiation through different types of curricula has thus been replaced by internal curricular differentiation by means of different forms of curricular knowledge connected to socialization into different and polarized types of mentalities (Goodson 1992:72ff.). Forms of curricular knowledge can thus be understood as "the ideological heartland where subjectivities are constructed" (Goodson 1995:368), whereas school subjects should be studied "in connection with the history of the social forces which brought them into the educational curriculum" (Goodson 1990:11).

Summing up, one could say that forms of curricular knowledge are ideologically *productive*, on the one hand, while nonetheless mirroring more fundamental social structures, power relations, and conflicts that are *reproduced* in the educational system.

Another approach that still more radically stresses the productive aspects of curricular knowledge is Thomas S. Popkewitz's Foucauldian "social epistemology of schooling," in which "the sociology of curriculum knowledge" becomes an object of analysis (Popkewitz 2001:152). In the work of Popkewitz, curriculum ("curricula") is understood as "[…] historically formed within systems of ideas that inscribe styles of reasoning, standards, and conceptual distinctions in school practices and its subjects" (Popkewitz 2001:151).

Since curriculum is conceived as rules for "telling the truth," it does not only form the objects that teachers and pupils observe and experience in schooling, but also functions as a disciplining technology, directing how the individual is supposed to act, and acquire knowledge not only of "the world" but also of "our 'self'" (Popkewitz 2001:152). Thus, curriculum can be seen as historically formed technologies of power which inscribe certain forms of reason into the subjects of schooling, such as teacher and pupil subjects respectively. Based on the conceptual relation between knowledge and subject as productive power, as derived from Foucault (Chapter 3), such systems of reason are to be understood as "governing practice" (Popkewitz 2001:152). Consequently, curricular forms of knowledge and the formations of which they are part are studied as elements that structure social practice. In other words, curriculum is conceptualized as a regulative system of knowledge, a historically formed knowledge, which inscribes rules and standards "by which we 'reason' about the world and our 'self' as a productive member of that world" (Popkewitz 2001:152). Not only does curriculum form curricular objects, but sentient, observing, and acting subjects – teachers and pupils (see also Popkewitz 1998).

In Popkewitz's approach, in other words, we can say that the content of schooling – the curricular forms of knowledge – may be seen as productive or, perhaps, rather as part of a productive game, whereas the approach outlined by Goodson puts the emphasis on the reproductive side of curriculum and school knowledge, particularly, how social interests and conflicts are reproduced. Common to both approaches, however, is that curriculum is understood in the light of power and differentiation. The two approaches also exemplify aspects of fundamental understandings of curriculum as an object of research which are combined in my study: Namely, the productive versus the reproductive dimensions of curriculum as power technology and means of social distribution.

2.4 Top-down or micro-politics? Locating curriculum through the concept of recontextualizing

But where should curriculum for studies of this sort be empirically located? Goodson argues that studies of the contents of education and instruction, of curriculum and school subject areas, for instance, should employ a broader understanding of curriculum than as a political or bureaucratic text and its production, and should include not least 'school practice and process': "In addition, more broadly conceived notions of curriculum will have to be explored – the hidden curriculum, the curriculum conceived of as topic and activities […]" (Goodson 1995:368). This points to the question of how we can study curriculum as classroom practice, as practiced text, and consequently, how relations between institutional curricular levels can be understood.

The Swedish curriculum historian and curriculum theorist Ulf P. Lundgren has provided a framework for posing analytical questions that connects questions concerning the content of schooling and instruction with questions regarding how knowledge is selected, organized, and included in curriculum at different social levels (levels of society). In Lundgren's understanding, the concept of curriculum does not only include documents that make up the legal frame around school and its subject matters (either with mandatory or supervisory status for the level of practice), produced by the political system and its institutions. Rather, the concept of curriculum seeks to analytically capture the entire philosophy and the conceptions behind concrete curricula in a society on all institutional levels. Such general conceptions or systems of principles, Lundgren defines as *läroplanskod* – curricular code – underlying and unifying principles in governing texts which, in different historical and social contexts and processes, organize 'the world' as knowledge for the educational system; as educational or curricular knowledge (Lundgren 1981:21).

Three levels of analysis are sketched out, which (drawing on Lundgren 1981:21-22) can be explained as follows:

- Questions concerning how knowledge is the object of negotiation and struggle in society: How are valuation, knowledge, and experience selected and organized (i.e. as social and political structure and struggle in society)? This also concerns which agencies, in a broad sense, 'outside' the educational system, are used to legitimate the organization and selection of knowledge, e.g. religion/religious institutions, the nation, modes of production/division of labor. Thus, one kind of question could concern, for instance, from which agencies legitimation is derived, and how this impacts the ways that boundaries are drawn between school subjects.

- Questions concerning how the concrete curriculum is formed as a governing document (that is, in political, bureaucratic, and legal processes).
- Questions concerning how the curriculum is formed in the process of education (i.e. the classroom). Here, the means of control is located in the organization of instruction in topics and themes and forms of activities such as group work, teacher's presentation, turn-taking systems, etc.

Although Lundgren's analysis of curricular codes may be understood, in a research disciplinary sense, as a history of curriculum, his differentiated conceptualization of curriculum as a theoretical and methodological concept opens up the study of curriculum at the classroom level in a curriculum-sociological sense. Which curriculum appears in the classroom, and which organization and selection of valuation, knowledge, and experience is at stake here? And which external agencies/interests are mirrored in this practiced organization of curriculum? Thus Lundgren's three-dimensional approach for analyzing institutional practice around curriculum can be understood as an extension of the concept of recontextualizing: Curriculum becomes possible to analytically locate in concrete institutional instruction practice, but this practice is seen as (part of) the broader social space. This concept of curriculum – an extension of the overarching theoretical framing of curriculum as recontextualized and pedagogized knowledge – is fundamental to the way this study understands and explores curricular knowledge.

Recontextualizing, as a theoretical frame, makes it possible to understand how knowledge in the educational system is not only reproduced, but rather formed and produced in a manner that is relatively autonomous due to the institutional logic of the school itself. Furthermore, it clarifies that school knowledge cannot be reduced to a question of transfer from other (e.g. more dominant and higher-ranking) fields, whereas Lundgren's way of posing analytical questions makes possible an empirical distinction among the institutional levels of curriculum, and connects the knowledge production of the classroom to questions concerning the selection and organizing of knowledge on a social level. Nevertheless, with respect to the question of reproduction versus production, this study's perspective on curriculum is closer to the approach of Popkewitz. Following a Foucauldian conception of power as decentral and productive (which will be further developed in Chapter 3), pedagogies and politics are seen in this study as inseparable: Curricular and knowledge politics are understood to be produced in the classroom, and likewise function to co-produce subjectivities in the classroom. The pedagogical politics of the classroom is consequently seen as not only knowledge politics, but also as *identity politics*, forming experiences and subjects in conjunction with school knowledge.

Consequently, this book explores how knowledge formation concerning 'religion' and 'subjects' takes place in the classroom as *transformation*; a transformation of knowledge about 'religion' produced not only in the classroom but also outside the educational system. The question then becomes how these forms of knowledge are shaped and produced – or in other words, pedagogized – within the social structure of the classroom. Summing up, this study is therefore about the micropolitical technologies around knowledge of 'religion' and the subjects produced in the classroom, where the classroom is seen not as a space where social interests are reproduced, but rather as a space where social categories, interests, and knowledge are produced in the first instance, as well as where knowledge and social structure are interdependent, and co-produce and define one another.

2.5 Recontextualizing knowledge about 'religion,' 'culture,' and 'identity'– an initial localization as a framework for asking questions in the classroom

Exploring curricular phenomena at the classroom level as recontextualized forms of knowledge demands an initial localization of the types of knowledge that have been relocated in the pedagogic practice under study. The following reading of the historical context, with an emphasis on the production of meaning related to knowledge about 'religion,' 'culture' and 'identity,' serves to initially diagnose formations of knowledge which can be observed outside the classroom.

The initial empirical focus includes, in extension of the research questions, speech about the school subject *Kristendomskundskab*, speech about 'religion' and 'culture,' and speech about education and identity, as well as where these types of speech intersect. It also includes speech about children of migrants in relation to schooling, as 'the immigrant child' in shifting historical forms, from the 1970s onwards, has been projected as a particular object of schooling and as such has been a recurring figure in professional as well as public debates (for a definition of the concept of figure in a Foucauldian sense, as it is used in this book, see Chapter 3).

In public debate, the *Folkeskole* subject of *Kristendomskundskab* has frequently been a stage for what could be called moral panics (e.g. Jenkins 1998) or, in a Foucauldian understanding, an object of persistent ethical concern. Other than in professional circles, such panics around this school subject have taken place, for instance, in the mass media and in parliamentary political debate. They occurred frequently during the 20th century and have been concerned not least with whether or not the school subject should take the form of preaching (Bugge 1968, 1979, Buchardt 2011a). Beneath this debate, however, the question of the cultural status of Christianity and its relation to the state has also been at stake (Buchardt 2011a, 2013a).

In 1993, the statutory definition of *Kristendomskundskab* was defined as a school subject dealing with how "[…] *the religious dimension* influences the vital principles of the human being and its relation to other (human beings/MB)." In that sense, the school subject could be read as pluralistic and non-confessional, dealing with questions concerning Christianity as well as so-called non-Christian religions, as well as with philosophy and ethics. At the same time, nevertheless, this school subject is obligated to give priority to the teaching of Christianity (*Fælles mål. Faghæfte 4: Kristendomskundskab* 2004, *Act of the Folkeskole* of 1993). This contradiction in the subject's legal curricular basis has contributed to a chasm between various (often irreconcilable) interpretations of the curriculum among teachers and religious education scholars as well as in the public political arena, and has fueled the continuing public panics surrounding it.

By the end of the 1990s, one such panic got started on the occasion of the so-called Aalholm case, where the Copenhagen school Aalholm, among other issues, fought for the right to call the school subject Religion (Buchardt 2006a). Though the explicit and concrete reason for the debate was whether or not the school subject should be called *Religion* instead of *Kristendomskundskab*, the debate was not least an expression of an ongoing discussion and struggle over whether the multicultural development of Danish society was desirable or not. This was articulated as a dispute about whether the school subject should transmit and uphold the religion and culture of the majority – meaning a 'Christian/Lutheran-Evangelical cultural heritage' – or be developed into a subject which mirrored what was seen as Denmark's multicultural and multireligious reality, and consequently transmit and affirm an understanding of an equal relationship among religions and cultures. In light of a Bernsteinian understanding, one could say that the battle has mainly been fought over classification, meaning that it has been targeting where boundaries regarding knowledge and identities ought to be drawn, more than a battle concerning framing, whereby it might concern what forms of activities and thus what forms of control ought to be implemented.

The main positions in this public panic often had their parallels in professional circles, among school teachers, teachers college professors, and university scholars involved in instruction or the study of religion, as articulated in subject matter didactical literature. These debates often revolved around the (much older but persistent) discussion about whether academic theology or comparative religious studies should form the knowledge base (the so-called *basisfag* meaning the basic academic disciplines) of the school subject (Buchardt et al. 2006).

The primary polemical positions involve competing understandings of the concept of religion, its relation to 'culture,' and not least, the consequences of this for the status of Christianity, but the divergent arguments are also connected to the epistemological foundations of the two academic disciplines in question (e.g. Buchardt 2004).

The anthropologist Cecilie Rubow, who has conducted several field studies of religious practice in relation to the Evangelical-Lutheran People's Church in Denmark, suggests a framework for understanding this. Comparative Religion studies its object 'religion' as a cultural phenomenon, meaning as culturally as well as socially constructed. To identify which type of culture and thus which type of religion is basically the result of the research, not its point of departure. In contrast, Theology, as an academic discipline – due to its historical institutional relation to Christianity and the Church – takes the relation between Christianity and culture for granted. Thus, theology takes its scholarly point of departure in the assumption that a relation between Christianity and culture exists, and that it makes sense to study it. In other words, it presupposes that there exists a relation between Christianity on the one hand and Danish (and European) culture and identity on the other (Rubow 2000. See also Rubow 1993, 2008).

When applying this framework to the debate about *Kristendomskundskab*, one might add that this epistemological structure seems to be recontextualized into and related to the dispute about religion as school knowledge, namely, as a discussion about whether 'religion' and 'culture' are to be perceived as perpetual and static entities, possessing a certain essence, or as mutable historical constructs (Buchardt 2004, 2006b).

Seen as a discursive order, there nevertheless seems to be a certain resemblance between the two opposites: In both cases, 'culture' forms a crucial site for which the discussions and struggles continuously provide meaning; likewise, knowledge about 'religion' tends to inscribe 'culture' into it, creating a comprehensive categorical complex of 'religion/culture.' This process of recontextualizing – what happens when, as in this instance, concepts and discussions from the academic field are transferred to another field, in this case the field of education – can also be described as a process that simultaneously moves in the opposite direction: A case of (disputed) school knowledge circulates as knowledge production in the broader social space.

By extension, one could say that school subjects are not isolated islands in the educational system, but should be understood in relation to the general structure of curriculum as well as in relation to other social phenomena and social structuring (cf. Goodson 1992, Callewaert 2003). Consequently, the articulations and positionings around school and religion and its instruction should be seen in relation to educational political speech in other specific senses and wider contexts. Here, the discovery and occurrence of 'the immigrant child' in its multiple and shifting configurations, especially since the 1970s, are of importance.

2.6 The emergence of 'the immigrant pupil'

In 1970, the first official formulation regarding so-called foreign children appeared in a departmental circular stipulating that children residing more than six months in Denmark were to be covered by the statutes on compulsory education (Ministry of Education 1970). Over the ensuing decade, a particular area of schooling within state schooling seems to have emerged. By the late 1970s and the early 1980s, the children of migrants came to be mainly described in relation to and understood in light of their parents' relation to the labor market, namely as 'foreign workers' in often unskilled jobs, and tended to be associated with rural life and 'traditional family patterns,' and characterized by their (lack of) language skills (Buchardt 2011a, 2013c).

In the decades that followed, the 'migrant pupils' have repeatedly emerged as a heated topic in Danish educational politics. While not much legislation on school strategies directed towards the children of migrants was adopted in the 1980s, the decade saw the emergence of a changed debate on what was increasingly labeled as 'Muslim immigrants,' particularly following the media coverage of the Iranian Revolution and the civil war in Lebanon (Würtz Sørensen 1988, Pedersen 1988). During the conservative-liberal government (1982-1993), predominant ideological signals concerning the politics of education were inspired by the US scholar Harold Bloom's notions of a canon of 'Western culture,' or the so-called canon approach (Rasmussen 1996).

Part of the changing political environment was also the rise of a growing field of experts in the teaching of 'foreign language pupils,' or – as they were increasingly dubbed, 'bilingual pupils.' These experts were invested in 'culture' as a pedagogical category, particularly as a way to promote multicultural education and an interest in the 'cultural background' of the pupils (Buchardt 2011a, 2013c).

These professional investments in 'culture' also brought 'religion' to the fore. *The multicultural school. About intercultural, anti-racist education* (my translation), a 1986 handbook for teachers, provides an instructive example of this (Clausen 1986). In this handbook, religion is on the one hand presented as a resource; for instance, immigrant parents can be invited to talk about everyday Islam or social discrimination (in a structural sense) (Clausen 1986:63-64). On the other hand, religion is described as an obstacle within schooling, causing "cultural clashes in school," for instance, in the form of immigrant parents' presumed attitudes to sexual education and dressing (Clausen 1986:65).

Islam had now become part of the cultural difference defining 'immigrant parents' and their children, while culture was becoming the central descriptive category, replacing the earlier terms that had underscored a specific relation to the labor market. At the same time, the interest in the language of migrant pupils became both professionalized and increasingly connected to 'culture' (Buchardt 2011a, 2013c).

During the same decades, the 1970s and 1980s, especially following the 1975 *Act of the Folkeskole*, this school institution was assigned an increasing number of tasks which in everyday pedagogical discourse are often called *dannelsesopgaver* (tasks concerning *Bildung*/formation). It became a school duty to qualify the life project of each individual pupil and his or her future as a citizen in the wider community of society. As the so-called critical pedagogy became dominant among opinion-making teachers, the individual and his/her *experience* became a pedagogical and curricular focus along with experiments with project-oriented and problem-based education (Øland 2010, Østergaard Andersen 2012, Kampmann 2012, Buchardt 2012).

During the 1990s and 2000s, at least two main tendencies can be said to be at stake. On the one hand, a tendency oriented toward *competence*, in which the pupil is framed as an agent in a democracy, and thus should be 'brought up' as such in school (e.g. Schnack 2004, Hermann 2003, Saugstad 2011). On the other hand, a tendency oriented toward *nation* and *culture* which seeks to strengthen the pupil's sense of belonging to *Danish* culture (Buchardt 2006b). By the turn of the 21st century, these tendencies were further strengthened and may be found in the legal basis of the *Folkeskole*, e.g. in the official purpose of the *Folkeskole*, as stipulated in the *Acts of the Folkeskole* from 1993 and 2006, respectively, and can be interpreted as a sign of the state's persistent attempts to implement identity politics (Haas 2003, 2004, Buchardt 2006b).

Legal implementation of project-based work, the so-called *undervisnings-differentiering* (differentiation of instruction), has similarly increased the focus on the individual pupil, a move which should be seen in relation to new pedagogical doxas about "The pupil as responsible for her/his learning process" ("*Ansvar for egen læring*") and the so-called shift (of paradigm) "From teaching to learning" (Hermann 2003). Since the *Act of the Folkeskole* in 2006, the introduction of individual plans for each pupil (*elevplaner*) and mandatory national tests has underpinned the focus on the individual pupil in the *Folkeskole*. These tendencies in Danish educational policy point to a broader trend of focusing on the individual in terms of inculcating a sense of collective identity (culture), as well as in the sense of cultivating individual competence and personal identity. Popkewitz describes this trend in terms of double inscriptions in the registers of individuality and collective belonging, connected to what he calls the overlapping registers of modernity, concerned simultaneously with freedom and social administration (Popkewitz 2006).

With this initial localization of meaning and knowledge in relation to 'religion,' 'culture,' 'identity,' and 'school' in and around the educational system, I will argue that it is possible to distinguish certain *monuments* (Popkewitz 2001, e.g. 152, see also Foucault 2003b). The relation between these monuments, or the discursive formation of these monuments, can now be summed up as the relation between *religion* ('Christianity' and 'Islam,' 'Christianity' and 'the other religions'), the *identity of the pupil* (individual development versus collective belonging), and the school as transmitter of *knowledge and skills*.

These regularities – dots on the map of schooling and society – serve as my initial sketch of a discursive formation of religion and schooling. The question to explore further is what happens to this discursive formation of the relations among the 'religion,' 'culture,' and 'identity' of groups and individuals in and through school instruction when the topic is supposedly 'religion'? How does such a formation of knowledge operate, and what shape does it assume at the classroom level where the agents are teachers and pupils? How is such a formation of knowledge recontextualized, and what is then produced in the practiced classroom curriculum?

2.7 Research on religion in schools and its impact on this study

In Denmark, the tradition of doing research on school classroom practice in relation to the question of religion has been less extensive than in Norway and Sweden (Skeie & Bråten 2014, Osbeck & Skeie 2014, Buchardt 2014). In that regard, the

PhD dissertation which forms the basis of this book is among the first of its kind in the Danish context, along with Laura Gilliam's PhD dissertation defended in 2007 in educational anthropology (Buchardt 2008, Gilliam 2009). Gilliam has explored the social practice, self-perception, and teachers' categorizations of Muslim pupils, pointing to, for instance, the ways in which the category of 'the Muslim pupil' has become identified with 'trouble-making' in social practice within the school institution (Gilliam 2009). In addition to this work, Thomas Gitz Johansen's work on multicultural classrooms (2006), although not specifically focused on religion, has contributed an important analysis concerning the meaning of cultural difference in school practice. School practice in the context of a confessional Islamic school, furthermore, has been explored by Annette Haaber Ihle (2007) and Marta Padovan-Özdemir (2012), providing Danish analogues to Jenny Berglund's research in the Swedish context (2010).

The scholarly work on *Kristendomskundskab* in Denmark done in the disciplinary fields of history and the history of ideas, regarding school and education is also worth mentioning. K. E. Bugge's groundbreaking work on the state's organization of religious education and the historical development of professional circles of teachers specialized in the teaching of religion has formed an important base for understanding struggles around the school subject during the 20th century (Bugge 1968, 1979, 1994). Niels Reeh's study in the historical sociology of religion concerning the intersections among the external relations of the Danish state, the shifting forms of governing, and religion- and school politics (covering the period 1721-1975) has also been important (Reeh 2006. See also 2009a, b). Working in the history of ideas, Pia Rose Böwadt's study of German and Danish philosophies of life and how these were pedagogized in Danish school traditions (for instance, in the written curriculum of the school subject *Kristendomskundskab*, both in ministerial texts and in the school subject's didactical literature) has similarly provided significant insight into the background of the present study (Böwadt 2007, see also 2009).

Although Bugge, Reeh, and Böwadt neither use classroom data, nor situate their work within the disciplinary frame of curriculum sociology and -history, these scholars investigate the history of the school subject in question as part of broader social and political processes and idea- and knowledge-related phenomena. Reeh's work contributes to a clearer focus on how state-organized religious instruction has served as an instrument to the pursuit of state interests, such as military and foreign political purposes. This perspective has sharpened my focus when analyzing speech about religion in schools and the ethical concerns surrounding nationhood in the form of 'Danishness versus Muslimness' and culture as an expression for nation in this context. Böwadt's analysis of the child as a symbol of authenticity recontextualized – particularly in Danish traditions of normative didactics of philosophy and religion, in which the child/pupil is ascribed qualities such as spontaneity and authenticity – has highlighted the importance of the identity formation of the pupil in the Danish field of education, an aspect I have similarly emphasized in this chapter.

More recently, I have conducted further research on the category of culture in the practiced curriculum in a range of school subjects in the humanities, together with Liv Fabrin (Buchardt & Fabrin 2010, 2012), which have pointed to similarities with other school subjects with regard to the findings in this study. I have also expanded my historical research on the category of culture in relation to welfare-state schooling across the Nordic countries (Buchardt, Markkola & Valtonen 2013). In this context, the study of the emergence of 'the Muslim pupil' in Danish state schooling from 1970s onwards has been of importance for this study (e.g. Buchardt 2011a, 2013c).

2.8 'Religion'/'culture' as knowledge and identity politics

Identity politics is mostly understood in educational research as linked to the central administrative state, e.g. in state politics regarding the nation (e.g. Haas 2003, Korsgaard 2004, Skeie 2001). Skeie connects the question of identity politics to what he sees as the emergence of different cultural groups in the Nordic multicultural societies, and suggests that "[...] cultural politics are replacing class politics, and as part of this, national identities are weakening while different group identities are becoming more prominent" (Skeie 2001:237). In this account, this "cultural turn" is followed by a "return of religion" for majority as well as minority groups, presenting new challenges to many European states, including questions regarding state-organized religious education, something which is handled differently depending on the historical forming of the states in question (Skeie 2001:240ff.). This calls for greater attention to the relations among multiculturalism (including group identity politics), religious education, and the nation-state as an area for research.

Sunier and Baumann (et al.) explore religious education in the context of the nation-state, particularly education aimed at *civil enculturation* in relation to the handling of religious and so-called ethnic differences, comparatively, in the British and Dutch contexts (Schiffauer et al. 2004). Sunier's work, in particular, investigates religious education in state curricular documents, in text books, and also at the classroom level (Baumann 2004, Baumann & Sunier 2004, Sunier 2009). Their research is based on the assumption that features of 'civil culture' are transferred into schooling, and underscores the importance of the school as an instrument of northwestern European states: "Without state schools, there would be no nations as we know them in northwestern Europe, no national *conscience collective*, and no effective means of inculcating and rehearsing the conventions of dominant political culture" (Baumann 2004:2).

In these approaches to studying the identity politics of state and nation in relation to religion and religious instruction in school, the emphasis is put on the *central state's* organization of the school curriculum, which is to say, on the political decision-making level and in relation to central state bureaucracy. This is especially the case with Sunier and Baumann, who see the state as an entity facilitating a seepage of 'the nation' down through the educational system and into the classroom. This implies an understanding of politics as tied to central state bodies, from which politics seeps – in a top-down manner – to the micro-level. Skeie adopts a different perspective, adding an "individual level" to what he calls "the level of identity politics" where groups and states are the agents (Skeie 2001:247).

The study presented in this book is an extension of these approaches in the sense that it addresses 'identity' as politics in relation to 'religion,' 'culture,' and instruction. However, by means of a Foucauldian understanding of the subject and power, the study takes a different angle on politics, and thus on the politics of identities. By extension, power (including power strategies and politics) is viewed as decentral and productive. Thus, it is possible to locate power *everywhere* (something I will discuss further in Chapter 3). In the words of Deleuze and Guattari: "Everything is political, but every politics is simultaneously a macro politics and a micro politics" (Deleuze & Guattari 2004:235). The production of religion in relation to the nation-state in this study, therefore, is not explored as something which is implemented by the state and inserted into other institutional levels, nor as an inculcation and rehearsal of nationhood and citizenship. Instead, this study makes use of a concept of politics that locates power at the level of micro-politics, which can simultaneously be understood in light of, and in itself as, macro-politics.

When identity production, as in this study, is viewed in terms of differentiating practices and thus as connected to power (Chapter 3), identity politics becomes a key concept typifying the micropolitics of the classroom (cf. Foucault 1997, 2000b). In this light, the crucial research interest of this study is to explore how religion as a knowledge category operates in relation to the identity politics of the classroom: How is knowledge about religion – as regime – connected to subjects? And in what ways does religion play a role in the politics of social distribution in the classroom? In order to orchestrate such explorations, an architecture of operational conceptualizations is necessary.

3. Conceptual architecture: recontextualizing and the pedagogic field of practice studied as discursive regularity and social economy

In this chapter, a conceptual architecture will be unfolded, developing Bernstein's concept of recontextualizing by way of theoretical inspiration from Foucault's understanding of the relation between knowledge, subjects, and power, and Bourdieu's concepts of *social space* and *capitals*.

3.1 Operationalizing the Bernsteinian understanding of field and discourse

Bernstein's conceptualization of the educational system is based on an understanding of its institutional practice as relatively autonomous in relation to other social fields beyond the school. This autonomy is what makes it possible to transform forms of knowledge produced elsewhere into the logic of the pedagogical field, yet this autonomy is precisely no more than relative. Pedagogic practice is thus understood to encompass social mechanisms of distribution which relate to and mirror the division of labor in society with a corresponding system of valuation (Bernstein 1997, 1990).

By way of Bourdieu, the pedagogic field can be understood as a social field and thus, as bound to other social fields in relations of homology (Bourdieu 1993:183, 185, 1998a:136, 1998e:5, 2004a:175). What is valued – for instance, which school subjects are viewed as most important (as described by Callewaert [2003]), and what counts as good achievement on the parts of the pupils (as described by Moldenhawer [2001, 2007a], for example) – can thus be explained through the homology with social structuring and valuations from other social fields.

This can also be described through Bourdieu's concept for society; *social space*, which in the words of Callewaert is "the space of general class relations" (Callewaert 2002:494. My translation. See also e.g. Bourdieu 1998e). The social structuring of the social fields neither renders them equal to each other, nor is it reducible to "the space of general class relations," but these do correspond (Callewaert 2003:262). Homology can be understood as something that is brought into play by agents in certain social fields through their respective embodied possessions of distinct capitals. It is thus through the agents that relational struggles on the field are related to other social fields (see also Callewaert 1997:85, 2003:264).

Consequently, the concept of *capitals* (and connected to this the concept of *habitus*) makes it possible to analytically capture the social-historical dimension of the agents, namely, how their embodied social history, their *dispositions* (meaning: their embodied capital possessions) are seen and recognized in a particular social field, in this case, the pedagogic field, as captured analytically in and around the classroom.

By extension, I operationalize Bernstein's overarching concept of recontextualizing with a Bourdieuian understanding in the sense that the classroom is seen as homologous and as a concrete manifestation of social space. The aim is to analyze how the social histories of the agents are interpreted in the classroom – what is recognized and what is not – in an interplay through which positions in the classroom are or become accessible to some, while not to others. The question is who is occupying which positions. This means that the concept of capitals, to which I will return later in this chapter, is employed in this study as s concrete analytical tool from Bourdieu's theory of field, practice, and social space, which I put to work as one of two primary analytical tracks.

The other key analytical track is an operationalization of the Bernsteinian concept of discourse, where I develop an analytical strategy based on the Foucauldian understanding of *discursive regularity,* especially drawing on the archaeology of knowledge, with the purpose of targeting the content of education and instruction, the forms of knowledge, and the relations of these to the production of subjects. My aim is to find and examine the threads connecting knowledge production and the production of social structuring, or rather (with Bourdieu), social classification processes in the classroom: How can categories of knowledge be understood in relation to social categories when played out and produced in the classroom and thus in pedagogized form?

The two analytical strategies conjoined by the concept of recontextualizing can be represented as follows:

Model II

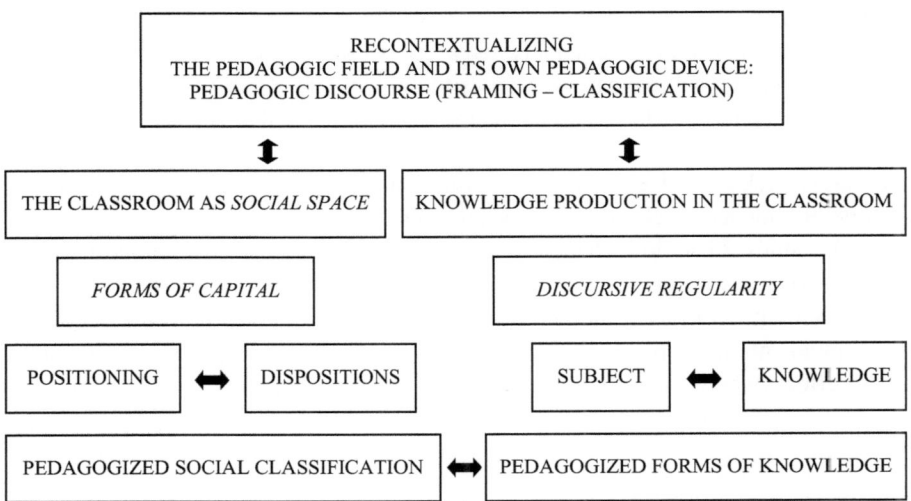

3.2 Pedagogic discourse and discursive regularity

The conceptual model of recontextualizing – or more specifically, the concept of pedagogic discourse – is what makes possible an analysis of the forms of knowledge and communication about the field of pedagogic practice in relation to a more classic Bourdieuian sociology of education (using the concept of capitals as the central educational sociological tool, as discussed later in this chapter). Simultaneously, the conceptual frame opens up a deeper study of how recontextualized discourse is transformed by the logic of the field through a process in which knowledge and subjects are subjected to power (classification) and control (framing). The conceptualization of recontextualizing thus makes it possible to study the relations among the production of knowledge, the production of subjects, and power in pedagogic practice.

When adding the conceptual relations among subject, knowledge, and power to the optics of recontextualizing, I draw on the work of Foucault in the sense of "[a] history of different modes by which [...] human beings are made subjects" (Foucault 2000:326).

In Foucault's work, the subject is viewed as decentered and thus, not as an autonomous and bounded entity which can be the originator of discourse. Through this lens, the subject is not ascribed an intentionality which generates the statement (e.g. Foucault 2003b:30-31). What appears as intentionality is instead to be understood as an effect of power. The subject is viewed as an installation, an effect of power, and an empty seat: It is 'the seat' or the space which produces the subjects, and not the other way around. This implies an understanding of 'power' as produced and relational, and not for instance as something that can be possessed, nor as an external force. Power does not exist in itself but only as appearance and emergence, as relations and technologies (e.g. Foucault 2000:336). Power relations are thus seen as productive, namely, as ways to create orders and to differentiate. By extension, the subject can be seen as the object and effect of differentiating or 'dividing practices,' which simultaneously constitute and subjugate it (Foucault 2000:326, Mills 1997:21). What comes to the fore in such an analysis is "[...] the way in which knowledge circulates and functions, its relation to power. In short, the regime of knowledge [*Savoir*]"[7] (Foucault 2000:331).

In this study, I use 'knowledge' to designate subject-matter content and its forms and relations to subjects, as well as knowledge conceptualized in terms of a regime and technology of power. The latter is captured and interpreted through the general conceptualization of knowledge as regime/power, by which subjects are understood as an effect, where the first and most basic level of this analytical incision is an

---

7 Foucault distinguishes between *connaissance* (knowledge as it circulates and functions, e.g. science and forms of knowledge as "the relation of the subject to the object and the formal rules that govern it" (2003b:16, reference 3)), and *savoir* (knowledge as regime, indicating the totality of *connaissance* as well as the conditions under which it emerges) (Foucault 1971, 2003b).

analysis not of discourse, but rather of *discursive regularity*: the rules governing the formation of knowledge to which concrete statements refer.

The actual reading strategies thus draw mainly on what in the Foucault-reception is sometimes called the archeological phase (e.g. Dreyfus & Rabinow 1986, Howarth 2000). In this part of the oeuvre the object of study is *statements* (l'énonceé/enunciation, Foucault 1971, 2003b), with the purpose of analyzing the rules of formation that structure discourse. What is undertaken in this study, therefore, is not a discourse analysis of language, understood as a primary and formative structure in social practice or as the key to understanding social practice, but rather an analysis of statements or enunciations with the purpose of using what discursively emerges as a site from which to discern and explore the rules of formation for discursive practices; the rules of formation for what can be thought, said and done. Foucault's analytical foci for analyzing discursive regularity are to be found in *The Archaeology of Knowledge* where he defines this term as encompassing systems of rules that constitute *objects*, *subjects* (enunciative modalities), *concepts*, and *strategies* (1971). This study will focus on how objects and subjects are produced in the enunciations of the classroom: What subjects and objects are produced? What regularity can be read from the dispersion of statements? (Besides Foucault 2003b, inspired by Foucault 1994, 2003c, Bjerke 2005, Villadsen 2002).[8] In addition to these basic archeological concepts I will use a concept of *figures* inspired by Foucault pointing to elements and circles of meaning constituting a domain of abnormality (Foucault 2003a).[9]

As a whole, this implies two important and interconnected premises for the analysis of discursive regularity: The study is not concerned with subjects as such, but rather with an analysis of how subjects become subjects as an effect of knowledge production, whether as objects of knowledge or through the enunciative modality of self-knowledge. Hence, no autonomous agency is ascribed to the produced subject, which also means that acts of resistance are not interpreted as something outside the discursive regularities and knowledge formation. Rather, within a Foucauldian optic, resistances are to be understood as operating within, and as part of, the productive power (Foucault 2000:330, 1998).

In summary: When reading the Bernsteinian concept of pedagogic discourse (including the connected rules of framing and classification) in the light of

---

8 In developing this analytical strategy, Foucault 1993 and 2001 have also been central, as has Foucault 1991. This is explicated in the dissertation, Buchardt 2008.

9 In a College de France lecture from January 22, 1975, Foucault speaks of how "the domain of abnormality" is constituted by three entities: "figures," "elements" and "circles" (Foucault 2003a:55). The concept of figure aims to grasp the multiple meanings ("a number of ambiguities," p. 324) in the emergence of the domain of abnormality, as it is phrased in his "course summary." The "characters," understood as personified roles, that appear as an ambiguous constitution of the field (p. 56, 59) or domain (e.g. p. 56) are "the Monster," "the individual to be corrected," and "the masturbating child" (pp. 55-75, 323-329). The concept of figure is framed within an "archaeology of abnormality," and thus in a framework of an archaeology of knowledge.

Foucault's concept of discursive regularity and his understanding of the relations of knowledge-subject-power, pedagogic discourse can be used to grasp and explore the formative rules regulating knowledge and conjoining subjects to each other through a certain disciplinary device; the pedagogic device (cf. Chouliaraki 2001). Thus, it becomes possible to explore the conditions and spaces of possibilities and limitations in a particular societal institution which relates to what is specifically produced in it, namely, knowledge and subjects and the relation between them. Or, when reversing the order of analytical tracks: Reading the concept of discursive regularity in light of the concept of recontextualizing, it becomes possible to understand the regularities that appear in the analysis as connected to a relatively autonomous field which in turn can be seen in continuation with regularities appearing in other social fields.

A systematic study of recontextualizing processes tracing the transformation of forms of knowledge between the field of pedagogic practice and, for example, the intellectual and political fields, is not possible within the frame of this book, nor is it the purpose. Rather, the analytical aim is to explore how speech about 'religion' and 'culture' in the educational setting and speech about 'the migrant pupil,' which can also be identified in other social fields, is announced in the discursive regularity which can be analytically unfolded by studying the classroom text.

3.3 The grammar of the classroom: language as social practice

Bernstein's optic on the field of education as a whole and on the field of pedagogic practice, in particular, enables an understanding of how the content in the field – the specialized pedagogic communication – is not simply a reproduction of knowledge and social structure, but also a field-specific production. This directs the analytical attention to "the intrinsic grammar of pedagogic discourse" (Bernstein 1990:180, Chouliaraki 2001:48) and implies an interest in 'the grammar' of the classroom and its communicative patterns. Such a focus can be compared in a sense with the analytical status of the statement/enunciation in the archaeology of knowledge: Grammar is not what governs the rules for what is produced, but grammar can render visible the rules for what is produced (cf. Foucault 2003b:29-30).

While Foucault is rather distant from linguistic analysis, Bernstein grants communication a status as material from which social practice can be analyzed. His conceptual apparatus does not include tools for linking grammatical features and linguistic patterns to the study of the regularity of pedagogic practices. Such tools, developed precisely in dialogue with the work of Bernstein, among others, can be found in the analytical framework of the sociolinguist Norman Fairclough – the so-called textually-oriented discourse analysis (TODA) or Critical Discourse Analysis (CDA) – that connects the study of language as discourse to the study of discourse in a Foucauldian sense (Fairclough 1992, 1995, 2001, 2003, n.d., Chouliaraki & Fairclough 1999). Fairclough suggests an analytical distinction between three interrelated dimensions, namely *text*, including the concrete use of language; *discursive practice*; and *social practice* (Fairclough 1992:37-61, 73). Language is consequently seen, in line with Bernstein, as a powerful and manifest part of social practice, albeit not the only part.

Concrete linguistic data (*text*) is used to explore how certain linguistic features, such as grammatical features, are applied in a specific text, and how the text can be understood in relation to the *activity type* of which it is a part (for instance, in classroom practice, teachers' presentations, turn-taking, etc.). The question of genre and intertextuality/interdiscursivity – how a text draws on other texts and genres – is also important (Fairclough 1992). An example of this would be how teacher-pupil communication increasingly draws upon genres from the private sphere with the effect of an intimization of linguistic practice in the classroom, with possible consequences for the relations between pupils and teachers (Chouliaraki 1998). In other words, social change is explored by means of language as data. In the study of concrete language, Fairclough points to and draws on *systemic functional linguistics*, as developed by M. A. K. Halliday (e.g. Halliday & Matthiessen 2004). With Fairclough's analytical framework as link and selection tool, grammatical traits according to this tradition will be the operative tools for my reading strategy of the classroom text (see also Chouliaraki & Fairclough 1999:139-155).

Systemic functional linguistics (SFL) is a theory of language as system and structure as well as functional language use (Andersen et al. 2001, Halliday & Matthiessen 2004, Frimann Trads 2000, Frimann 2004, Hestbæk Andersen & Smedegaard 2005). Concrete use of language is understood as *instantiation*: actualization of resources (Andersen et al. 2001:24-26). SFL describes the functions of language that are simultaneously at stake in the utterance, and thus, the focus is the use of functions and resources that speakers employ when exchanging information, for instance. The grammar system of SFL is a so-called lexico-grammar: Grammar is seen as interwoven with semantics, i.e. meaning (e.g. Frimann Trads 2000:36). Since multiple resources and combinations of resources are available, a central premise in this context is that it is possible to understand the concrete use of language as interpretations that produce representations of *the world* and organize *relations* within it. The question is then: What meaning is created?

SFL distinguishes between three meta-functions of language, present in each utterance (a distinction also incorporated in Fairclough's CDA-framework):

- The interpersonal function: Who communicates and which relations are established between them? (In CDA, this is a source for exploring which *identities* are established in the text).
- The ideational function: What is the communication about? How is the world represented? (In CDA, this is a source for exploring how knowledge about the world is established).

- The textual function: This function organizes meaning created through the two other functions as coherent language. In other words, how is coherence established in the text?

To each of the three functions, a range of lexico-grammatical resources are connected. Among these, the system modality, a resource connected to the interpersonal function of language, will be of special importance in this study. In particular, the focus will be on how the text establishes varying degrees of commitment to *truth* and *necessity* and, primarily in light of this, how it includes ideational resources. How this plays out in specific contexts will be described in Chapter 4, in connection with the description of the research material and the concrete tools for analysis.

It is important from the outset, however, to emphasize that although linguistics are applied in my analysis, this is not done for the purpose of a linguistic analysis as such. Rather, linguistics is employed as a tool for a systematic reading of how meaning is produced. Thus, the analytical procedure will be that detailed readings of concrete texts by means of lexico-grammatical tools are continuously analyzed and interpreted in light of Foucault's conceptualizations of the production of and relations among knowledge, subjects, and power. Consequently, the concept of choice between linguistic resources, which is a central underlying premise in SFL, will not be adopted in this analysis: The intentionality and subjectivity established in speech will, following the Foucauldian analytical track, be seen as what creates the speaker, and not the other way around.

3.4 Classroom as social space: positioning and dispositions of the agents

I will now turn to the other main analytical strategy of the study, namely the conceptualization of the classroom as social space, inspired by Bourdieu's sociology. This strategy works up a different type of analysis focused on the ways in which pupils (as agents with distinct social histories) are seen as legitimate or not; how their strategies in the classroom are subject to recognition or non-recognition; and how their respective social histories are interpreted in this context. Notably, by *agents*, I do not mean to suggest a landscape of persons with different degrees of independent agency (in an interactionist and voluntaristic sense, cf. Chouliaraki 2001), but merely a landscape of persons doing and saying different things, with different effects, which relate to the ways in which their social histories are interpreted and utilized. In contrast to the Foucauldian focus on discursive regularity and the production of knowledge and subjects, the Bourdieuian analytical strategy does approach power as possession; that is to say in the meaning of social distribution between the agents and thus how the social categories appearing in the classroom can be seen as parts of social classification processes.

The pivotal analytical tool operative here is the concept of capitals which again is connected to the concept of habitus. Capitals describe the types of material and symbolic resources recognized within the field studied. Habitus denotes the embodied capitals, connected to and possessed by each specific agent, including resources that are not seen, or not recognized in the particular field.[10] In this book, the concept of *field* is not operational, but merely serves as a framing and theoretical premise behind the operational concepts in order to make the Bourdieuian concept of capitals function in a Bernsteinian frame. It is the concept of capitals which will be most actively used in the analysis, but the concept of habitus serves as theoretical background for the way the concept of capitals is put to work in the study.

The empirical focus is thus on the classroom as social space which is consequently seen as an arena for social classification and distribution. Here, the study emphasizes how distributions and classifications can be seen as transformed in the classroom – as pedagogized – and thus, the productive side (rather than the reproductive aspect) is brought to the fore.

This epistemological ground leads to two types of sub-analysis within the larger Bourdieuian strategy, both focusing on what is institutionally recognized and what is not. On the one hand, a sub-analysis of the *positioning* of the agents, looking at how the pupils struggle to occupy *positions* in the classroom in relation to what is seen as legitimate, and how successful they are, empirically focused on turn-taking practice (to be elaborated in Chapter 4) (Bourdieu 1993, e.g. 182-183, 2004b[11], 2005, Lindblad & Sahlström 2002). On the other hand, a sub-analysis focusing on the social history of the pupils, their so-called *dispositions*, and how these appear between recognition or non-recognition (e.g. Bourdieu 1997, 1998a:30-41, Øland 2007). The empirical focus of this sub-analysis is the categorization practice of the teacher, conceptualized as institutional agent.

3.5 Forms of capital: The economy of the symbolic – the symbolism of economy

I understand capital – or rather, forms of capital – as a multi-dimensional concept of types of resources, specifically, resources which are recognized as legitimate and acceptable. Through various forms of capitals, Bourdieu aims to address the valuations and thus the social classifications within social space. As such, forms of

---

10 Other examples of what we can call a "light" usage of the concept of *field* include Mottelson 2003 and Moldenhawer 2001, both of which are written in the tradition of Bourdieu as his work has been applied in educational research, and as it has developed in the tradition of Staf Callewaert's scholarly work from the 1980s onwards (see e.g. 1997, 2002, 2003), in particular at University of Copenhagen, where the dissertation project behind this book was likewise conducted. This tradition also affects my conceptualization of Bourdieu with regard to the classroom, without a broader field analysis of relations between institutions. My research is nevertheless of a different character due to its use of a Bernsteinian framework and its double analytical strategy, one of which is derived from the work of Foucault.
11 Bourdieu 1975 and Bourdieu, Chamboredon & Passeron 1991 have also formed an important background for developing this analytical strategy. This is explicated in the dissertation, Buchardt 2008.

capital are always connected to the specific social fields in which they take on particular forms and are recognized – and thus, are produced and reproduced – in field-specific ways (Bourdieu 1997, 1998e, f).

A general distinction between forms of capital is between economic capital and symbolic capital, where the former includes concrete possessions (income, properties, assets), while the latter, in contrast, is to be understood as "what is recognized," which is to say, "what social groups recognize as valuable and which is ascribed value" (Broady 2002:458, my translation). Symbolic resources, in other words, must be recognized in order to become capital. Indeed, those who occupy the perceiving position must be predisposed to intercept particular resources as capital, that is to say: Those resources must be familiar to the perceiver before they potentially can be recognized and valued. In this sense, economic resources can also serve as symbolic capital, just as symbolic capital can have a material basis (e.g. Moldenhawer 2001:72-74). With regard to symbolic forms of capital, the analysis in this study focuses specifically on cultural capital. Inspired by Broady, who explains this form of capital as *"Bildung* capital" (*"Dannelseskapital,"* Broady 2002:461), I conceptualize it as *cultural Bildung capital* with a range of materialized sub-formations, including what Börjesson calls field-specific capital (in this context, school-capital and education-capital) (Börjesson 2005:51-52). In this study, school-capital signifies capital that is transferred or transmitted (via parents and family) as well as acquired by and attached primarily to pupils, and put in relation to education-capital, primarily attached to parents.

The concept of education-capital is also used to describe how the parents' capital is valued as more or less useful, problematic, or not problematic. But the concept of cultural Bildung capital also bears a broader meaning, namely, as valuation of what is perceived to be cultivated or cultured. In this sense, the cultural Bildung-form of capital refers to culture in the singular: *Culture* in this instance designates what is deemed legitimate and therefore what is dominant, inflected in hierarchies and distributed unevenly in relation to what is recognized as 'the right culture.' The ability to master a certain style of behavior, language, etc. is an intrinsic part of this.

This becomes central with regard to categorization practices in the classroom. Inspired by Bourdieu's analysis of "academic forms of classification," the evaluative words that teachers use when describing their pupils can be said to be not only about their concrete achievements but also about their ways of being and acting in a broader sense (Bourdieu 1998a:30-41, 1998c:26). The hierarchy of categorizations ascribed to the pupils – distributing the pupils across this hierarchy – corresponds to the socioeconomic history of the pupils and their dispositions – their possessions of capital. Nevertheless, the possession of particular resources needs to be seen and recognized in order to become capital (and thus, recognized institutionally). Though both relate to the overarching field of power, and thus are in homologous relation to dominant patterns of recognition in the social space in general, economic as well as cultural Bildung capital is recognized to different degrees, depending on the field in question and the disposition for seeing and valuing on the parts of those who manage or administer the power to recognize.

Cultural Bildung capital, in the sense of having Bildung and being cultured, is thus pursued by the university-educated middle class, whereas the economic middle class (e.g. white-collar workers with short- or medium-long education, employed in public offices, banks, etc.) instead values education as a means of optimizing economic capital (Muschinsky 1991). These two entities could be designated the cultural middle class and the economic-technical middle class.

The question at stake in this study's Bourdieu-inspired analysis does not concern the identification of social classes and valuation in general. Rather, the analysis adresses the shapes that class and valuation assume when social space is located in the classroom. How do pedagogized forms of economic and cultural capital appear when ascribed to pupils? What connections can be made between the categorization of pupils and their dispositions? How is their possession of resources related to economy and cultural Bildung? And what role is ascribed to 'religion' (and 'religion' as 'culture') in this context? In light of the concept of cultural Bildung capital (and in connection with this, the concept of economic capital), the theoretical optic of the study is to read 'class' as social classification which is one the one hand created in the classroom as social space, and on the other hand related to broader social structures (cf. homology), formed and translated into the social economy of the school and the school class: a pedagogized social economy. The purpose of this analytical strategy is to break down categories such as 'religion' and 'religion as culture' by means of the analytical perspective of social classification, thereby enabling not only a critical distance and relativization of such categories, but also an understanding of 'religion' as part of such a social economy.

3.6 Conceptualizing the classroom: social classification and knowledge

By operationalizing Bernstein's concept of recontextualization within a Bourdieuian analytical strategy with the concepts of social space and forms of capital, as well as within a Foucauldian analytical strategy concerning discursive regularity, I seek to analyze power as hierarchies in relation to social distribution, but also as the formation of knowledge and subjects, and thus to conceptualize the classroom through this dual strategy. More precisely, the purpose is to conceptualize the classroom curriculum in a manner whereby the production of pupil-subjects and the interpretations and valuations of the social histories of the pupils are seen as part of the practiced curriculum.

How the different types of analysis will be used in relation to different types of data will be described in Chapter 4. In sum, this study will examine how social categorization and the categorization of knowledge are produced in a complex interplay, and what – in light of distribution of capitals, recognition, and dispersion of knowledge – can be said about the social economy of the classroom, specifically in relation to its production of knowledge about 'religion' and 'religion as culture,' and vice versa. Through these distinct theoretical lenses I conceptualize, construct, and analyze the same object: The classroom and the social relations it generates and sustains between content and persons; school knowledge and (especially) pupils.

4. Two classrooms in the socioeconomic landscape. Constructing the empirical material

In this chapter, the operationalization of the analytical tracks, strategies, and incisions presented in the preceding chapters will be unfolded, as will the data material – the empirical foundation of the study. When approaching the schools and the classrooms in this study, my focus is the micro-practices and micro-politics as they are displayed in the classroom. Insofar as the classroom is part of the school institution, exploring the practices and the politics of the classroom is an empirical sample of the institutional logic of the school. The classroom is thus read, on the one hand, as a micro-political arena of identity politics and, on the other hand, as a space of possibilities which, in light of the concept of social space, can be understood as a coordinate of positions which the agents struggle to occupy.

4.1 Constructing the data – constructing the classroom

The primary data are various types of material collected through observations of two delimited educational modules on the school subject *Kristendomskundskab* in two school classes (in fact three, but two of them are taught together) at two schools. Both classes are so-called middle-level classes (namely 4th and 5th grades), and no pupils are exempted from instruction in the school subject. There are majority and minority pupils[12] at both schools, which geographically recruit from the surrounding areas and, in a broad sense, may be considered to be located in the same part of Copenhagen – or the same "social city district" as the municipality of Copenhagen phrases it. At the outset of the study, the two schools are also placed in the same school district. Notably, the school districts were later changed, primarily with the aim of changing the proportions of minority-majority pupils enrolled in the schools. The two schools thus show some similarities, but there are also a range of differences between them that justifies selecting them. It is important to note, however, that the idea behind making observations at two different schools is not to make comparisons as such, but rather to elucidate the research questions by putting them to work in two different settings, thus unfolding them in the context of two different ways of organizing the school and classroom. The point, therefore, is to sharpen as well as to complicate the discussion of the research questions and findings.

---

12 I apply the term 'majority pupil' to denote the group of pupils not defined by the teachers in terms of their (relation to) migration history, and 'minority pupil' to denote those who were (be that as 'bilingual,' 'Muslim,' 'Turkish,' etc.). Further explanation later.

4.1.1 The dissimilarity of the school sociogeography and the socioeconomy of the school classes

The area (*bydel*) in which the two schools are located is one of the (at the time) 15 Copenhagen areas that, in 2003 (when the study took place), has a share of "immigrants and descendants" above average (18.3%) for the municipality as a whole, namely approximately one in four (Municipality of Copenhagen 2004a, b). The local neighborhood of the two schools is historically a working-class neighborhood with social housing of which some of the former rental apartments have been converted into cooperative housing.[13] There is a smaller residential area of privately owned houses as well. While a relatively large share of the residents of the rental and cooperative apartments have a migration history, and as such belong to the 'minority' category, the privately owned houses are primarily occupied by higher-educated non-migrant middle-class people with non-migrant parentage, or, in other words 'majority.' Notably, this is where the recruiting bases of the two schools differ.

The school district (*skoledistrikt*) and thus the recruitment area of the B-school includes the social housing as well as the formerly rental (now cooperative) apartments, including the part of the residential area known in public debate as 'the ghetto'[14] – equaling the US expression 'the projects' – where a large share of the residents are associated with migrant histories. At the beginning of the school year in which I started the observations, the share of minority pupils at this school, measured from the category 'bilingual pupils,' is about 60%.

The school district and thus recruitment area of the C-school covers residential areas of privately owned houses in addition to the same type of housing as in the recruitment area of the B-school. Remarkably, the rental and cooperative housing geographically closest to the C-school belong to the recruitment area of yet another school. Among the teachers in the school district, the C-school is known as a relatively 'white' school – albeit not as 'white' as a third school in the district which has an even lower share of minority pupils – with a limited share of minority pupils (less than 25% at the beginning of the school year in which I started the observations).

The two schools thus show dissimilarities in not just the proportions of minority-majority pupils, but also in the composition of expected capital distribution,

---

13 Cooperative housing is a particular kind of ownership in the Danish real estate market, placed in between rented and owned apartments: A number of apartments are owned collectively by a cooperative, and each resident buys a share in the cooperative, equaling one apartment, while most major expenses connected to the maintenance of the apartments and the building are shared among the residents.

14 In Denmark, social housing is a much more extensive category of housing than in, for instance, the US; it is thus not at all always the same as what is referred to as 'the projects.' Throughout the decades of social democratic welfare state-administration, a large body of social housing was constructed to facilitate a broad selection of the population, and whereas some of this housing was or became known as 'ghettos' (the projects) much of this housing remains highly attractive, with some of it being so attractive that one has to sign up on waiting lists decades before being offered an apartment in these particular social housing facilities.

measured in economic capital (in terms of residential ownership, assuming a correlation between types of housing and income) as well as cultural Bildung capital (for instance, in terms of educational capital and the cultural capital that is associated with access to a private garden).

These types of general dissimilarities between the two schools in terms of pupil body composition and the recruitment bases are likewise reflected in the groups of pupils and parents in the particular classrooms studied.

In the analysis of the two classrooms the categorization of the pupils in respectively majority/minority is based on how they are described in the teachers' speech; if they are connected to a migration history (of their own or of their parents), for instance by describing the pupil through a non-Danish nation-ness or not, or if they are described as bilingual and/or as participating in the school subject Danish as Second Language or not.[15] At the C-school, moreover, information from the parents through the questionnaire has also been used.

The school class observed at the B-school is a 5th grade comprise of 17 pupils, 9 girl-categorized and 8 boy-categorized (from here onwards: girls and boys). Ten of them are minority pupils – many of them not migrants themselves, but with migrant parents and/or grandparents. No pupils in this school class has parents with academic degrees. One pupil has a parent employed in a white-collar job: a mother working in an organization in a middle-management position that matches her IT- and office education. This parent is born in Denmark to migrant parents. The rest of the parents of this school class are either skilled or unskilled workers, among whom several are unemployed, regardless of majority or minority. They all live in apartment blocks, and several of the minority pupils lives in the social housing, labeled in public debate as 'the ghetto'/'the projects.'

At the C-school, around one in four of the total of 50 pupils in the two observed 4th grade school classes belong to the minority category – including a category of pupils I count as 'half-minority': pupils about whom the teachers highlight that

---

15 Regarding the category of 'bilingual pupil,' etc.: One of the teachers at the C-school, Jens, describes which pupils are attending the course Danish as Second language. When I, in extension of this, ask him whether the pupil Anders, whose mother is from Thailand whereas the father is from Denmark, also attends this course, Jens replies: "no he doesn't … you have to be from specific places to be … I mean because actually … Paula and … Anders and Benjamin are half bilingual so to say … right … they all have one of the two parents to be non-Danish" (referring to Paula's mother being from Chile and Benjamin's father from the US). While Jens in the first part of the utterance distances himself from the practice of pupils having to be "from specific places," the rest of the teacher's utterance follows exactly this logic by the use of the term "half bilingual." The 'half' here refers to the migration history of the parents and not to language skills. "Bilingual pupil" and who attends courses in 'Danish as Second Language' can thus be said to be connected to the pupils' own or the parents' migration history, more specifically to where this migration is geographically and geopolitically attached, and to the degrees of this attachment rather than practical linguistic criteria. The category "bilingual pupil" thus functions as a minoritizing category in a symbolic-economic sense (see also Laursen & Holm 2010, Buchardt & Fabrin 2010).

they have one 'non-Danish' parent (further in Chapter 10). Of the 47 pupils present during the educational module, 26 are girls and 21 boys.

A little more than one in five pupils have parents with academic degrees (Higher Education), a little more than one in five have parents with college-level education (for instance, primary and lower secondary school or preschool teachers, called medium-long education) or white-collar jobs with matching specialized educational qualifications. Around one in five have parents who are either skilled workers, have short-term technical educations (for instance, SOSU [*Social og Sundhed*/Social and Health] – low-paid workers at old people's homes, hospitals, etc.) or are unskilled workers, home-based or unemployed. This leaves around 30% of the pupils about whom it has not been possible to obtain information concerning the parents' backgrounds.[16]

In terms of housing, around 52% live in cooperative housing apartments or rental apartments, whereas around 48% live in privately owned apartments/houses.[17]

All pupils whose parents have academic degrees are majority, whereas two minority parents are found among the group of parents with medium-long college-level education, though only one has a job that matches that educational background. In terms of the distribution of economic and educational Bildung capital, a more differentiated socioeconomic landscape appears at the C-school than at the B-school. The C-school has more majority than minority pupils while the socioeconomic dispersion is greater.

4.1.2   The official self-articulation of the schools

There are also a number of dissimilarities in the ways in which the two schools present themselves, for instance, in the materials they produce in print or publish on their websites. For example, the categories 'culture,' 'individuality' and 'collectivities' – which, like 'religion,' are among the empirical keywords of the study – are used in different ways and to different degrees, whereas the category of 'religion' only appears in the self-articulation of the B-school. Another central dissimilarity between the schools involves the ways in which teachers' work is organized and the ways in which the teachers organize the teaching, something that also to some extent is reflected in the promotional material presenting the schools publicly.[18] At the B-school, the teachers are formally organized in teams, but in

---

16 The percentages on work and education are counted from the 33 out of the 47 pupils present in more than half of the module, where parents filled out questionnaires and/or the information was provided through interviews with teachers and/or pupils. In other words, the counts cover 70.21% of the 47 present pupils, and 66% of the total number of pupils (50) in the two classes.

17 This percentage covers the 27 pupils – or 57.5% of the 47 present pupils – about whom I could obtain this information.

18 The following draws on two types of documents. In the case of the B-school, an introductory folder that parents, new teachers, substitute teachers, and interns received and, in the case of the C-school, the "development plan" of the school. As such the documents represent different genres, but they have been selected because these are the documents from the two respective schools that contain the most elaborated articulations of their pedagogical profiles.

practice it seems more common that the teachers plan their teaching individually – and during the module I followed, quite loosely – with no systematic debriefing, and the forms of cooperation with colleagues appears quite informal.

In the introductory material to new parents, the school conveys an institutional self-image and policy in which the categories 'religion' and 'culture' are explicated: "At the [...] school we have a basic vision of all children and grown-ups as equal and everyone is entitled to respect regardless of background." 'Background' is further qualified by the categories "socially, culturally, religiously and ethnically," which appear as parallel but distinct categories.

Further elaborating on the ambition of ensuring equality across these categories, it states: "This is why striving to provide equal opportunities to every one of our children and meeting them with the respect to which they are entitled is more important than ever." Thus, the text implies that there are aggravating circumstances in relation to differences in 'backgrounds' that requires extra attention in order to be leveled out. The quest for equality is further content-filled with a double emphasis on the school as 'inclusive,' as well as with a demand for 'discipline.' Finally, it states that "even though we're a school with children from more than 20 different nations, it is important that children as well as adults understand and accept that we are a Danish school." A "Danish school" is then defined as one that "builds on Danish traditions and a wish to provide the children with the social and vocational qualifications that are necessary in Denmark." By using the terms 'children' and 'adults' instead of 'pupils' and 'teachers,' the text suggests that 'adults' denotes not only teachers but also the parents that this material addresses. This should be seen in the context of the different types of distinction-making that are at stake in the introductory material, for instance, in the description of "school-home-cooperation" that includes a section titled "Particularly to Muslim homes." In this section, it is stated that the teaching of religion "is of importance to the pupils' understanding of Danish culture as well as other cultures," thus orienting the teaching toward 'culture' and justifying it in the context of a juxtaposition between "Danish culture" and "other cultures." It is also worth noting that the school here chooses to call the school subject *Religion* and not, as in the ministerial texts, *Kristendomskundskab*.[19]

What appears as the core of this institutional self-articulation is, in short: a 'Danish' school with multicultural users, where not just pupils and teachers but parents as well are part of the equation, and where 'religion' unfolds as 'culture' and related to 'Muslim,' 'Danish,' and 'other' cultures.

To ensure the anonymity of the schools, teachers, and pupils, these documents have solely been annexed to the assessment jury that reviewed the PhD dissertation in 2008.

19 "Religion" is the term used in the introductory material, although during the period of observations the school subject is often referred to as *Kristendomskundskab*. It is also stated that "Religion" is primarily taught in interdisciplinary modules: blocks of humanities and natural science school subjects respectively; however, in practice, the teaching in general appears to a large extent to be divided into separate school subjects.

The C-school – which has larger average classes of 25 pupils against just over 18 at the B-school – is divided in three sections, covering the primary school years, middle, and secondary levels, with two classes per grade. The mid-level, the one I observed, covers grades 3 through 5. These levels are organized in "self-managing teams" combined with "flexible planning" as it is phrased in the 'development plan' (accessible on the school website). The teacher teams of each section plan 10 weeks ahead, and the forms of instruction in each module are a mix of plenary presentation-based courses and project-based courses. This organization is spelled out in the development plan, as well as in other local institutional texts. In addition, both teachers and pupils use the intranet where, for instance, parts of the instruction material are uploaded, and the parents receive a newsletter every week. In general, written material and material that describes the future modules and teaching is quite extensive at the C-school. My quantity of written data from this observation period is thus quite substantial.

The C-school emphasizes and profiles itself as strong in the natural sciences, something that is affiliated with terms such as "sustainability" and "green approaches." In the context of this vocational focus, the development plan furthermore articulates a goal of taking "the pupils' experiences in and experiences of [*oplevelser og erfaringer*][20] the world" as a point of departure on a level with "intellectual abstractions." Experiments in teaching should consequently begin from "the pupils' backgrounds and everyday knowledge" and in this way create "overlaps between everyday knowledge and school knowledge": the Faculty of Science in pedagogized form. The parents are also mentioned in relation to a series of meetings called "parent courses" aimed at providing a better understanding of the pedagogy of the school.

The word 'culture' appears in the written material, for instance, in the context of "art and culture as areas providing a sound development base for creativity" and in the context of an aim of "establishing a democratic culture in which both the individual and the collective enjoy space and respect." Culture thus appears with the connotation of 'higher culture' and also as practiced 'democracy.' 'Background' and 'difference' are also emphasized, namely in the context of "developing inclusiveness and understanding" regardless of "backgrounds and different needs," and in the context of "respecting others;" something you can only do if you "respect yourself." The latter is associated with proficiencies in terms of "working independently" and "being responsible for your own learning." Individualities are thus projected as the pivotal base from which the collective can be managed, a perspective that is reflected in the emphasis on using a variety of approaches to learning, utilizing the pupils' "multiple intelligences." Finally, "bilingual pupils" are singled out as particular objects of attention in relation to enrollment processes

---

20 In Danish, the two words distinguish between 'experiences (in)' [*oplevelser*], meaning things that occur in your life and things that you seek out (also used in the 'excess department': 'experience' in the sense of 'adventure'); and 'experience (of)' [*erfaring*], meaning things that you learned, for instance, through your own activity or through observation.

in which the school aims to be "thorough" in order to "better know the children and their backgrounds."

A number of differences in the self-articulations of the two schools thus appear. The C-school projects culture as 'school culture,' 'higher culture,' 'democratic culture,' etc. while the B-school attaches culture to 'religion' and 'background' and correlates this with 'tradition' and 'nation'/'nationality.' While difference is tied specifically to 'the social,' 'the cultural,' 'the religious,' and 'ethnicity' at the B-school, the C-school's self-articulation does not elaborate much on where this perceived difference is manifest. It is implicitly attached, however, to "multiple intelligences" and the preconditions for learning, as well as in relation to the specifically identifying bilingual pupils as a particular object of knowledge production; this is manifested both in terms of the school's aim of installing knowledge in the pupils and their parents about the school, as well as in terms of extracting knowledge from their "backgrounds."

With regard to the organization of teachers and teaching, the B-school describes a practice that in a Danish context would be considered traditional and to be expected, and not many words are spent on this matter. The C-school, in contrast, elaborates quite extensively on this particular aspect of the institutional profile. The school-organized framework of teachers and classes is weakly framed at the B-school, whereas differences among pupils' and parents' backgrounds are strongly classified. At the C-school, one sees precisely the opposite: the framework of teaching is strongly framed, whereas the projection of differences and pupil backgrounds appears as weakly classified. Nonetheless, minority parents/families are particularly highlighted at both schools, respectively addressed as "Muslim homes" and "bilingual children and parents."

4.1.3   Producing the material

The methodological design for the construction of the material for analysis is basically the same for the two schools, involving the collection of three different types of material. Two of these types of data consist of spoken words: recordings of speech in the classroom, as well as interviews with teachers and pupils. The third type consists of my observations and annotations of practices, particularly practices connected to the ways in which the pupils seek to 'conquer' the right to speak, or indeed, not quite conquer the right to speak. In classroom research, this is called turn-taking and the turn-taking system (e.g. Mehan 1979), something that Sahlström defines as an economy of interaction (Sahlström 1999:87ff.).

At the C-school, a questionnaire to the parents regarding their socioeconomic background information was also produced – more on this later in this chapter.

The types of material are each correlated to the different aspects of the analytical strategies of the study upon which this book is based. The recordings of *the official text of the classroom*[21] provide the foundation of the analysis of discursive

---

21 Because the analytical focus is on the official text of the classroom, the sound recording

regularity, concerning the production of knowledge and subjects/subjectivities attached to 'religion' and 'culture,' and as such these provide the empirical basis for the Foucauldian analytical track. In the case of the B-school, I also draw in educational material used by the teacher during the module and, to various extents, appearing in the teacher's speech.

I define the official text of the classroom as the speech that takes place in the plenary sessions: the teacher instruction and the speech that take place between the instructing teacher and pupils, who either speak upon teacher approval or in other ways conquer the right to speak in plenary.

The interviews with teachers and pupils are (primarily) used to analyze the socioeconomic backgrounds of the pupils and the ways in which their capital and habitus are recognized or not recognized in the teachers' descriptions of the pupils. This corresponds to the Bourdieuian track of the analysis. More specifically, I use this material to analyze how dispositions appear in the social space of the classroom. At the C-school, this material is extended to include questionnaires to the parents.

The third type of material – the systematic registration of the practices of the turn-taking system during the plenary sessions – is used to analyze the strategies of the agents in terms of conquering or not conquering the right to speak, which is to say: How the agents variously seek to occupy different positions in the classroom. This is also connected to the Bourdieu-inspired analysis of positions in the classroom, but this type of finding will not appear as an independent analytical dimension, but will instead be included in the analysis of discursive regularity as well the analysis of how dispositions come to be recognized. The movements and placements of the pupils have also been registered, but this is solely used as a backdrop for the analysis of the turn-taking practices.

The interviews with the teachers are used, furthermore, to gain insight into the teacher planning of the modules.

4.2 The official text of the classroom

The primary data when analyzing the content of instruction is classroom speech as this unfolds between teachers and pupils: the official text of the classroom. My analytical questions when processing this material are directed at how the teachers project subject matter content when the teacher speech occurs without interruption and when pupil speech blends in.

---

equipment was at both schools physically placed so that the teacher speech would be closest to the microphone, and the pupil speech recordable would be the pupil speech said out loudly enough for the instructing teacher to hear. In cases where the pupil speech is too quiet to be detected properly, it would thus most often be in situations where the instructing teacher could not hear it either, whereupon he or she has for instance asked the pupil to repeat it, reprimanded the disturbance, or simply not responded to it. The communication that takes place outside of the official text of the classroom (for instance two pupils speaking among themselves during instruction) is not my analytical priority and has thus not been recorded.

These questions are centered on: 1) the ways in which the teacher speech produces the content of the school subject, namely Christianity and Islam (and at the B-school, Judaism as well): What characteristics are attributed? 2) the relations between subject matter content and the individual pupils within teacher speech: What identities and characteristics are attached to what pupils? 3) the relation between pupil speech and teacher speech, including moments of conflict: When and where do parallel or divergent meanings emerge? The focus is on knowledge formation between 'religion' and 'culture,' and how this relates to migrant history ('immigrant'-/'non-immigrant'-ness), and 'ethnic,' 'social,' and 'national' differences and meanings, as well as how it relates to various categories of individuality/ties and collectivity/ties.

In processing the data, where I listened to the tapes several times and transcribed large amounts of speech, a number of thematics emerged. These can be summed up according to the following considerations: the ways in which teacher speech organizes and prioritizes pupil experience; the ways in which knowledge is authorized amidst the struggle for knowledge-authority between teacher and pupil; how pupils are installed as subjects and objects in relation to religion.

Finally, one text sample from the official text of the classroom at the B-school and two text samples from the same lesson at the C-school have been selected for detailed analysis, using the tools described below. A larger portion of the data has been processed and analyzed in detail, which serves to qualify the questions and findings presented in this book. The reason for telescoping in on a relatively restricted part of the data for such detailed analysis is that the overarching conceptual guideline for this study is attention to micro-processes. Thus, I do not seek to argue for validity based on frequency or scope, but rather by means of getting as close as possible to the production of knowledge and subjects in order to render visible a micro-political texture.

4.2.1   *Fairclough-inspired reading strategies*
When analyzing the official text of the classroom – and preparing it for an analysis of how subjects and objects are organized in the knowledge production – I employ reading strategies inspired by Fairclough.

In my analysis of the relation between text and context, I draw on Fairclough's conceptualization of text as interwoven with social practice, and thus consisting of words not solely written or spoken but also embedded, for instance, in common assumptions, conventions, and social order. *Intertextuality* as an analytical concept seeks to capture the heterogloss. Text draws on others texts, by: 1) responding to other text; 2) transmitting or referring to other text; and 3) by inferring meaning from text outside of the text.

At the level of concrete analysis, intertextuality is closely linked to the concept of *presupposition*, of which I distinguish three types:

1) The conjunction between clauses within the same series of statements. For instance: at the B-school, the pupil Sulayman (Chapter 7) responds to his teacher's utterance about ablution before prayer in the mosque by saying: "you [man[22]] don't always have to wash in a mosque (A) maybe you [man] did it at home (B)." The pronoun "it" in clause B presupposes "wash" in clause A.
2) There is yet another type of presupposition in Sulayman's clause A. By "don't always have to," Sulayman implies that the teacher expressed the opposite in her prior utterance, namely that ablution in the mosque is something one should do, and thus always does. This type of presupposition thus involves response to and interpretation of other utterances.
3) A third type of presupposition is referral to text outside of the text in question. It could be through direct or indirect quotation of a specific *alien text* ('other' or 'alien text,' Fairclough 1992:121, indicating that the concept 'alien' is drawn from Bakhtin), for example, educational material or what Fairclough calls "not an individual specified or identifiable other text, but a more nebulous 'text' corresponding to general opinion" (Fairclough 1992:121). For instance, the teacher Jette at the B-School responds to the pupil Meriam by such a nebulous intertextual presupposition: Meriam has stated "there is an order in which you [man] do these things" (and has thus used presuppositions of types 1 and 2) to which Jette responds: "maybe it says so." The verb "says" in conjunction with "it" presupposes that Meriam's utterance refers to a written text, and since the thematic context of the utterances is Islam, this presupposition implies that "it" is the Qur'an to which Meriam is referring. The proposition of the teacher thus presupposes another text than the one found in Meriam's utterance, namely a nebulous text corresponding to general opinion: That Muslims speak and act according to what is written (in the Qur'an). In other words a presupposition that identifies Meriam with the 'common notion' that 'Muslims' are scripture fundamentalists, and that the actions of Muslims (be they material or spoken) are generated by or derived from the Qur'an. In Jette's presupposition, a chain of meanings is at play that is associated not only with the nebulous text 'Muslims are scripture fundamentalists' but also with another nebulous text: Namely that Meriam speaks *as a Muslim* rather than as a pupil in the course of being a contributing participant in classroom content instruction on religion.

Intertextuality and presupposition thus cannot be analyzed without bringing hegemony/power into the equation, including a consideration of which types of text can potently conjoin particular texts and identities to other texts and identities. Intertextuality cannot be reduced to presupposition, but in my analysis this is the concept that primarily structures my reading of intertextuality, with particular

---

22 Danish word for plural indefinite, see full explanation in Chapter 7.

attention to knowledge formations linked to 'religion' and 'culture' outside, but woven into, the official classroom text.

Throughout this book, the concept of intertextuality is therefore to be understood as a concrete text-analytical counterpart to the overarching analytical framing concept: re-contextualization.

4.3   The detailed focal points in analyzing classroom conversation

I have chosen grammar-semantic concepts from especially Systemic Functional Linguistics, or more precisely: lexicogrammar, as tools with which to dig into the micro-politics of what is said in the classroom. These tools are put into operation through my research questions which translate into the following four overall analytical concerns.

Coherence and ruptures in the speech in relation to the genre/type of activity

By examining coherence – and lack of coherence – in speech I seek to shed light on relations between content and participants; between what, inspired by the Foucauldian conceptualization, I call connections among knowledge, experience, truth, and prescription in relation to religions and subjects. How are certain substantive topics pursued? How do they slide back, disappear, and reappear? How do themes play out among speakers, within and in-between the utterance of speakers? By conceptualizing the relation between text (concrete linguistic practice) and context (discursive/social practice) – drawing on Fairclough – I consequently analyze speech/text in the classroom in relation to the broader social practice of the classroom, and thus the 'activity type' by which the classroom is characterized and the specific genres of the classroom.

In order to analyze the textual practices in light of the broader *grammar of the classroom*, and thus taking the analysis beyond the level of clauses, I examine the text in light of the turn-taking system, which, administered by the teacher, can be seen as a foundational structure for distribution speech. On the other hand, I look at the text in light of the Initiation-Response-Evaluation-format (IRE), referring to the classical finding that classroom communication in teacher-controlled instruction is dominated by a pattern of speaking turns, where the teacher *initiates* (with a question), and a pupil *responds*, followed by an *evaluation* by the teacher. This pattern does vary, though, not least due to an increasing use of new pupil-centered forms of instruction, such as group work.

Moreover, classroom research has pointed to the impact, for example, of pupil-pupil communication, as well as greater variation in the relations, in particular, between initiation and response. Nevertheless, it seems that evaluation still rests widely with the teacher (Sinclair and Coulthard 1975, Lindblad & Sahlström 2002:254-256, 265, 271, 273, Chouliaraki 1998:18).

To further zoom in on the ways in which speech structures the relations between speakers and content, I operationalize a concept of Topically Related Themes (TRT) drawn from Mehan and Chouliaraki (Mehan 1979, Chouliaraki 1998). In this manner, I explore the ways in which meaning is delineated – supplemented by the IRE model – as a way to examine the patterns of the genre-specific conventions of the classroom.

In the texts of the two classrooms, I find relatively few teacher-initiated questions in my empirical material, just as pupil initiations often take the form of additions or objections rather than answers. The IRE pattern (in its classical form) is thus weighed against the data, and elements such as *initiation, response,* and *evaluation* become analytical tools not assumed a priori to be linked to either teacher or pupil.

The evaluating utterance from the teacher is then analyzed – inspired by Ahrenkiel – as implicit/explicit and negative/positive evaluation respectively (Sinclair & Coulthard 1975, Ahrenkiel 2004:185ff.). In this process, I also examine to what degree speakers include the utterance of the other, for instance, reformulating or including as well as excluding other speakers or voices (for instance, that of the textbook or texts of a more nebulous character, such as "one says that ...") (cf. French & Maclure 1981). When digging into evaluations and the inclusion/exclusion of utterances, I look closely at the workings of presupposition.

In the text samples chosen for detailed analysis, I make an overall distinction between sequences of presentation (in most cases, the teacher introducing a topic), and sequences of interaction, where different speakers take the floor (which can also include elements of presentation).

The persons populating the speech (the interpersonal function)
At the level of concrete clauses, a pivotal focal point is the designation of persons; person deixis – for instance, what persons are designated by nominals (such as 'pastor') or by personal pronouns identified as responsible for the content of a statement as an operationalization of the SFL concept of *mood person* – which is linked in my framework, inspired by Frimann Trads, to the *interpersonal function* (Frimann Trads 2000:131; see also 127-142). The mood person of a clause in some ways corresponds to the grammatical subject – the it/they that does something. Drawing on Frimann Trads, I distinguish between an indefinite/diffuse mood person (one, someone, you) and a definite mood person, which can be distinguished furthermore in the *conversational interactant* (I, we, you [single], you [plural]) and *non-interactants* (he, she, it, they) (Frimann 2004:160-163).

To give an example from the classroom that shows the complexity of the designations of persons, not least in spoken utterances (in contrast to written ones): At the B-school, the pupil Sulayman asks, "What does ritual mean?" and the teacher Jette answers: "Ritual is that (hesitates) every time you [du] are in (hesitates) the mosque with someone on Fridays (pause) then you [I; definite plural] actually do the same things."[23] The content is attached to the recipient and conversational interactant Sulayman ("every time *you* [du] are in the mosque")

---

23 The use of [ ] containing the Danish pronouns 'man,' 'du,' and 'I' is explained in detail in Chapter 7.

through the personal pronoun "you," the mood person of the clause: the one who is held responsible for the actions (in this case, going to the mosque and 'doing the same things'). However, "you" can also be understood as a diffuse mood person, as another way of saying 'one.' I would argue that both meanings of "you" are at play, complementing and interacting with each other, in this particular example. Precisely because "you" can be understood as 'one,' the character of the statement is maintained as general, in other words as general knowledge, while the content at the same time is attached to the conversational interactant who then becomes generalized. Thus, the general knowledge of the proposition (in this case knowledge of Islamic prayer) is flavored with intimacy and subjectivity.

The concept of deictic terms pointing at persons, as indicated, does entail more than the concept of mood person – and we will need this 'more' to understand what happens when for instance the mood person "you" is in the mosque with "someone." "You" in connection with "someone" attaches the practices of Sulayman (to whom "you" refers) to those of diffuse 'others,' while a new collective mood person – held responsible for the actions – is established in the last sentence of the statement: "then you [I; definite plural] actually do the same things." Through this designated "someone" the conversational interactant Sulayman is attached to a new definite plural "you" that is no longer situated in the conversation, but in "the mosque."

Deixis thus denotes how text is entrenched in context – or conjures up a context. The many representational elements at play in classroom speech are not just text-situated in the concrete context in which the speech takes place; the speech also creates context outside of the classroom to which the mood persons are attached, as the examples above illustrate. This leads to analytical questions directed at the persons designated by the text; where these persons are placed spatially; the degree to which the conjured context is attached to the concrete context (the class) – and thus, the ways in which school knowledge is attached to the persons within the classroom.

The use of modality in the speech (the interpersonal function)
The use of *modality* is of pivotal importance to my text analysis of the classroom speech. In the SFL system, *mood* is understood as a resource connected to the interpersonal function of language, which concerns who it is that communicates as well as the relations established between the speakers grammatically. As a grammatical resource, modality installs relations among speakers as well as between the speakers and the ideational (what is the communication about? How is the world represented?) information, exchanged by means of inflecting speech: through *modal verbs* (e.g. had to, could, would, should) as well as through a range of adverbs called *mood adjuncts* (e.g. certainly, maybe, always, sometimes, cf. Halliday & Matthiessen 2004:128).

Modality denotes what is at stake in inflected speech, in the "space between yes and no" (Andersen et al. 2001:73, my translation). Expressed in the terms of SFL, modality is when utterances are neither *categorically positive* (for instance: I do/yes) nor *categorically negative* (for instance: I don't/no), but are inflected to a high degree (for instance: I must do this), a medium or median degree (for instance: I will do this), or a low degree (for instance: I could do this). There is, in Halliday and Matthiessen's words, "more than one road" between positive and negative polarity (Halliday & Matthiessen 2004:147). It is these roads, and the ways in which these roads flavor persons and objects and install relations between them, that are central to the analysis, and also provide a point of departure for the ensuing Foucault-inspired interpretations.

Modality can be further divided into different types: *epistemic* and *deontic*. Epistemic modality is attached to claims, or in other words, utterances that can be the object of argument (propositions): statements that seek to bring forward information or request information. When epistemic modality appears in propositions, it concerns the space between claiming and denying: it expresses degrees of *probability* and *usuality*. How likely, or how certain is it? How usual or how common is it? Epistemic modality (*episteme*: knowledge) therefore involves the extent to which the utterance claims to be true and certain knowledge, in other words the (claimed) relation between the utterance and the category of *truth*.

Deontic modality is attached to incitements and offers, or in other words, utterances that deal with the exchange of things and services (proposals). When deontic modality appears in proposals it concerns the space between 'do it' and 'don't do it,' between prescribing and prohibiting (Frimann 2004:152), relating to degrees of *obligation* and *inclination*. To what extent should, would or can I/you do this? Deontic modality (*deon*: duty, incumbent) thus relates the utterance to degrees of prescription, or the (prescribed) relation of the utterance to the category of *necessity*.

The interpersonal function of language in general terms concerns the ways in which the preservation, production, and development of social relations appear through grammatical choices and how this relates to the ideational (What is the communication about? How is the world represented?). In consequence of my research questions, I utilize SFL tools for analyzing grammatical resources – with special attention to the organization of modality in classroom speech – as a way to scrutinize speech and its organization of relations between bodies which must/will/can do something and the knowledge/truth of which they are made the object and to which they are subjected. In this sense – where the game between the prohibited and the prescribed as well as the game of truth take place and are inflected in speech – the analysis of modality becomes a cardinal point in the subsequent Foucault-inspired interpretations of the detailed readings. Attention to the use of modality serves to open the text to relations between the ideational and the interpersonal, rather than to say something about relations between the speakers as agents.

The representations of speech: realization of processes 'of the world'
As a supplement to the analytical incisions described above, I include in the analysis the ways in which verbs represent the world and knowledge about the

world, depending on the types of processes chosen. I include the use of words in general as well – for example, the meaning of nominals – particularly in cases where speech does not organize meaning by means of modality. In the context of SFL, this concerns the ideational function of language which is attached to the content of communication. The ways in which ideational meaning is organized thus has to do with organization of *experience*: how persons and things as well as activities or acts, occurrences, and modes are represented. The grammatical resource *agency* and the system of *transitivity* are significant here.

Transitivity organizes how acts in the world are represented in a given text. Which processes (in other words, 'something' one can do) do the verbs represent? And is this process of a mental, material action-oriented, verbal, or relational character? In this analysis, I direct my attention toward questions such as how speech about the content (in this case, religions in different shapes) and speech about experience (in this case, how it is attached to speakers: teachers and pupils) represent the subject of that speech through various types of processes: What kind of enterprise is attributed to 'the content' and 'the experience'? And is this represented as something 'someone' is doing (active) or as something that just happens (passive)? I do not systematically focus on the total occurrence of different types of such processes. Transitivity is merely a supplementary point of reading that serves to sharpen the reading of specific utterances, in line with the use of words in general: Is the theme Christianity represented by "the pastor" or by "Niels' mother"? Or by opposition to an entity such as 'the Muslim tradition'? And to what degree does this contribute to the attachment between what is spoken of and, for example, institutions or the intimate?

Objects and subjects and beyond

To sum up: The reading strategies and analytical focal points of the analysis thus operate in the field between what Fairclough calls the textual level and the discursive practice. Alternately, with Foucault, it is the speech itself, and the ways in which this speech carves out a space for speakers, that is the focus. By taking a closer look at speech and the different kinds of utterances, I seek to identify which sites for being 'someone' are available, and how this availability produces 'someone.' What regulative space – what space of opportunities and limitations, what possibilities and constraints – are made available to be and to become a speaker within it? And what space is available to be and become a pupil subject?

Whereas pupil subjects in this analytical track have appeared as objects of speech and effects of speech, the question now arises – as this analytical track exhausts its explanatory force – what conditions, departing from the analysis of knowledge and subjects, have been generated for pupils and their respective strategies?

At this point, the linguistic-analytical findings interpreted through the concept of discursive regularity must be discussed in relation to findings from the position- and disposition-oriented analytical work, interpreted in light of the concept of capitals. As sketched out earlier, the latter draws on other types of empirical material, to which I will now turn.

4.4 Practices of the turn-taking system

The set of data relating to the other main analytical track of the study, the Bourdieuian position- and disposition-analysis, focuses on the practices of the agents – teachers and pupils, and the social histories of pupils and how they are interpreted by the teacher as an institutional agent. While the keyword of the regularity-oriented analysis was 'the official text of the classroom,' the keyword is now 'the practices of the classroom.' Thus, Bourdieu's concept of practice is used to construct a different type of incision than the Foucauldian analysis, where the focus is on the classroom as speech and text. Consequently, another type of data is demanded.

The first part of this analysis focuses on *position mapping*. The ways in which agents in the classroom occupy (or attempt to occupy) various positions is investigated through material gathered from observation, consisting of systematic registrations structured around pre-constructed categories of behavior. These categories are based on assumptions about the institutional organization of the school, not least the turn-taking system. My focus has been on pupil strategies distributed across the following categories: 1) hand-raising, 2) being assigned the right to speak upon raising one's hand, 3) being assigned the word without having expressed a wish to speak, and 4) conquering the right to speak without prior approval – either on the occasion of a general teacher question with no explicit address to a particular pupil, or without any such obvious occasion. In addition, I have registered reprimands during plenary sessions in which the teacher manages the pupils' rights to speak, as well as the patterns of movement in the classroom (for instance, a pupil leaving his/her seat, or sliding under the table) and the teacher's way of managing the patterns of such movements: Which types of movements are treated as legitimate, and which are not? Finally I have noted the physical distribution of pupils in the room.

The rigidity of this data material deserves consideration in itself. When analyzing the official text of the classroom, the samples selected for detailed elaboration in this book inherently mirror what has taken place: Only the speakers – and primarily, the most frequently speaking among the pupils – are visible. But not all pupils speak, and not all pupils speak with the teacher. The idea behind producing a data set consisting of registrations of turn-taking practices is therefore to render visible all pupils and all types of strategies in the classroom; from the speaking and moving and the speaking but not moving to the not-speaking but moving and the not-speaking and not-moving pupils. These types of observations direct my analytical attention to pupils whom I do not otherwise notice in the midst of the logic and traverse of the classroom: The invisible pupil, so to speak, becomes visible through her/his invisibility. The rigidly systematic nature of this type of observation is thus a prerequisite for being able to analyze differences as generated relationally which must consequently be analyzed as relational.

The product of these observations takes the form of numbers and percentages, which could lead one to believe that this is a type of quantification or micro-statistics aimed at recording volume and frequency. This is not the case. The numbers are to be understood as the output of systematized observations: a way of conceptualizing the classroom in order to render some things visible while other aspects are subtracted from the equation. An example of the latter could be the interactions between the pupils outside of the official text of the classroom. What is brought to the fore, however, is not so much who talks a lot and who does not, but rather the pupils' ways of filling up the space, or indeed, not filling it up, and how these compare when interpreted in relation to one another. The numbers then become a point of departure for analyzing pupil strategies read through difference, and through the lens of this analytical strategy the difference that emerges is understood to be relational. In other words, the numbers are not findings in themselves, but rather serve as eye-openers making possible various ruptures in the analysis by forcing me to see each and every pupil in the classroom, and producing a kind of data that makes it possible to analyze the pupils by relating their strategies to one another.

4.5 The socioeconomic backgrounds of the pupils: teacher, pupil, and parent descriptions and information

The Bourdieu-inspired analysis of classroom practice cuts two ways (also empirically): a position analysis in which the agents' positionings – their attempts to occupy the positions of the room – are explored through a mapping of the turn-taking practices of the classroom; and an analysis of dispositions conducted on the basis of the pupils' self-descriptions in concert with a disposition analysis empirically based on the teachers' descriptions of pupils, as well as socioeconomic information about and from the pupils' parents. This type of incision aims to make possible an understanding of socioeconomic background in connection with pupils' strategies of seeking recognition in the classroom, as well as an assessment of the degree of success in these pursuits. The central place for this reading is the teachers' categorization practices, analyzed in relation to the two other types of data: the socioeconomic background of the actors, both as they themselves and their parents respectively describe it.

Positioning and recognition are keywords in both ends of the incision.

The analytical lens on pupil dispositions is specifically connected, theoretically and conceptually, to the concept of capitals. The first application of this perspective is the selection, as described, of the two schools based on their respective socioeconomic composition and the differences between them.

A central type of data related to socioeconomic variables and the recognition or lack of recognition of capital (and consequently, habitus) comes from my interviews with pupils and teachers. With the Bourdieuian perspective, drawing on the conceptualization of the classroom as *social space*, I seek to add to the analysis what the Foucauldian framework neither is able nor attempts to capture: Namely that agents situated in social history who, with their bodies and persons, bring this social history with them when entering a space in whose context they can be studied.

The teachers were interviewed before, during, and after the observed educational modules in order to access their articulations of the curriculum, the organizational and institutional framework of the school, as well as their descriptions of the pupils. The pupils were interviewed individually with the aim of getting them to present themselves, their families, their school situations, and their thoughts about the educational module on religion.

At the B-school, the number of pupils who followed the educational module was relatively limited. I conducted interviews with 15 out of the total 17 pupils, but in one case it later turned out that the audio equipment had failed. The other two missing pupils were one who was entirely absent during the educational module, and one who declined to participate in an interview. In other words: 14 pupil interviews were successfully conducted in this school class. Upon subsequent analysis, however, the interview data proved to contain several problems. Many of the pupils had not been able to explain what their parents did for a living, for instance. This fact is of analytical interest in itself: Which pupils are able and prioritize to account for their parents' jobs and educational backgrounds, and which are not? Though possible to reconstruct, this absence in the one body of data meant that I missed a comparative component, and at the C-school, I chose to supplement the interview material with a questionnaire distributed among the parents. Not all of the pupils present during the main part of the module at the C-school were interviewed, as there were 47 out of a total 50. Instead, I chose to follow the pupils in three working groups, as composed by the teachers (on basis of criteria that will be elaborated in Part 3), and interviewed all of the pupils who were placed in these groups (a total of 15).

All of the interviews were semi-structured and guided by the intention to ask questions in as open-ended a manner and with as little direction from the interviewer as possible. This also means that, to a great extent, I let the pupils (and to some extent, also the teachers) speak about whatever they wanted, and asked questions relating to what they opted to prioritize within the broad topics that I outlined at the beginning of the interviews.

4.6 Between and across the analysis of dispositions, positions, and positioning and the analysis of knowledge- and subject production

The analysis of the social space as a point of departure for analyzing the social classification of agents thus works in two ways. When considering dispositions, the agents are analyzed on the basis of how they are categorized and recognized and how this can be understood in relation to valuation, conceptualized as capitals. In this endeavor, the teachers' descriptions, the pupils' self-descriptions, and the responses to the questionnaires supply the empirical basis.

Though the linguistically oriented analytical tools are primarily used to analyze the speech of the classroom, I also do use elements of the Fairclough-inspired reading strategies when analyzing the interview data in the analysis of dispositions, for instance I pay attention to presuppositions. Also the question of what is pulled to the fore and what serves as background has played a central role in the way I have worked with the empirical material when analyzing dispositions. As such the Foucauldian analytical focus on the statement (what is announced) and "its correlation with other statements that may be connected with it, and show what other forms of statement it excludes" is part of my way of doing the Bourdieu-oriented analysis of what is recognized and what is not (Foucault 2003b:30-31). It is, however, important to underline that in the context of the analysis of dispositions, the Fairclough- and Foucault-inspired reading strategies serve mainly as a language for describing how what with Jette Kofoed could be called 'pupilness' (*elevhed*, Kofoed 2003) is produced. The analytical explanations, however, are drawn from a different theoretical universe, namely from the concepts of capitals and social space, and thus form part of analyzing how social class is produced in the classroom.

In the analysis of practices, the concept of position is used to distinguish practices that were accessible, and which pupils attempted to occupy, as well as the degrees of success in this enterprise.[24] This analysis focuses on the struggle around the right to speak as this appears when looking at the system of turn-taking in the context of the type of instruction that could be called 'the teacher presentation-focused plenary session.' This particular type of analysis does not constitute an independent part of the book, as it did in the original PhD dissertation. Instead, it is primarily included to support and add perspective to the analysis of discursive regularity and the hierarchies of recognition. It does, however, still form an important basis for the way the complete analysis has been empirically constructed.

In contrast to these two forms of analysis of social space is the reading of the forms of knowledge and the to-knowledge-attached and produced pupil subjects and subjectivities. My purpose is to unfold the analysis through two main analytical tracks – and to unfold both of these in two different institutional settings – in two schools with different socioeconomic terrain and somewhat distinct types of organization.

The point is not to validate my claims by identifying the frequency of occurrences; in such an endeavor, two schools would have been far too few. Likewise, my point is not to compare them in order to discern similarities and discrepancies in the effort to justify generalizations. Rather, my intention is to unfold complex processes connected to the forms of knowledge and the production

---

24 Though it does appear in the oeuvre of Foucault, and has come to be of importance in the Foucault-inspired tradition of poststructuralism, I analytically reserve the use of the concept of 'position' to the Bourdieu-oriented analysis.

of social classification in order to get closer to the divergent as well as homologous dynamics of these two analytical layers: the classroom as a micropolitical arena and as a social space. Thus, I will demonstrate how social structure and the politics of identity and knowledge intertwine when recontextualized in the classroom. Across these analytical layers, a central analytical interest is *problematization* (Foucault 1992, as introduced in Chapter 1) which plays a framing role for my research interest, together with the overarching framing concept of recontextualizing: How objects, be that practices, persons, or phenomena such as religions are made to appear as a result of being subject to *moral solicitude* and *ethical concern*, and how this is shaped in specific ways when recontexualized in school and thus appears in pedagogized form.

PART 2
DIFFERENTIATED 'MUSLIM' CLASS STRUCTURE

In this part of the book, the analysis of material from the B-school is developed in three chapters, organized by two analytical incisions. One incision (Chapter 6) explores the ways in which pupils are acknowledged, or precisely not acknowledged, on the basis of the teacher's descriptions of the pupils. The point of departure are the categorizations of the pupils, building upon the subject matter-related categories of 'religion'/'culture' as they appear in the teacher's speech: How do the pupils become recognizable as pupils? Which dispositions and hence capitals are ascribed to them, and thus which are viewed as worthy of recognition?

The other incision (Chapter 7) focuses on the official classroom text. An analysis of the knowledge production of the classroom is developed through reading strategies inspired by Fairclough and structuring concepts inspired by Foucault. What knowledge about 'religion,' which relations to subjects, and which spaces for them, are generated in the official classroom text? What spaces for subjects appear through the production of knowledge?

These incisions, following the two main analytical tracks of the book, are further informed by and elaborated through position mappings, e.g. of the pupils' strategies in relation to the turn-taking system and their relative degrees of success.

Subsequently these incisions will be discussed in relation to one another, focusing on the questions of how social classification appears, how the socioeconomic landscape of the classroom looks when translated into practices of the classroom and the various forms of teacher recognition, and how this can shed light on the spaces for subjects that are thereby made available, and consequently, how knowledge about 'religion'/'culture' can be understood as it plays out in the classroom.

5. The teacher articulation of the official classroom text

This chapter opens up the analysis through the teacher's speech concerning curriculum at the B-school. At this school, the data material is constructed around an educational module of "Religion," as the teacher calls the school subject *Kristendomskundskab*, and consists of observations and registrations in the classroom, three interviews with the teacher Jette conducted before, during, and after the educational module, as well as interviews with the pupils.

Jette is the primary of four teachers engaged with this particular school class. She teaches various school subjects in the field of the humanities, namely Danish, English, and Religion (*Kristendomskundskab*). She wishes to include several religions in the educational module that she has planned, an objective she motivates during the interviews. Her main subjects of study from the teacher training college are Danish and a foreign language, while her formal qualification for teaching Religion is from the (at the time of her education) mandatory common core subject *Kristendomskundskab*.

Jette has taught this particular school class since the 1st grade. She is in her mid-30s, born and raised in a medium-sized provincial town, and being a teacher she is better educated than her parents. This is not, however, among the components she includes in the description of the classroom curriculum, but as we shall see, other features connected to her person are.

5.1 A differentiated ideal of respect

One of the central characteristics of how the teacher describes the educational module is that she installs herself as part of her arguments and, in this process, also projects a specific concept of diversity, centered on the notion 'respect.'

Early on during the interviews, the teacher points out the fact that she is expecting a child, while being single, and returns to this subject several times. She also brings up this fact about her personal life during the teaching sessions, and thus situates it as part of the content. Jette depicts single parenting as something which is "acceptable in Denmark" as opposed to "many places in the world," and speaks about how she expects "respect" from the pupils, even if someone else ("they") might tell the pupils that single parenting is not acceptable.

> "And if they can't accept that this is how society is in Denmark … I mean of course you have a right to believe in whatever you want but you shouldn't judge others, but I think that you should pay appropriate respect."

Jette here presupposes a 'someone' – who could be inside or could be outside of the classroom, or both – who would not respect her. In her speech, she attaches this someone to "many places in the world" in which single parenting is not acceptable. When she elaborates on this, it becomes clear that the "they" whom she suspects might fail to accept her single parenting are grown-ups/parents:

> "You could say to your girls: 'uhm, maybe Jette is expecting a child and she's not married but that doesn't mean you should go do the same' ... I don't respect you if you have a child out of wedlock ... but I might still respect Jette."

The utterance can be interpreted as Jette arguing for her own legitimacy, for being worthy of a recognition that she apparently does not take for granted. But it can also be read as the articulation of a dual and differentiated ideal, in which the teacher posits respect for herself – as a teacher associated with the place "Denmark" – as potentially different from how a subject attached to "many places in the world," "your girls," can earn respect. In the teacher's speech, "respect" is thus respect for "society in ... Denmark" and not respect for having children out of wedlock, as such. Simultaneously, it is presupposed that it is legitimate not to respect "girls" doing what she is doing if they happen to be less attached to "Denmark." A differentiated ideal of respect can thus be seen as related to 'respecting diversity.'

The educational module on Religion that Jette taught was distributed over seven days during a period of 25 days, with a total of 16 lessons of 45 minutes each. The teaching sessions were organized in five sessions of two lessons and two sessions of three lessons – a compact version of the mandatory one hour per week lesson in the school subject *Kristendomskundskab*. Thus this educational module planned by Jette made up the total content for a full school year's worth of teaching in religion.

As a framework for the educational module Jette had chosen a particular text book (Meidahl 1989) in which six religions are presented: Judaism, Islam, African religion (vol. 1), Hinduism, Buddhism, and Christianity (vol. 2). The text book also includes a teacher's guide, but Jette worked neither with a detailed plan nor with any specified priorities of content, time-wise.

She did, however, have specific ideas about how and why to teach about each of the religions from the text book. Buddhism, Hinduism, and African religions are important to mention because "Muslims," she says, perceive these religions as pagan.

> " ... Islam traditionally has respect for what you call religions of the scripture meaning exactly Judaism and Christianity [...] whereas uhm African religions Hindus and Buddhists, really, but absolutely are totally heathens within... them, right ... and when we're at a school with so many Muslims then it's actually quite important to- I mean the other big religions I mean just to sort of mention that there are more than just these three which actually have more or less the same geographical point of origin, right ... so anyway that when you compare the world then it's not that far from each other."

Thus, it is particularly the "many Muslims" in the school class who need to learn about other religions than Christianity and Judaism. Not just to learn respect for those whom Jette suspects they regard as "totally heathens," but also so that the "many Muslims" can appreciate the fact that the three "religions of the scripture" are in fact not all that different – they have "more or less the same geographical point of origin" and are "not that far from each other."

Comparison as a didactic strategy is a recurring figure in Jette's speech about educational planning. Furthermore, comparison operates in the teacher's prioritizing of the content, closely linked to her expectations of an identification from the pupils with the content.

5.2 'The Muslim pupil' as a structuring figure

When I, before the module starts, ask Jette how much space she plans for each religion to occupy, she replies: "Well that also depends on what they want to say something about." The pupil's contributions or expected contributions become a central feature in the practiced curriculum, as will be unfolded throughout the following chapters.

During the course of the educational module Jette realizes that she has already spent six lessons on Judaism alone and revises her plan to include only Judaism, Islam, and Christianity, leaving five lessons each for the latter two religions. In the interview halfway through the educational module, Jette motivates this revision, saying that she had even wanted initially to prioritize Islam and Christianity as more important than Buddhism, Hinduism, and "African religions."

> "... It's also Judaism actually because- because Judaism- there aren't really any Jews but they ought to get the explanations anyway and it's the one that is most connected to or that- that actually Islam and Christianity in general are based upon so it's quite important ... that they know what it is and that it's not just those kind of people who run around shooting at Palestinians, right."

There are several presuppositions at play here. One presupposition is that what is important in terms of concrete school content is connected to what kinds of pupils actually populate the classroom and to which religions these pupils can be attached. Even though there "aren't really any Jews" in the school class, Jette finds it important to spend a third of the entire educational module on Religion focused on Judaism alone, exactly because Islam and Christianity – the religions to which she assumes the pupils are in fact attached – ought to be understood in relation to Judaism. Furthermore, as another presupposition in her speech, she judges this to be important because she assumes that someone in the class might happen to think of Jews as "just those kind of people who run around shooting at Palestinians."

'The Muslim pupil/s' is a recurring structuring figure in Jette's descriptions of how and why she has organized the content of the educational module in specific ways.

The pupils with their perceived affiliations and attachments also appear as the motivating factor when the teacher further elaborates her use of comparison and paralleling between the religions. For instance, she describes how she thinks that parallels help the pupils understand the content better because they attach the pupils to the content:

> "I actually think they hung in there quite nicely during both Judaism and Islam. Also because I ... I made it a point very early on to draw parallels ... but of course especially during Islam because there are in fact ten out of seventeen who has another ethnic background of whom the ... seven or ... eight ... have a Muslim background right ... if it isn't- if it isn't in fact as many as nine."

5.3 Separate and stable, yet flexibly changeable

During the interviews, Jette continuously circles around the subject of respect, and returns to this when asked to describe what she expects or hopes that the pupils will gain from the educational module.

> "I hope that uhm, some- some respect will come out of it, because I guess I actually think that in school we unfortunately have more often referred to Islam and said 'well, Muslims do this and this' where we might not have succeeded in properly explaining what exactly the Christian religion is really about ... and why it is the way it is ..."

Hence, on the one hand, Jette articulates an intention of breaking up the teachers' implicit way of dealing with "the Christian religion" – meaning: not actually dealing with it, but instead dealing a lot with Islam – and on the other hand, Jette presupposes that some pupils lack respect for Christianity, something that she, as a teacher, has a professional and subject matter-related responsibility to change. Who these pupils might be is not explicitly asserted, but in other utterances from Jette – for instance about "African religions" being perceived as heathen – the recurring object in need of being taught respect is projected as the pupils whom Jette supposes are Muslim.

Another key feature – closely linked to "respect" – in the teacher's utterances about the educational module planning and motivations for it is to introduce a concept of 'difference.'

> "So that's something to do with – I mean again – all people have different religions and different ... something that suits you ... something that suits another and you- you usually take something with you from back home but that's not necessarily what you always end up keeping."

While attaching religion and difference to something you bring with you "from back home," Jette also opens up another dimension, namely that you do not necessarily keep the things that you brought "from back home." The background-attached 'suitability' is thus changeable.

When looking at the teacher speech about the curriculum of the educational module by means of the concepts of classification and framing, a landscape of decidedly separated religions appears. However, this apparently *strong classification* is simultaneously decomposed in the articulations both prior to and during the practiced educational module.

The unstable and fluid character of the relation between the content areas, kept apart by the concept of "different religions," appears in the utterances about 'parallels' and the priority given to interaction in the classroom and "what [the pupils] want to say something about." And yet the unstable and fluid draws upon strong classifications, along the lines of the (culture- and nation-differentiated) concept of respect. This becomes visible in the speech about the disparity of religions as a precondition for drawing parallels and making comparisons, something which is intensified when the speech about religion as content slides into speech about religion as attached to and equated with pupils and their parents. Clearly delineated, classifiable entities now appear, parallel while also connected to the concept of respect, differentiated by the distinction between "Denmark" and "many places in the world," respectively. Furthermore 'Muslim' pupils emerge as particularly marked contributors, as well as special objects of the teacher's ambition to foster 'respect.'

This combination of diffuse and yet apparently strong demarcation recurs in what can be understood as *framing*. On the one hand, the teacher manages the course of the module and the interaction with the pupils on the basis of a specific text book. On the other hand, the teacher's speech opens the possibility of a weakly managed process due to the unpredictable character of the pupils' contributions.

6. Muslimness as differentiated school capital

This chapter deals with the socioeconomy of the classroom and unfolds an analysis of how the pupils' dispositions and their social history are translated and subjected to recognition or lack of recognition by the teacher in relation to school conduct. I examine the ways in which the teacher describes and categorizes pupils, focusing first and foremost on how this categorization operates in connection with religion as a category of school content. Secondly, the analysis focuses on the ways in which the teacher, in the descriptions of the pupils, prioritizes and values various skills differently. The social histories and categorizations of certain pupils are selected for further examination in order to delve deeper into various ways of evaluating cultural Bildung capital and recognizing dispositions, including how categories of religion play out in connection with (recognition of) economic capital and cultural Bildung capital.

The empirical material consists of: A) interviews with the teacher before, during, and after the educational module (in which the teacher describes the individual pupils, uses the pupils to describe the educational module taught, and elaborates on which pupils she considers and expects to be contributing, not contributing or contributing in problematic ways to the educational module); B) interviews with pupils in the class, in which they present themselves and describe their families as well as their school situations;[25] and C) observations and registration of movements and reprimands, turn-taking, and speaking turns in the classroom.[26]

What becomes clear when analyzing the teacher's categorizations and descriptions is that majority pupils are generally placed outside the category of religion, whereas the category of religion moves to the foreground in utterances about minority pupils. Furthermore, a specific pattern in the classroom landscape of religion-culture-background appears: Muslimness can be more or less cultivated and more or less strong with regard to the form of capitals: the more cultural Bildung capital ascribed to the pupil, the more legitimate the perceived Muslimness of the pupil seems to be.

How this landscape is generated will be explored in the following analysis of how particular pupils appear through the utterances of the teacher Jette, in relation

---

[25] As previously described, interviews were made with 14 of the 17 pupils. The three missing pupils were a pupil who was entirely absent, a pupil who was interviewed but for whom I later discovered that the audio recording equipment had failed, and finally Xiang, who declined to participate.

[26] The classroom mappings consist of registrations of the spatial locations of the individual pupils, their movements, and the reprimands that they received, as well as counts of 'pupil raising hand,' turn-taking, and speaking turns. The school class had a total of 17 pupils, of whom one was absent during the entire educational module, one was absent in 14 out of 16 lessons, and two were absent respectively half of the time and in 12 out of 16 lessons. The two entirely/almost entirely absent pupils are not part of the classroom counts and registrations. The two other pupils are counted in, while taking their half/more than half-absence into account.

to the ways in which the pupils present themselves and the ways in which the pupils' positionings play out when looking closer at turn-taking practices.²⁷

6.1 Culture as religion, religion as culture in the teacher's characterizations

When asked to motivate her planning of the educational module on Religion, one of the things that the teacher Jette replies is:

> "... I just think somehow that speaking about the different religions, that this was just as relevant as speaking only about Christianity when facing, when facing children from many different religious and cultural backgrounds."

Jette here expresses a lens through which she sees the pupils. Starting from the category of "religions" as content of instruction, the emphasis is on the pupils' "different religious and cultural backgrounds." Religion and culture are equated, and at the same time function as mutual content providers. At another point of the interview, Jette again operates with this equation – only now she phrases it the other way around: Asked whether she would describe her class as "multicultural," she replies:

> "Yes … no doubt about it … but then there are also … I mean there are also big differences within the- within the religions …"

In the utterance above, Jette suggests that the complex of religion-culture is more differentiated in her class than the concept of multiculturalism captures, which is implied to be something more homogenous. This utterance becomes a point of

---

27 The classroom in which the educational module Religion took place was architecturally a closed space. At one end was the door leading to the hallway, and next to this were a board and a selection of maps. Neither was used much during teaching. In front was the teacher's desk (where the audio equipment was placed), and Jette usually stayed in this spot while teaching the lessons. In front of the teacher's desk, the pupils' tables were organized in six groups; some for boys and some for girls. The teacher allocated the pupils a place to sit, and being moved from one seat to another worked as a form of sanction. For instance, the pupil Bilal was no longer allowed to sit next to Ahmed (who, as it happened, was absent during the entire module). The 'girls' tables' were closest to the teacher's desk, while the 'boys' tables' formed a second row. When the teaching was organized as a plenary session, which it was most of the time, the direction in which the pupils were seated was quite different with regard to the persistent 'control tower' of the classroom: the teacher's desk. Some were seated facing frontward, others in the opposite direction, or sideways. Similarly, some pupils could see most of the other pupils whereas others could only see a selection. Three of the four pupils who had almost no speaking turns during the module – Christina, Catharina, and Gaja, all female majority pupils – were seated with their backs to the teacher's desk. So did Gry, who was absent during most of the module, and, according to the teacher, in many other modules as well. The three most frequently contributing pupils were all faced towards the teacher's desk: Sulayman, Hassan, and Meriam, two male minority pupils and one female minority pupil, respectively. Furthermore, Hassan and Sulayman were seated in a way that allowed them to see most of the other pupils.

departure for Jette to continue with a number of utterances in which she piles together selected pupils in categories subsequently differentiated through disparities connected to religion.

> ".. I know that Gaja is baptized ... and I know that Andreas is not baptized ... but the other children ... I actually don't know if they are baptized, I mean those children who otherwise have two Danish parents ... uhm, I know who of them are Muslims and- and the only one of the bilingual children who is not Muslim ... well, that's Xiang ..."

In this sequence of utterances, two overall categories appear: "Muslims" attached to bilingual pupils, with Xiang being the only exception, and pupils with "two Danish parents." This latter category is subdivided into the baptized and non-baptized. This category of Danishness is presumptively populated by Christians, inasmuch as it is contrasted with "Muslims" and as the thematic context is religion. While baptism is the differentiating marker within the category which one might dub 'the two Danish parents-religion,' the differentiating marker of the "Muslim" category is the headscarf, as we shall see below.

6.1.1 A landscape of differentiations

In a longer sequence of utterances, a landscape of differentiations connected to 'Muslims in the class' is drawn up by Jette through descriptions and interpretations of the use of – or potential use of – the headscarf by four pupils and/or their mothers.

> MB: So you are saying that in reality there can be quite big differences among the religions ... in the class?
> Jette: Yes ... absolutely ... I mean I do think that ... I don't think I've seen Zainab's mother ... Sulayman's mother wears a headscarf ... Meriam's mother uses that slightly more kind of modern headscarf ... and come to think of it those are the only two mothers who wear headscarf ... I don't think Leila will begin wearing headscarf, the one I would be more inclined to believe would begin wearing headscarf ... that's Zainab but uhm I've seen Meriam with headscarf one Saturday when she came walking along with her mother so she might choose it as well ... but I'm pretty sure that ... I'm pretty sure that if Meriam she shows up with a headscarf then it's definitely a choice she made ... and she'd been ... she'd been informed about- about her choice ... but I'm more inclined to believe that she'd wea- begin to wear headscarf once she's married ... I'm not sure she'll do it during puberty ... I don't know about Zainab ...
> MB: And Leila you can't imagine that?
> Jette: No her mother is too- her mother is too chic ... I mean personally I feel a bit like if a woman wears make-up and then also wears headscarf, then I think it's, from what I know about the rules about uhm why you wear headscarf, if you're wearing make-up as well then, I'm just thinking 'this here ... this here is somehow a little farfetched,' I think that's two opposites clashing right there ... I mean the way I see it they might just as well wear headscarf and then appear in a bikini

showing it off ... I mean it's- it's almost the same, I know that's really exaggerated, but it's like it's something to do with not being supposed to attract attention to yourself ... and then if you're all beautifully painted up while wearing headscarf it's a bit, you know...

The differentiated meanings, implications, and predictions of (potential) headscarf-wearing that are at play in this sequence – as well as in other utterances in which Jette returns to the theme of religious affinity and the headscarf as a marker – will be unfolded in what follows through the examples of Zainab, Meriam, and Leila as these pupils appear in the teacher's utterances.

6.1.2 The predictable headscarf user

Jette initially describes Zainab's potential use of the headscarf by juxtaposing Zainab with Leila, whom the teacher does not imagine will begin wearing the headscarf, and with Meriam, whom the teacher thinks might begin wearing the headscarf, although most likely not before she will have married – and even if she were to do so, Jette is convinced it would be based upon choice. Zainab, on the other hand, is the one whom Jette would be "more inclined to believe" would begin wearing headscarf, implying that Zainab might already begin wearing it during her adolescent years, indicating a lesser degree of deliberation and choice.

In a later interview, Jette uses the phrase "very devout" in relation to a differentiation of the pupils, and when asked whom she is referring to, the teacher returns to the headscarf as a marker: "Uhm, Zainab, of course, because well she's now chosen to wear the scarf." When asked whether Jette then believes that wearing the headscarf is a choice made by Zainab, she says that she could not be sure. She motivates this doubt with reference to the degree of coverage by Zainab's particular scarf and the degree of uniformity between Zainab's and her mother's way of wearing it – by this time, Jette has met Zainab's mother, she says, and Zainab's mother "wears the scarf in the same way as her, where she uses that kind of beanie, the one that covers the whole neck and then with the scarf on top."

On one occasion while the teacher is describing her planning of the educational module on Religion, Jette mentions Zainab as someone who "might surprise" in terms of contributing to the content matter:

> "... because I think that maybe she might be more religious than one usually reckons ... but then again because in the 1st grade, the instant we started on Christianity she just plugged her fingers in her ears ... it was terrible."

Along with the pupil Bilal, who is diagnosed with ADHD and described by the teacher as the son of two illiterates, Zainab is characterized by Jette as a suspected defender of a 'true Islam.'

> ".. I think that Zainab – well she's hanging in there, but – but Zainab is terribly quiet during school hours ... very very quiet and ... and sometimes it's difficult to

figure out … and then she, well then apparently she picks up a lot more than you think, because she really isn't stupid … she's absolutely not stupid … but she- she also, once in a while I get this feeling that … for instance with Tülay whom she sits next to at the moment … that she kind of does this 'good Muslims do so and so,' I haven't actually heard her say that but that's just kind of the feeling I get, that she might you know in some way try to exert influence …"

Jette also mentions that she once overheard another pupil in the schoolyard say 'if you don't do this you will go to hell,' and even if Jette has never heard Zainab make a similar statement, the teacher has "this feeling" that she might.

In Zainab's case, her suspected 'true Islam'-preaching is supported by what Jette experiences as an unwillingness to learn about Christianity – something which the teacher describes as problematic. But at the same time, it is precisely through Zainab's (and Bilal's) perceived strong faith that Jette invests hope in their ability to contribute to the content matter, to "surprise" and "bring in something."

Besides her perceived 'strong Muslimness,' Zainab's 'Palestinianness' is placed in the foreground in Jette's descriptions. Zainab is also mentioned as problematically frequently absent, due to travels with her family. Jette suggests that these school absences might bring about the consequence that her parents, who live "in the ghetto," would be punished economically – thus presupposing that they depend on state benefits.[28] From Zainab's own description of what her parents do, however – for instance, that her father owns a grocery store – this does not in fact seem to be the case.

Something that appears repeatedly in the teacher's descriptions of Zainab is her quietness, something which "irritates" the teacher.

" … she's quiet, but I think – I mean this is what irritates me the most – that is that she goes to our language center where she of course steadily improves her skills … she's also quite technically gifted … we discovered this when we went to LEGO Dacta[29] … but she's too shy to ask those questions .. and that irritates me … because asking doesn't make you more stupid …"

---

28 In 2000, the mayor of the city Elsinore (north of Copenhagen) announced that he would deduct an amount from the unemployment benefits of parents every time their children were absent from school without legitimate reason. This was aimed particularly at so-called 'gypsies' in the municipality, and was heavily criticized as discriminatory and potentially illegal. The municipality of Elsinore did go ahead, but the practice was declared in conflict with the existing laws regulating unemployment benefits and stopped two years later. At the time of the interview with Jette, it was neither legal nor practiced to make such deductions in social benefits due to children school absence, but the debate has been ongoing ever since, as the national-populist Danish People's Party in particular has frequently put forward the proposal.

29 LEGO Dacta is the name of a brand of bricks from the Danish toy company LEGO produced with educational purposes, and the educational division of LEGO as such used to be called LEGO Dacta.

Though the teacher repeatedly describes Zainab's 'quietness' as problematic, the picture, however, looks different when considering the observations and registrations of speaking turns in the classroom. Zainab does not belong to the most quiet part of the class. The almost completely non-speaking are four majority pupils – Catharina, Christina, Marc, and Gaja – who, even though they make up one fourth of the total school class, are almost invisible in the counts of 'pupil raising hand' and successfully achieved speaking turns.[30] The quietness of these four pupils, along with Tülay and Kira, who also have fewer speaking turns than Zainab, are however never described as problematic by Jette.

Approximately two thirds of the 'hand-raising' (66.21%) and more than two thirds of the speaking turns (71.54%) are occupied by three pupils – Sulayman, Meriam, and Hassan – belonging to what I call the steering-group (*Styregruppe*. Dahllöf 1967, Lundgren 1972, Lindblad & Sahlström 2002:259) of the school class. Zainab belongs to the group of pupils that speaks less than this 'steering-group,' but she does speak, and when she does, she does so partly with teacher approval upon hand-raising and partly without prior teacher approval. The latter practice is, in general, the most accessible way of gaining a speaking turn, as it makes up 82.01% of the total 717 speaking turns that take place during the educational module. The rate of success is 60.14% by hand-raising and at least 75.34% for speaking without prior approval.

When Zainab maneuvers in this landscape, her way of using speaking turn strategies places her in the middle group of pupils with regard to numbers of speaking turns, but nonetheless the teacher deems her school behavior problematically quiet. Apart from this Jette describes Zainab as "rather well liked" and then adds that she is "probably the … the most Muslim of our girls … at least that's the impression you get."

In Zainab's self-descriptions, her 'Muslimness' also appears, namely, when I ask her to evaluate the educational module on Religion. She says that she found it "quite interesting" because they "could learn something about the Jews," about whom she did not "know anything *at all*" before, "only that they were Israelis and things like that." She also learned things about Islam that she had not known before even though "I'm Muslims."[31] More than being Muslim, however, she speaks quite extensively about the migration history of her family, particularly, when explaining about her family and their movements after the war in Lebanon, a situation that had scattered the family members in France, Sweden, and Denmark.

---

30 Pupils' speech took place in one of the following ways: A pupil was assigned a speaking turn upon hand-raising (12.41% of the total speaking turns); a pupil was assigned a speaking turn without prior hand-raising (5.58% of the total speaking turns); a pupil spoke without prior approval from the teacher, but as a reaction to something the teacher had just said (12.69% of the total speaking turns); a pupil spoke without prior approval from the teacher, and with no apparent prompt (69.32% of the total speaking turns).

31 Using the gramatically incorrect, yet in socio-dialect common singular plural [in Danish: *Jeg er muslimer*], as explained earlier.

Regarding school in general, Zainab says that she enjoys it, particularly the school subjects Needlework and Woodwork, where one can actually do things, but she also likes Math, English, and Danish. During the interviews, she seems attentive and amused by the situation. Compared to the other pupils, her answers are fairly long and she is very eager to get to listen to the interview afterwards. There is one thing, though, that Zainab does not enjoy about school, and that is when the teachers "scream." They mostly scream at the boys, but sometimes also at Tülay and herself:

> "So we're just sitting there, talking ... and then one time we were sitting in a group ... this group right ... and then it was Meriam she was talking ... I don't know who with ... and then it happened that she [the teacher, MB] just starts to scream at me ... and I haven't say – I haven't said anything at all."

What Zainab articulates here is not a critical evaluation of Jette's teaching and planning as such; rather, I interpret it as disapproval of the teacher's unrestrained behavior. Indirectly, Zainab thus questions the teacher's cultural Bildung capital – not on a subject matter-related professional level, but in terms of proper social conduct. For her part, the teacher describes Zainab in a similar way: It is her quiet behavior – not her skills – that are problematic.

6.1.3   The cultivated headscarf user

The first thing that Jette points out about Meriam's potential use of the headscarf is that her mother uses "that slightly more kind of modern headscarf" (in contrast to Sulayman's mother who just "wears a headscarf"). Jette's description of the occasion when she had in fact seen Meriam with a headscarf serves as a point of departure for emphasizing that, should Meriam eventually begin wearing headscarf, it would definitely be an act of choice, and furthermore, the result of an informed choice.

Jette is preoccupied with the special way that Meriam's mother wears her headscarf, namely as "an ordinary scarf tied in the nape," and emphasizes that Meriam's mother does not cover her neck. The teacher compares the scarf-wearing practice of Meriam's mother to "the way we would see it with Danish rural women in the fifties." With this image, she implies on the one hand a resemblance with a local Danish tradition, and on the other hand, she keeps the distance between herself and the 'backwardness' of the Muslim headscarf, which she assigns not only to the past, but also to a rural context, separated from herself by the phrasing "the way *we would see it* with Danish rural women." Meriam's mother thus appears in the teacher speech as (relatively) "modern," as well as more closely attached to "Denmark" than the other minority parents, while her Muslimness at the same time ties her to a past time and space.

The modernity aspect of Meriam's mother, as she appears in the teacher speech, rests on Jette's emphasis on the fact that Meriam's mother does not cover her neck. The lesser the extent of coverage by the scarf, the stronger the degree of supposed modernity and thus legitimacy, it appears, not least when contrasted with Jette's description of the headscarf worn by Zainab's mother and later also Zainab – "the one that covers the whole neck" – a headscarf practice that makes Jette doubtful of the existence of (informed) choice.

Still in context of the headscarf, Jette mentions that Meriam's mother was once interviewed by her labor union magazine, and in this interview she expressed an affinity to religion that surprised Jette. The fact that it was surprising becomes part of the legitimacy of the religious affinity, precisely because it signals the opposite kind of Muslimness than the 'preaching Muslimness' of which Jette suspects Zainab: Meriam's mother is devout, but manages her devotion with discretion.

Further elaborating on her Saturday encounter with Meriam and her mother, where Meriam wore a headscarf, Jette adds that she interpreted Meriam's wearing of a headscarf as located somewhere between child's play and an adolescent's experimentation.

> "[I'm] pretty sure that some of those young people when they get closer to- when they are close to completing their education and then are about to move on that they sometimes feel the need to make a statement ... both about them being both Muslims but also that they are good Muslims by wearing that scarf ... well, I think it's- that it's unnecessary ... but it's kind of I think that there is a- it seems that there is a movement underway in some places and that those who begin wearing it late in life actually seem to be, how can I put it, seem to be rather intelligent ... as if they are saying 'well they are not going to tell me that I can't, so I'll just go ahead and do it.'"

In these utterances, potential use of the headscarf is connected to educational aspirations and to people who are "rather intelligent," as well as it is interpreted as a form of resistance. Even if Jette finds it "unnecessary," should Meriam choose to wear the scarf to "make a statement," Jette connects this fictitious prospective scenario to a capacity to choose and to cultural and cultivated capital. Jette emphasizes that "if they have a, a choice that they can motivate and that is behind this, then it is quite alright." The legitimacy of headscarf wearing is thus dependent on degrees of educational capital and cultivation in the shape of choice and awareness.

Meriam belongs to the steering-group of the school class, along with the two minority boys Sulayman and Hassan. She is the second-most frequently speaking pupil in the class, and she succeeds in gaining a speaking turn by raising her hand almost three out of four times – which makes her more successful in this practice than Sulayman, who has the highest total number of speaking turns. Meriam is also highly successful in terms of speaking without prior teacher approval, as at least 90% of her attempts go without reprimands.[32] However, the teacher does not nearly

---

[32] During my registrations I did not note the specific occasion for each reprimand. Thus, I cannot say whether the reprimands were given for speaking without prior approval or for something else (for instance, speaking with the neighboring pupil). However, by deducting the number of

as often ask for Meriam's contributions on her own initiative (5 times) as she does with Sulayman (12 times). The positions and functions of these two steering-group pupils in the classroom text are indeed quite different, as will be elaborated in the next chapter. When Meriam enters the official text of the classroom, the high level of recognition that she receives from Jette when the teacher describes Meriam's (potential) use of headscarf plays out quite differently, as we shall see in Chapter 7.

6.1.4   The headscarf user who cannot be taken seriously

Opposite Meriam in the (potential) headscarf-wearing landscape delineated in the teacher descriptions, Jette places the pupil Leila. Jette does not find it likely that Leila would begin wearing the headscarf – and if she did, it could not be taken seriously. The reason for this judgment by Jette appears in her utterances as connected to Leila's mother who is "too chic"; more specifically, this is a particular kind of chicness that involves wearing make-up, something which Jette interprets as negating the very meaning of the headscarf: Something that shows off your body in a vulgar way, like wearing a bikini.

In Jette's other descriptions, Leila is likewise presented as neither acceptable in school terms nor as a Muslim. Her potential scarf-wearing could not be taken seriously, while her contributions or "stories," as the teacher phrases it, are treated by Jette as being off the mark. In the teacher speech, Leila is described as fundamentally lacking cultural Bildung capital in the form of an ability to conduct herself in accordance with social codes as well as the ability to form coherent sentences ("she's not all that articulate"). She is grouped by Jette at the bottom of the socioeconomic spectrum, along with the majority pupil Gry who is a "second-timer" (meaning that she has had to do the same grade twice), who is often absent, and about whose parents Jette says that the father has a criminal record and an addiction and the mother is an unskilled worker suffering from depression.

Besides describing Leila's school behavior and school appropriateness through comparisons with majority pupils at the socioeconomic bottom of the class, one of the main components in the teacher's assessment of Leila is the fact that she "like all of our other Palestinian children plus our Chinese boy" lives in 'the ghetto,' meaning the housing projects near the school.

Leila's interactions in the classroom are generally not acknowledged as valid contributions by Jette – not even as disturbing contributions, such as it is the case, for instance, with the ADHD-diagnosed, 'correct Islam preacher'-suspected Bilal. What Jette says about Leila is, for instance:

> "Leila is … a strange child … she can be like completely in her own world and look at her pencil and just like sit there and fiddle with it and you- sometimes you just kind of think 'what … is she daydreaming or is she completely indifferent to the rest of us or what's going on."

---

reprimands from the number of not prior-approved speaking turns, it is possible to conclude how many definitely went without reprimands, namely at least 75.35 on average.

When Leila does in fact participate in classroom conversations, Jette describes it as unusually out of context:

> "I mean, I think that – well I don't think that no matter who says something ... then I never think that it's something that you can't use ... or I mean, when- when Leila says 'what's that for?' and then you're just like 'OK then, we actually just went over this' and I just thought that we had been through this so many times ... so that everyone would have kind of gotten the point by now ..."

Like Zainab, Leila receives a relatively high number of reprimands compared to how much, or how little, she speaks (70.59% of her speaking turns without prior approval, and 55.55% in Zainab's case). The not-explicitly approved, but in practice legitimate way of conquering the right to speak, is apparently not as available to Zainab and Leila as it is to other pupils. Likewise, their behavior is regarded as inappropriate by the teacher in other ways. Both Leila and Zainab belong to the non-dominant, yet frequently speaking group, and they also more often than average use hand-raising as a strategy for gaining the right to speak. They both succeed in around half of their attempts.

At another point in the interview, when Jette is asked about the pupil contributions and which ones she finds useful, she answers with an example of what she does *not* find useful. In this example, Leila appears in comparison with the majority pupil Kira.

> "Well, Leila tells, the last time, then Leila starts to tell about the experiences of her parents[33] during the war [in Lebanon, MB] and that her mother's hair had turned grey and things like that ... right, and that is of course relevant, but- but she's not all that articulate ... and in her language ... so that her story actually becomes interesting to listen to ... but it was relevant ... but it was kind of, she- rhetorically said it in such a- such a strange way ... so you really needed to pay attention to her to figure out that it was actually relevant and not just some kind of blablablabla story ... right ... Kira sometimes pops out with these utterances that are not exactly totally irrelevant but sometimes it's like, 'OK, that might be just a bit too far out,' right ... not quite multi-relevant, but not un-relevant either."

Kira's socioeconomic background is described both by Jette and Kira herself with reference to the situation of her parents about whom they both say that the father is a craftsman and the mother is ill. Kira is one of the newer arrivals in the class, and is otherwise labeled by the teacher as "a weak girl." Kira is one of the few pupils who does not speak without prior approval from the teacher, but nonetheless she receives nine reprimands. Both Kira and Leila have difficulties being seen and recognized as pupils – and in Leila's case, she is also not recognized as 'a Muslim.' Leila's parents are not explicitly mentioned by Jette, which is unusual compared to

---

[33] It was in fact not Leila's parents, but her grandparents who, as Palestinian refugees, experienced the war in Lebanon.

the teacher's descriptions of the other pupils. The only thing Jette says about Leila's parents concerned her mother being chic in a manner that appeared to make headscarf-wearing unlikely as well as inappropriate.

Leila, for her part, describes the occupations of her parents with a degree of detail that makes her more comparable to Meriam than to the pupils with whom the teacher is inclined to group her. Her mother, Leila says, is "sort of a designer, only at home," and she also "works with child upbringing and those things at a college for social education."[34] Her father, who does not live with them, is a taxi driver.

A father who is employed, and a mother who does design from home and either teaches or studies at a teachers college for social education, would otherwise have been expected to equip Leila with a fair amount of educational capital, as compared to the rest of the school class. Apart from Meriam's middle-manager mother, all minority parents are either unskilled workers, small shop owners, unemployed, home-based, and/or attending language classes, while the majority parents are unemployed, on sick leave, home-based, or unskilled or skilled workers. The capitals of Leila's parents however, are neither emphasized nor attributed to Leila by the teacher. On the contrary, she is mostly described as irrelevant in relation to the subject matter, and also socially problematic, with a cultural Bildung capital somewhere between plainly counterproductive and non-existent. This is the context in which the talk of her prospectively inappropriate or non-serious use of the headscarf may be understood: Leila is placed at the bottom of 'the Muslim class (room) universe,' where the lack of acknowledgment of her educational capital and potential is matched by her perceived lack of Bildung potential as a Muslim.

6.2 To be or not to be legitimate, to be or not to be 'subject matter-relevant'

When differentiating the Muslim pupils by the headscarf as a marker, the teacher attaches capitals of a cultural (in the sense of cultivated) nature to Meriam, something that interacts with the (potential) practice of headscarf-wearing and adds legitimacy to it. In the case of Leila, in contrast, the same practice is described as not legitimate and not even to be taken seriously. Zainab's use of the headscarf is described as predictable and attached to piety – it is not illegitimate (as with Leila), but neither is it connected to cultural Bildung (as in the case of Meriam).

In the teacher's descriptions, legitimacy is closely tied to what she sees as the presence or absence of choice, and furthermore, the ability to motivate choice. The teacher thus connects legitimate use of the headscarf with educational capital and Bildung in the shape of choice and deliberation.

The use of juxtaposition to describe the pupils, as with Zainab and Meriam, is a feature that appears in several of the teacher's descriptions of the class. In what follows, Jette has named those of the pupils who have "other ethnic background"

---

34 "Pædagogseminarium": Educational training, today the equivalent of a bachelor's degree, for professions in day care institutions (pre-school).

(10 out of 17), and then she goes on to focus on those whom she believes to be Muslims, namely, all of them except "our Chinese" Xiang.

> "So then nine out of ten are Muslims ... and as far as I know they are all believers but- but I don't think- I think that those who I think are most devout ... well that's Sulayman, Zainab, and Meriam ... but then again they are also the ones to question things ... I mean Sulayman and Meriam and then Hassan ... and I find that healthy ... that they have a- they can definitely uhm justify why they think that their religion is the best and I think that's healthy too ..."

Zainab is equated here with Meriam and Sulayman as being among the "more devout," and is left out of the equation in the naming of those who "question things" and are able to "justify ... their religion," something which in the teacher's utterances is highly acknowledged. With the use of "but," however, the teacher implies that there is otherwise a contrast between being a devout Muslim and questioning things – with Sulayman and Meriam as exceptions.

As was the case with the utterances differentiating headscarf-wearing practices, the meaning of the content slips in the comment: What starts out as a category of religion and degrees of religious affinity is transformed into classifications attached to the school capital of the individual pupils. The "healthy" and legitimate qualities that are acknowledged in Meriam and Sulayman, are connected to the presumed ability to choose, to justify one's choices and "to question things." While these skills and qualities are also attributed to the third steering-group pupil Hassan (who is not attached to a strong degree of faith), they are not associated with Zainab. Neither is the opposite quality, however. Zainab is simply removed from the equation with the utterance, "I mean Sulayman and Meriam and then Hassan."

6.2.1   Qualifying in a subject matter sense, qualifying as religious – or not at all

The same pattern appears when looking into utterances that take their point of departure not in religion but in educational achievement-oriented categories.

Sulayman, Hassan, and Meriam are highlighted as particularly contributing pupils in all three teacher interviews – and as mentioned, do indeed account for two-thirds of the speaking turns, although they comprise less than one fifth of the total school class. When I ask Jette, prior to the beginning of the educational module, whom she expects to be contributing, she immediately names these three pupils. She then goes on to mention Yasin and Ahmed as pupils who will most likely say "some foolish thing or another," while she expects Zainab to "surprise" due to her presumed strong religious beliefs. Another possible surprise-contributing pupil is Gaja, according to Jette, again attributing this to Gaja's presumed devotion: "because she is, I think, perhaps the most Christian of the children ... at least she attends some kind of- some Church-hubbub ... some sort of scout-like thing you know."

The teacher then mentions Bilal as a potentially contributing pupil and justifies this expectation by saying: "He'll be like 'this is not good enough' and 'this is not Islam' and 'oh this is so terrible' … and 'this is not properly explained.'"

As a whole, the teacher names five pupils whom she connects with being qualified in a subject matter-related and educational achievement sense (in Danish: 'faglig') – subdivided between the qualified Hassan, Sulayman, and Meriam, and the unqualified Yasin and Ahmed – while three others are named as religiously qualified: Zainab and Bilal as devout Muslims and possible defenders of 'true Islam' and Gaja as "the most Christian of the children."

Gaja seems to be aware that she is perceived to be particularly Christian inasmuch as she explicitly dissociates herself from this notion when interviewed. She does not "believe in our own" – she believes in Buddha, she says. When asked how she knows about Buddha, she explains that her friend had been on a journey and came home with stories about how "other people" "sort of pray" and had brought books about Buddha, something which captivated Gaja: "Then I wanted to believe in it," an utterance immediately followed by another dissociation: "I have never been a Christian … that's just my grandmother."

To Jette's surprise, as expressed during a later interview, Gaja does not contribute at all during the entire educational module on Religion. Based on my registrations and observations, Gaja in fact does not attempt to occupy any kind of position in the classroom. Not once does she raise her hand or speak without prior teacher approval, and she has only one speaking turn – initiated by the teacher who explicitly directs a question to her. She receives a total number of three reprimands, and leaves her seat five times.

Gaja nonetheless does express appreciation of the educational module, and this pupil – whom the teacher primarily describes as "a bit odd," as a child with hygiene problems, and as someone who is, for the moment, "taking a leave mentally" – elaborates quite extensively on why she likes Religion as school content:

> "For instance Judaism sounds very interesting … and I'm also really excited about Islam because … I never heard anything about Islam (MB: no) and I think it's important to know something about them in any case the classmates, what they believe in (MB: yes) know a lot about it … so that you can have a shared conversation about it so that you don't just say 'oh, how stupid you are' and things like that … about things … because you don't know that if you haven't heard about it."

In the teacher's utterances about Gaja's ability to contribute to the content, however, the expectations invested in the pupil are attached to her perceived religious affiliation – expectations that are not met. The same is the case with Gaja's school capital in general, which was described by the teacher as acceptable but poorly utilized, while her cultural Bildung capital in terms of social conduct is described as remarkably low due to bad hygiene and an odd personality.

The only other 'majority' pupil who is explicitly attached to religion in the utterances of the teacher is Andreas, who is described as "completely Danish" and "not baptized." As with Meriam, the legitimacy of his religious (non-)affiliation is *choice* – his parents have "chosen not to baptize" Andreas in order for him to be able to "make the decision himself." In the socioeconomic landscape of the classroom, Andreas is placed in the sound end. His father is a craftsman and his mother is a trained office worker. The teacher places Meriam in the same part of the socioeconomic spectrum with a "modern" mother who is a middle manager and a father who might be uneducated, but does have a job and "smiles a lot."

While Andreas is considered to be qualified (in school terms) due to his explicit non-religion, Xiang – the only minority pupil whom the teacher does not think is Muslim – is considered to be neither qualified in a school- and subject matter sense nor religiously qualified: Xiang has problems expressing himself in Danish and, as far as Jette knows, cannot explain to which religion he belongs or does not belong. Xiang did once state that he thought he might be Hindu, but this was not something Jette took seriously. Judging by the briefness of the teacher's descriptions of the "kind and smiling" Xiang, it seems that she finds Xiang's qualifications or lack of qualifications as a pupil neither problematic nor very interesting.

6.3   Those in whom one can invest expectations

The three steering-group pupils – Meriam, Sulayman, and Hassan – are often highlighted by the teacher in the interviews, and often in relation to one another. For instance, during the description of Sulayman, Jette says:

> "He [Sulayman, MB] is quick-witted and he's articulate but he's learned to raise his hand as well ... and then we also have Hassan ... he's also quick-witted and articulate ... that's our Pakistani boy ... and then we have Meriam ... she's also quite quick-witted."

While many of the same categories are attached to Meriam and Sulayman, there are also a number of discrepancies. On the one hand, as in this comment, the quality of speediness, being "quick-witted" as well as the ability to articulate oneself is slightly less emphasized in relation to Meriam than to Sulayman. On the other hand, Meriam is explicitly marked as strong in Bildung capital in the descriptions of her possible future use of the headscarf. Sulayman is not as strongly attached to, or determined by, his mother's headscarf wearing as Meriam and the other female marked pupils are by the relation between 'the headscarf' and their respective mothers: This does not form part of the teacher's inflection of his Muslimness or his possession of various types of cultural Bildung capital.

6.3.1   *The adaptable unadapted*

"Sulayman ... is very bright ... Sulayman is king of the class." These are the words by which Jette opens her description of Sulayman – a description that goes on three times longer than the longest of the other pupil descriptions, and five times the description of Meriam, which is about average length.

In the classroom, Sulayman is one of the five pupils – among them also Hassan – seated in a position that faces both the teacher's desk and the majority of the other pupils. He squirms around on his chair and leaves his seat more often than any of the other pupils, and he has the highest number of speaking turns – substantially more than either of the other two steering-group pupils. He primarily seeks to gain speaking turns without prior approval from the teacher – mostly on his own initiative, but also with a high number of reactions to general questions posed by Jette during teaching. Around nine in ten of these not-explicitly-approved speaking turns are successful, which is to say, they are not reprimanded. Sulayman is also the pupil who receives the highest number of direct questions from the teacher. When Sulayman does raise his hand, however, he only gains a speaking turn about half the time, which makes his rate of success with this strategy lower than Hassan's and Meriam's.

The teacher explains Sulayman in two contradictory and yet complementary ways: On the one hand, he is having difficulties adjusting; on the other, he has precisely learned to adjust and, in this capacity, he contributes to maintaining order in the classroom. Sulayman is described as someone who enjoys a great deal of respect among his classmates – to such a degree that Jette thinks that they might be afraid of him – but he uses this respect to act as the teacher's mouthpiece, something of which Jette approves. As an example of this, Jette speaks of an episode during a fire drill in school where Sulayman took it upon himself to explain to another pupil why it was problematic that he had left school without mentioning it to the teachers.

> "... and then he said to him... 'because then they have to keep searching for you inside the school ... and then by having gone to the bakery without telling anyone you might end up causing the death of a firefighter' and I was just sitting there thinking, 'yes, that's in fact what I said last year' ... and then he just said and that was just really great."

She uses this example to show that her words have "a great impact" and goes on to say that it also shows that it is actually possible to put some sense into Sulayman, and that "he's one of those kind of pupils that- that you have to fight until they learn that you're in charge."

This sort of struggling with the "strong" Sulayman is also something that preoccupies Jette in the descriptions of Sulayman's family – descriptions that are unusually long and detailed. Sulayman's parents are divorced and Jette thinks that the mother "might not have been allowed to do a lot of things" while she was with the father, but that since the divorce the mother has "put quite a lot of effort into both getting out but also into learning Danish." Jette has the impression that the mother "might also try getting an education or at least learning enough Danish to get a job and be able to provide for herself and things like that." Such experiences are great, Jette says.

The teacher suspects that Sulayman might be quite a challenge for his mother. However, Jette invests hopes and expectations in her: Even if Sulayman's mother is poor in cultural Bildung as well as economic capital at the moment – with no job, no education, and limited skills in Danish – her aspirations to learn Danish and seek an education, or at least to be able to provide for herself, are described in acknowledging terms and thus recognized as relevant and legitimate in a cultural Bildung-sense by the teacher. The father, on the other hand, is described primarily as someone who has been hampering the potential of the mother – and in Jette's utterances, potential is equated with the capacity to speak Danish, with formal education, and with "getting out of the home."

The mother worries about Sulayman, Jette says, because the father and the older brother could be bad role models for him. The brother has "been through all kinds of provisions throughout his adolescent years" and ultimately ended up with "a striped view," meaning that the brother has been in prison. These potential maladjusted features and futures for Sulayman, in Jette's descriptions, are confined to the sphere of the boy's father.

Sulayman's self-descriptions are remarkably similar to the teacher's, as he interprets his own conduct as both maladjusted and legitimately adjusted.

When asked to present who he is, Sulayman replies:

> "I would say then that ... I am Sulayman ... I don't know what else I'd say, I'd say why do you ask that ... instead of just bringing some kind of who are you ... I already tried that and then I just said I'm Sulayman why do you ask ... and then I just say ... I just say, I'm a Muslim and ... I pray ... then that's it."

Sulayman likes the educational module on Religion because it allows him to learn more about other religions as well as his "own religion." He also likes "speaking English," and he "loves" to swim. Math and Nature-Technics are the school subjects that he likes the least, he says, and when I ask why, the following exchange takes place:

> S: Because the Math teacher is – she's always out to get me
> MB: How is she out to get you?
> S: I don't know because before I used to be cheeky (MB: yes) very cheeky. So she thinks I'm still cheeky and then she's out to get me
> MB: Did you stop being cheeky?
> S: Yes
> MB: Why?
> S: Because I thought long and hard ... I thought you never know if I'll be sent away to a children's home or something like that.

On the one hand, Sulayman here underlines his new adjusted self, and marks a before and an after in relation to this adjustment. On the other hand, he expresses having difficulties receiving the proper recognition of his new adjusted-ness.

For her part, Jette describes both Sulayman and his family in a double diagram: As a pupil, he is highlighted for his ability to express himself and for his intelligence. As such, he is described as having an intimidating effect on the other pupils, but this is leveled out by his willingness to utilize the fear-effect to enhance the disciplinary measures of the teacher. His maladjusted-ness lies in the fear he causes; this is what makes him unacceptable as a pupil (and at one point, this has actually been the cause for moving him to another school, something which he resisted, ultimately with success). His adjusted-ness lies in his ability and willingness to transmit discipline in accord with the teacher's efforts.

A similar diagram is at play in the teacher descriptions of Sulayman's parents, where the father represents fixity – restraining the mother from doing what she wants – and the danger of social maladjustment, with prison as the final destination, while the mother represents progressive motion, possibility, and the desire to adjust (= learning Danish). In fact, the father also attends school in order to learn Danish and improve his reading skills, but this is something Sulayman mentions, not Jette.

In Jette's descriptions, Sulayman's school legitimacy is attached to exactly his lack of school capital and his way of managing this. His background is attributed no educational capital whatsoever, and apart from economic capital in the shape of living in a four-room apartment that might be a cooperative ownership apartment, he does not possess much of this capital, either. His mother, however, is attributed some amount of cultural Bildung potential that derives from her being separated from the father. Within this double-sidedness, Sulayman appears as promising: against certain odds, attached to his father and brother, and with promising prospects in connection with the cultural Bildung potential attached to his mother, as well as his own ability – and willingness – to use his authority in the service of the teacher. The promising potential that the teacher attributes to the mother is also the context in which one should see Jette's lack of interest in the mother's headscarf: She is a bearer of the static, uneducated, and un-cultivated, but this is not necessarily permanent; the headscarf, thus, does not in itself become a determining marker in the teacher speech about Sulayman and his mother.

6.3.2   The cultivated and flexible Muslim

Both Sulayman's and Meriam's parents have migration histories related to Morocco, but in Sulayman's case, Jette only mentions it indirectly, whereas this Moroccan connection is the first thing the teacher highlights about Meriam: "Meriam is of Moroccan descent." Jette elaborates this by saying that the mother "grew up in Denmark," whereas the father "was brought here." She then continues describing Meriam's parents by saying that they are employed and "incredibly nice," and finally, by speaking of the mother's headscarf (something to which she continuously returns during the interviews).

In the descriptions of Meriam's parents, Jette places a lot of emphasis on the mother's stronger relation to Denmark – stronger than the father's and stronger than that of the other minority parents in the class. She is marked as non-Danish, but closer to Danish than others. She "functions well," Jette says. In the description of Meriam's mother being interviewed by her labor union magazine, Jette remarks:

> "She mentioned among other things that … it's not something she ever really said to me but I guess it was sort of implied that she prays the number of times she's supposed to … she might not always do it on the correct hours but then she'd catch up when she got home … so she's one of those devout Muslims I know of that- yes she wears the scarf but otherwise you don't really notice much that- that she's different."

Jette here emphasizes the flexibility of Meriam's mother's prayer practices – she is projected as a professional who adjust her religious practice to her working life. In this context, the headscarf becomes less problematic: Yes, she wears it, but "otherwise you don't really notice" that "she's different." The otherness that marks her is thus mitigated, characterized as not very remarkable after all. The positivity of this unremarkable otherness is emphasized in the following utterance:

> "her religion is important to her but- but it's also really a matter that stays between her and her God … she's not that kind of person who has to always correct others and those kinds of things and she definitely passes this on to her children."

The positive evaluation – and thus the legitimacy – of her non-remarkable religion is based on the fact that it "stays between her and her God," and by emphasizing that Meriam's mother is not the kind of person who corrects others, Jette implies that other Muslims do that: They correct others and are in various ways remarkable. Meriam's mother's remarkable headscarf instead becomes not all that remarkable, and it is in the context of this recognition-worthy way of managing otherness that the teacher interprets Meriam ("[the mother] definitely passes this on to her children"). Meriam is described as "incredibly skilled and incredibly ambitious, and incredibly pretty as well, and very sweet," and "very articulate and, and curious in the good sense." She is attributed optimal and unquestioned school capital, something which the teacher also derives from her interpretation of the mother, whose religiosity is flavored with Bildung. Or, rather, the way in which she practices her religion is interpreted in relation to her being evaluated as someone who is professional and "functions well." Meriam is also attributed ambitions, and thus she is the only pupil whom the teacher by presumption assigns an educational future.

The recognition of Meriam's school capital, however, does not seem to be reciprocated by Meriam when she describes her own relation to the teacher. Meriam is the only pupil who articulates a direct critique of the teaching content and organization. This is something she brings up while describing which school subjects she likes, and dislikes. Among the former are Danish, Physical Education, and Music. Meriam motivates her preference for Danish with the fact that she finds it challenging. Math, on the other hand, is "very easy," so she "finishes" quickly and "gets really bored." She says she likes to "be occupied … instead of just sitting there during classes drawing or something like that." The problem of boredom also comes up in her critique of the educational module on Religion – Meriam calls it "Christianity" – which "might be" the educational module she likes the least.

> "Because we just … first of all because we're not allowed to read by ourselves and then it's just because it's just that … well, we're just sitting there listening to what she's reading."

Meriam stresses, however, that even though she does not like the module, she still "pays attention." In these utterances she positions herself as someone who has the right to expect something from school instruction, and stresses her own ability to exercise legitimate school behavior by noting that she "pays attention" even in situations where she is bored. She lives up to the expectations of the instruction even if the instruction does not live up to hers. The teacher is only referred to as "she" and never by name, and is only mentioned in the context of criticizing the form of the activities included in the educational module. No other pupils articulate this kind of evaluation of the teacher's educational planning and practice.

In Meriam's case, a balanced Muslimness, represented by the ways of managing headscarf practice attached to her, and a high level of school legitimacy are connected. In the teacher's projections, the 'modern' headscarf becomes a sign of cultural Bildung capital in the shape of relation to Danishness, professionalism and the labor market. Whereas Meriam positions herself as someone who possesses the right to exercise recognition, Sulayman asks for recognition and is answered with recognition by the teacher for his attempts to adjust. When comparing the teacher's descriptions of Sulayman and Meriam, the latter is depicted sympathetically, but neither intensely nor emphatically (nor extensively), in contrast with Sulayman.

6.4 Summing up: the socioeconomic landscape

One pattern seems to be that minority pupils are first and foremost characterized by their non-complete Danishness. This can be overruled, however, by what the teacher describes as behavioral problems and thus social illnesses (such as the ADHD diagnosis). Where this is the case, references to non-Danish nationality and migration history recede. Considering the openings of each of the teacher's pupil descriptions, Jette says about minority pupils:

> "Zainab is Palestinian / Yasin is also of uhm Turkish descent / Then we have Hassan … Hassan is of Pakistani descent / Tülay is a Turkish girl / Ahmed is of Turkish descent / Xiang is Chinese."

About majority pupils, she says:

> "Christina has been with us all the way from pre-school class / Gaja is a somewhat strange girl / Gry has, like Leila, been part of the class from the end of 3rd grade / Catharina is probably the shortest in the class / Kira started around fall break in grade 4 / Marc is- lives alone with his mother, older sister and younger brother."

The only pupil descriptions that deviate from this pattern among the minority pupils is that of Sulayman, whose school- and social intelligence is in the foreground, and Bilal and Leila who are introduced respectively by way of a diagnosis and a comparison to a problematically absent majority pupil. Among the majority pupils, Andreas' non-baptized but complete Danishness is highlighted: "then we have Andreas … Andreas is completely Danish."

After describing around two thirds of the pupils, the teacher begins to reflect on the fact that she has not mentioned nationality and (lack of) migration history in relation to majority pupils. This happens during a description of the majority pupil Catharina:

> "School-wise [fagligt] she does quite well … her spelling is not magnificent, but when you ask her to give it another try then- then she usually gets it right … and is completely Danish … both parents are Danish there also … those children about whom I haven't mentioned their parents background they've been … as far as I know anyway … Danish both of them."

The exceptional opening "Andreas is completely Danish" appears after this reflection, and this particular pupil's relation to Danishness and Christianity becomes a prominent feature in the rest of the description. This is a feature that also characterizes the description of Gaja, who is highlighted for her status as baptized, and hence, for her affinity – in the teacher's, but not in Gaja's own view – to Christianity, and thus, her perceived school qualifications as a Christian; someone whom one can expect to contribute to the school content as a Christian. In the same way, the teacher invests school expectations in the otherwise problematically quiet Zainab, due to her supposedly strong affinity to Islam.

Compared to Leila, both Zainab and Bilal are placed on the acceptable side of Muslimness. Leila is neither acceptable school-wise nor as a Muslim. Her potential future headscarf would be inappropriate, her stories are off-topic, and she is projected as someone who possesses no cultural Bildung capital whatsoever: She has no proper social codes and no skills to articulate comprehensively. At the bottom of the socioeconomic landscape of the school class, she is located alongside the frequently absent majority girl Gry, with her criminal father and her mentally ill mother. Leila's working father and studying mother are admitted no place when capitals are counted.

The majority pupils generally appear outside the category of religion (with Gaja and Andreas as two exceptional figures in the teachers speech). In contrast, minority pupils are attached not only to their families' migration histories but also and not least to religion (in Xiang's case, by describing his lack of religion, after which he slips out of the landscape of religious categories). The pupils whom the teacher categorizes as Muslims in that respect differ from Xiang. The kind of Muslimness and the degree of acceptableness attributed to them appear as proportional to the degree of school capital and cultural Bildung capital, in a broader sense, attributed to them, while markers connected to Muslimness also form part of the attribution of Bildung capital. The degree of Bildung is also connected to the pupils' respective capabilities of adjusting, their relative dispositions for and capacities to choose, as well as their educational capital in the shape of their parents' educations and the pupils' own potential educational futures. Muslimness can be more or less cultivated and more or less strong in capital: the stronger in capital – the more passable and legitimate.

Muslimness can, in other words, be seen as a feature in the social classification structure of the school class; as inflected in the pupils' relations to forms of capital and as a contributing part of what is recognized or not recognized as capital. With regard to economic capital, all pupils in the school class bear quite low dispositions in relation to social space in a macro-sense, but recontextualized in the micro-social space, cultural Bildung capitals become particularly significant within the differentiated class structure of the classroom. In the pedagogized social economy, Muslimness becomes a parameter of social class, higher as well as lower.

7. Production of 'the Muslim subjects'

In this chapter I will turn to the official text of the classroom, where a selected text from plenary speech about the module content is analyzed in order to explore how curricular knowledge is produced through teacher and pupil speech, which is to say, how knowledge and subjects are produced in the practiced classroom curriculum. The text sample selected for this language-oriented analysis shows how "wedding ritual in Judaism" is transformed into 'Friday prayer in the mosque' when the teacher's presentation gets superseded by interaction with the pupils. Simultaneously, a pupil comes to be placed within the content: The teacher speech includes one of the pupils not as a pupil but as a Muslim, and situates this pupil as a participant in 'Friday prayer.' Another pupil is excluded from the category 'Muslim' through the teacher's disregard of her contribution though nonetheless incorporating it, albeit in a slightly but significantly altered form, by connecting the pupil's utterance to a nebulous text outside of the classroom. By installing pupils and their (assumed) experiences inside the curricular content, different spaces for being a 'Muslim subject' are produced.

More specifically, the analysis will show how comparison, when deployed as a strategy for handling religion, attains a special meaning when combined with the incorporation of pupil experience.

In addition to the teacher Jette, the speakers in the selected text sample are the pupils Sulayman and Meriam. The classroom conversation in the sample takes place after a longer teacher-initiated, one-way presentation from a text book, a presentation that is converted into a conversation by a content-related question from Sulayman. After an exchange between Jette and Sulayman, Meriam enters the official text of the classroom, namely by uttering opposition to what Jette presents as knowledge about Islamic rituals. Neither Sulayman nor Meriam positions themselves as Muslims in their utterances, but are addressed and incorporated as such in Jette's responses. The question that initiates this sample is thus not related to Islam, but to the topic of Jette's teaching on a more general level, namely 'ritual.' But Jette answers by placing Sulayman inside the content that now shifts from 'Jewish wedding' to 'prayer in Islam.'

The overarching analytical question to be explored in this chapter is how relations between the content of teaching and the agents in the teaching situation can be understood. The text sample is therefore read through a lens focusing on how the speech in the classroom produces both agents and content, as well as relations between the two; how 'religion' is transformed into knowledge, and how 'pupils' are both exposed to and made into knowledge themselves.

In the analysis, I focus on the double role of the agents as both speakers and content of speech. More specifically, I look into the relations between speakers and themes: How are topics and themes projected between content and speakers? In other words: How is the process of topic projection related to the shifts between speakers? I read the text sample with the use of classroom research concepts, such as Topic Related Themes (TRT) (Mehan 1979, as applied by Chouliaraki 1998) and elements of Initiation-Response-Evaluation (IRE) (Lindblad & Sahlström 2002:250), particularly focusing on negative and positive evaluation, respectively.

Another reading strategy is the exploration of relations between speech and context, examining how connections and ruptures between statements – and between statements and text outside of the text (intertextuality) – are established. Furthermore, I identify which persons and objects are designated by the speech, and to what or whom they are attached. And finally, I look at how the persons and objects are inflected – what is put in relation to *truth*, which degrees of connection to truth are established, and which degrees of *obligation* are installed between the persons and the objects appearing in the speech.

With the intermediary concept of figures (Chapter 3), I then interpret the analysis through a Foucauldian lens, rendering visible the ways in which subjects and objects appear in the speech.

Two Topic Related Themes (hereafter, TRT) appear in the text sample, and the grammatical analysis of these TRTs will concentrate on how content and persons – knowledge and subjects – are mutually inflected. In other words: How are speakers and themes organized between the categorical and the modal? And in this context: Which 'persons' appear in the speech, and to whom and what are they attached?

Consequently, the analysis focuses on the use of modality and on mood persons and other persons, as well as on the places to which the text points (person- and place deixis). These reading strategies are complemented by considering the meaning of nominals and verbs, not least transitivity – asking what is realized through verbal groups, and how this represents, for example, such categories as 'ritual,' 'Islam,' and 'pupils.' Other recurring analytical pivots will be intertextual references and the use of presuppositions.

7.1 Situating the text sample: educational module and lesson

On the day that the conversation in the selected sample plays out, the educational module has reached its third session, and it is the first lesson of the day. The general subject is (still) Judaism, and the teacher starts by summing up where they had left off in the previous lecture: the part of the Judaism chapter in the text book titled "From cradle to grave." Jette repeats what they had discussed previously on the subjects of circumcision and Bar and Bath Mitzvah, and then arrives at the topic: the wedding ritual. No pupils are engaged in the classroom speech yet – it is solely teacher presentation.

When Jette has completed the part about the wedding ritual, she sums up the different rituals and then turns to the funeral ritual. At this point, Sulayman initiates by asking: "What does ritual mean?" whereupon a series of interactions occur between the teacher and Sulayman, and then between the teacher and Meriam.

Lastly, the teacher returns to Sulayman. Over the course of these exchanges, the theme changes from 'Jewish wedding' to 'Friday prayer' and 'Islam.'

7.1.1 Comparisons, symbols, and embodiments

During the teacher presentation, Jette has presented circumcision as a 'covenant symbol,' through which one becomes Jewish – and compared it to circumcision as a covenant symbol in Islam. Bar and Bath Mitzvah are presented as 'rituals' and compared to confirmation, which is located "in church." For these two comparisons, the teacher alternates between reading from and commenting on or paraphrasing the text book section concerning the Jewish wedding ritual. She particularly focuses her attention on the crushing of glass, and then – taking a detour from the text book – adds the consumption of salt and bread as well as "some wine." The first element of the ritual is related to an act of remembrance – namely remembering the destruction of the temple – and the other, to a hope that the couple will always be able to feed themselves, she states. Both aspects are thus explained by the teacher as metaphors and symbols: practical and concrete actions pointing toward something else, or rather another level of meaning. From this dimension of ritual as phenomenon, Jette then turns to comment upon the biological necessity of salt: something "very important for humans," without which their bodies get "really strange" to the extent of "not really being able to function," she remarks, referring also to the expression "the salt of life."

The significance of the crushing of glass, as well as the theme of rituals serving as demarcations of key points in individuals' life cycles, are topics that the teacher draws from the text book. The speech about salt and bread – along with the explanation of the meaning of these elements – is something that Jette adds on her own initiative. With this addition, she confers a dimension of 'everyday life' and biological necessity to the text book understanding of rituals, in which rituals are described on a practical as well as a symbolic level.

I would characterize this addition by the teacher as an instance of the formation of knowledge in which the body as a material occurrence becomes central, in combination with a knowledge that presents ritual practice as something else and something more than simple concrete actions – something that reaches beyond the agents and their bodies. The questions are then: How do these understandings of rituals play out when pupils enter the stage?

7.1.2 Text sample

Note on translation: The translation of samples from the classroom text is to be understood as an illustration of the Danish-language original, seeking to match the way the speakers use language in the classroom. Where the text appears as incoherent or when there is an incorrect use of language, this mirrors the character of the spoken language in the Danish version of the text. Grammatical features such as modality, which is central to the analysis, are difficult to translate; therefore, the Danish words are included in the text sample, as well as in the quotes throughout the analysis, when necessary. Another issue concerns the fact that, in Danish, the speakers use two different pronouns that both translate to 'you':

'Du' primarily (and most frequently) refers to the singular definite 'you,' but – especially in Copenhagen – can also function as the plural indefinite. The word 'man' bears the meaning of the plural indefinite 'you.' Thus, the Danish word is noted in [ ] every time 'you' is used. (Translating the Danish 'man' as the indefinite 'one' in English would suggest a misleadingly high degree of formality, and furthermore, would render invisible the potential double meaning of 'du' in Danish). The third meaning of 'you' in English – plural definite – is 'I' in Danish.

For original Danish version: Appendix A.

<u>TRT1: Ritual becomes 'Friday prayer': Jette and Sulayman[35]</u>
1   Jette (teacher): Yes
2   Sulayman: What does ritual mean?
3   Jette: ritual is that (hesitates) every time you [du] are in (hesitates) the mosque with
4   someone on Fridays (pause) then you [I] actually do the same things
5   Sulayman: Yes.
6   Jette: What the imam sa- what the imam says varies a bit [lidt forskelligt = slightly
7   different] but you [du] start as a good Muslim you [du] start washing from your
8   hands to your elbows you [du] wash your face and you [du] wash your feet
9   you [du] leave your shoes outside and you [du] enter (pause) then maybe you [du]
10 more or less have a somewhat particular spot where you [du] go to sit where
11 you [du] prefer- like to sit when you [du] pray maybe you [du] also have a
12 (hesitates) little thingy on your head
13 Sulayman: I don't
14 Jette: no but many people do but maybe that's part of being a grown-up I don't
15 know but (hesitates) then what takes place- what takes place during Friday prayer
16 is something sort of that has to do with that you [du] could tell me that first we do
17 this and then we do that and then we do that and then the imam says something it
18 varies a bit [lidt forskelligt] and then this happens and then that happens. So some
19 things differ a bit [lidt forskellige] but the things that differ a bit [lidt forskellige]
20 are still the same because they occur at the same time during (pause) what takes
21 place (pause) so when you [man] say that there are some things that are very alike
22 that happen (pause) often then you [man] call it a ritual (pause) for instance it's
23 a ritual that- that (hesitates) Muslims before they pray must wash face and hands
24 and feet (pause) to show respect (pause) so you [man] begin with that (pause)
25 and (hesitates) I'd believe that if you [du] look at (hesitates) a lot of those people
26 you [du] know (pause) if you [du] just look at one of them you'll [(vil) du] see that
27 they have the same way of doing things (pause) maybe someone would start by
28 washing hands and then maybe they wash their left arm before they wash their
29 right and once you [man] start getting such habits about how exactly you [man] do
30 things then you [man] do it almost the same way every time.

---

35 The samples have been selected from recordings of all the sessions in the educational module which, as already mentioned, consisted of plenary sessions. These recordings have been transcribed selectively and synoptically and compiled with my observation notes.

TRT2: An order of things? Jette and Meriam (and Sulayman ...)[36]
31 Meriam: Jette it is something you [man] must do each time you [man] must
32 begin with-
33 Jette: yes
34 Meriam: ... then you [man] do
35 Jette: yes (pause) and // so that's a ritual //
36 Meriam: // Jette Jette it is actually // some-
37 Jette: // but it // doesn't actually say- it doesn't actually say that you [du]
38 must wash your feet first (hesitates) start with your big toe and finish with your
39 pinky toe or that you [du] must wash your face first but many people if you-
40 Meriam: there is an order in which you [man] do these things
41 Jette: there is an order in which you [man] do these things
42 Meriam: yes
43 Jette: but then it says- does it say that one hand comes before the other
44 or something?
45 Meriam: (hesitates) you [man] start with the right always
46 Jette: you [man] always start with the right (pause) so it is- maybe it says so but
47 otherwise some people might do it slightly differently [lidt forskelligt],
48 yes Sulayman
49 Sulayman: I mean (hesitates) you [man] don't always have to wash in a mosque
50 maybe you [man] did it at home (pause)
51 Jette: yes (pause) but then it's because they trust that you [du] have gone through
52 that ritual before you [du] arrive (pause)
53 Sulayman: but when I- when I enter I've already washed [...]

7.2 Ritual as the structuring theme – Sulayman as the content

From the moment that Sulayman poses his initiating question (2), 'ritual' in Jette's speech (3–30) becomes more than the topic: it becomes the structuring tool of the conversation. Ritual as an overarching topic of TRT1 is then filled with the content "you" [du] (referring to Sulayman) as well as material processes of acting ("do," "wash," etc.) attached to descriptions of Islamic prayer.

By referring back to 'ritual,' Sulayman ("you") is attached to "the imam" and "those people" who do all sorts of things in "the mosque" (wash themselves, pray, etc.). "You" (which does not only refer to the conversational interactant Sulayman, but also functions as the indefinite plural 'you'), along with the other designated persons and the actions carried out by them in the mosque, thus becomes the theme related to the topic 'ritual.'

When Meriam enters the conversation (31), her contribution does not, as with Sulayman's, become a point of departure for the teacher's response. When Sulayman asks, "what does ritual mean," he is transformed into thematic content by the teacher, as the Jewish wedding is turned into Islamic prayer, and the described religious practices are attached to the pupil, the interactant. The contribution of

---

36 The sign // indicates two speakers at the same time. The sign – indicates interruption or, when the same speaker continues to speak afterwards, self-interruption.

Meriam, however, is not tied into the conversational structure by the teacher, who instead returns to the topic 'ritual' as a way to close Meriam's speaking turn. Whereas 'ritual' structures both TRT1 and TRT2, it does so in different ways: by means of incorporation and attachment, and by means of exclusion, respectively. The content filled into 'ritual' also changes between TRT1 and TRT2. In the first case a "you" [du] attached to Sulayman, an "imam" and "those people"/"they" (the grown-ups, the 'Muslims') as well as a sample of them ("many," "someone") become the designated persons, the "mosque" becomes the space, and "Friday," the time. In TRT2, 'ritual' becomes content-filled with "must do" and "do" attached to "an order," and the teacher speech does not install the conversational interactant Meriam as part of the content, as with Sulayman in TRT1.

How exactly this plays out can be explored by taking a closer look at the ways in which the speech organizes speakers and themes.

7.2.1   TRT1: 'You' and 'someone' in the mosque on Fridays

TRT1 consists of seven speaking turns: Four are occupied by Jette and three by Sulayman. Content-wise, the TRT is initiated by Sulayman, to whom Jette assigns the right to speak, most likely as a reaction to Sulayman raising his hand. Sulayman pulls out the word 'ritual' from the last part of Jette's theme 'wedding' and the introduction to the next theme 'funeral.' While Sulayman simply asks "what does ritual mean," Jette, in her response, adds another theme: Something that takes place in the mosque on Fridays. At first, the mood person of the utterance is a singular definite "you" followed by a plural definite "you" ("every time you [du] are in (hesitates) the mosque with someone on Fridays (pause) then you [I] actually do the same things"). This can also be viewed as an implicit initiation directed at Sulayman, who responds with a confirming "yes" (5).

While maintaining her speaking turn, Jette continues to explain what takes place in the mosque, while keeping focus on what "you" [du] do (5–12). Another person – a non-interactant – is now designated: "the imam." Furthermore, in the next utterance, Jette's speech places a "little thingy" on Sulayman's head and thus initiates his third and last speaking turn, in which he objects to wearing the "little thingy" ("I don't") (13). By responding, he does however accept having been placed by the teacher's speech inside the mosque and thus having been made part of the content in the phenomenon 'ritual,' now transformed into Friday prayer.

At first, Jette evaluates his response positively by recognizing his objection ("no"), only then to introduce the demarcating "but," establishing both contradiction and alternative. This provides the basis for a continuation of her former claim about the "little thingy": "many people do but maybe that's part of being a grown-up." "Many" thus replace "you" as bearers of the "thingy," and the teacher then adds a reservation – "I don't know" (14–15) – which makes it more difficult to contradict the utterance. From then on, Jette continues elaborating what "takes place during Friday prayer" until the moment when Meriam interrupts her with another initiation.

In TRT1, 'ritual' becomes 'Friday prayer' flavored with persons that become attached to it and populate it. In particular, a 'you' that is both individual and general serves a double purpose. Installing the interactant Sulayman in the context brought to life in the utterances, the pronoun 'you' thus transforms him from a pupil asking a general question into a part of the content, which is no longer Judaism, but Islam. The fact that the designating 'you' [du] (in Danish, or more specifically, in Copenhagen dialect) simultaneously bears the meaning of a general (plural indefinite) 'you' adds a generalizing touch to the utterance.

When looking more closely at Jette's last, lengthy speaking turn in TRT1 – in which she speaks of things that "differ a bit" [lidt forskellige] but are "still the same," while installing Sulayman in the mosque along with the imam and the grown-ups doing all sorts of things – she uses the (primarily) singular definite 'you' [du] all along, except in the two instances of summing up. Here, she switches to the plural indefinite 'you' [man], thus using it to generalize the knowledge her speech has produced with the definite "you" as a central material:

> "so when you [man] say that there are some things that are very alike that happen (pause) often then you [man] call it a ritual" (21–22)
> "and once you [man] start getting such habits about how exactly you [man] do things then you [man] do it almost the same way every time." (29–30)

Sulayman, as the interactant, along with the non-interactants – the "many," the "they," the "some people," the "someone," and the "imam" (all mood persons attached to 'Muslims') – come to represent something about which one can possess a common knowledge: a common knowledge about a specific religious practice. The conversational interactant is thus held responsible for the actions described in the utterances, and as such he is made into both Muslim and knowledge.

7.2.2   TRT2: What you do and what it says

In TRT2, Jette and Meriam have six speaking turns each (before Sulayman enters the conversation). The TRT is initiated by Meriam's not-prior approved speaking turn (31), in which she calls attention to herself by uttering Jette's name.

The pupil does not wait for Jette's acknowledgment and assignment of the right to speak before she continues: "it is something you [man] must do each time you [man] must begin with-." The "yes" with which Jette then interrupts her has several functions. It is an attempt to close down Meriam's speaking turn, rather than a positive evaluation, and at the same time it neutralizes the potential conflict between what Jette has just said and the reaction from Meriam. Meriam nevertheless seeks to keep her speaking turn, an attempt Jette meets with a repeated "yes" and a return to 'ritual,' thus indicating that Sulayman's original question has now been answered and the topic is closed. Unlike with Sulayman's utterances in TRT1, Jette does not incorporate Meriam's utterances into her own speech.

When Meriam insists on regaining her speaking turn – again by uttering the name of the teacher (twice) (36) – the speaking turns go back and forth between them. Four speaking turns to Jette and three to Meriam play out with a number of interruptions and occasions with more than one speaker speaking at a time, indicating struggle.

When Jette, after Meriam's repeated insistence, responds with the demarcating "but," (37) the teacher recognizes that what Meriam says is in fact contradictory to what she said herself. This opens a space for Meriam to articulate her point, namely that "there is an order in which you [man] do these things." Jette then repeats Meriam's point – only to add: "but then it says- does it say that one hand comes before the other or something?" This question does not only signal skepticism but also introduces a new element: a reference to a nebulous text outside of the text. With "does it say …," Jette presupposes that Meriam is referring to something written, to enshrined scriptures in which 'the order of things' is prescribed, rather than to religious and ritual practices. Meriam, however, has not uttered anything about what is written. She speaks about what is done. She describes this 'doing' as relatively stable, but it is Jette who adds stability in the form of scripture.

The teacher then concludes that "maybe it says so" – attaching a low degree of usuality and probability to the recognition of Meriam's point, and through this weakening she adds an invalidation of the stability of ritual practice suggested by Meriam: "but otherwise some people might do it slightly differently" (47). In other words: There is no ritual order. Simultaneously, she maintains the interpretation of Meriam's utterance as referring to something stated in a written text ("it says so").

Jette thus maintains the meaning ascribed to Islamic rituals in TRT1 as something characterized by flexibility and attached to individual and personal choices. Jette allocates and attaches Meriam's objection to this instability to a Muslimness in which Islamic practice is identified with scriptures/holy scripture, in other words, rituals as prescribed by the Qur'an. By interpreting Meriam's argument as derived from scriptures, Jette presupposes an identification between Meriam and a literalist or fundamentalist Muslimness. After repeating and then re-articulating Meriam's utterance in a way that includes her point only to contradict it by returning to articulations from the teacher speech in TRT1, Jette emphatically returns the word to Sulayman by a double designation: "yes" and "Sulayman."

7.3 Intimacy and distance

A remarkable difference between TRT1 and TRT2 is the use of mood persons and the designation of persons. In TRT1, the teacher uses the definite singular "you" [du] which Sulayman accepts and implicitly recognizes by using "I." Jette furthermore uses a number of designations of persons (person deixis) – "those people," "many," "they," "someone" which all signal 'Muslims' – and, when summing up, the use of an indefinite plural 'you' functions as a diffuse mood person flavoring what has been said with the quality of something from which to generalize.

Meriam, in contrast, consequently uses the indefinite plural 'you' [man], indicating a distance, something which is underlined by the fact that she chooses not to elaborate on the personified speech of the teacher. Jette seemingly accepts this distance, although upon repeating Meriam's utterance she adds "some people" who "might do it slightly differently." The teacher does not explicitly place Meriam inside the content or as part of the content in the way that she does with the willing and cooperating Sulayman. However, by attaching Meriam's utterances to a nebulous text outside of the text, equating the pupil's insistence on stability of practiced rituals with adherence to enshrined scriptures, the teacher does indirectly install Meriam as part of the content. More specifically Meriam becomes the negation of the flexible and choice-flavored 'Muslim' that Jette – with Sulayman as interactant – projects in her teaching.

When Jette re-assigns Sulayman the right to speak at the end of TRT2, Sulayman starts off by adopting the grammatical choice of Meriam. He no longer situates himself inside the mosque where the teacher's speech left him, but speaks of an indefinite plural 'you' [man] who "don't always have to wash in a mosque maybe you [man] did it at home." His attempt at opposing the attachment of the educational content to his own body does not last for long, however. When Jette responds by re-installing Sulayman inside the content "then it's because they trust you [du] have gone through that ritual before you [du] arrive," he – after a slightly oppositional "but" – adopts the teacher's choice of singular definite 'you' [du], returning to his formulation in TRT1 as cooperating subject of the presented and discussed actions: "when I enter I've already washed [...]."

7.4 Modality at work

The differences in how ritual is filled with content in TRT1 and TRT2 becomes particularly visible when looking at the speakers' uses of modality. In TRT1, the teacher speech is characterized by the fact that actions and persons are formed and differentiated as flexible, unpredictable, and attached to intentionality. 'Islamic prayer practice' thus becomes something unstable and subjective. The only kind of stability ascribed is one attached to habits and as such connected to the bodies and preferences of subjects, just like the flexible intentionality. This is what Meriam objects to, by – so it seems – pulling the content back toward Jette's initial presentation from the text book. The contradictions and differentiations, the oppositional and cooperating strategies within the speech, emerge more clearly when further exploring the different uses of modality in the sample.

7.4.1 'Muslims' as flexible, unpredictable, and attached to intentionality

In order to fully grasp the role of modality in TRT2, it is necessary to take a closer look at the teacher speech in TRT1 – the speech to which Meriam's initiating objection is a reaction. Sulayman does not use degrees of modality in his utterances, but the teacher does, quite a lot. A recurrent feature of Jette's speech is the expression that "it varies a bit"/"differ a bit" [lidt forskelligt, lidt forskellige]. With this expression 'Islamic prayer' becomes flavored by flexibility and non-factuality. The same function is at play in the expression "very alike": things are

103

both the same and yet not the same, inasmuch as "very" in the space between 'yes' and 'no' exactly indicates something non-categorical. Circumstantial information – information describing the circumstances surrounding 'the things' – is in some of Jette's utterances used in such a way that the utterances contradict and more or less neutralize each other:

> "... the things that <u>differ a bit</u> [lidt forskellige] are still <u>the same</u>" (19–20)
> "once you start getting such habits about how <u>exactly</u> you [man] do things then you [man] do it <u>almost</u> the same way every time." (29–30)

In these utterances, "differ" (forskellige) and "same" (ens), "exactly" (præcis) and "almost" (næsten) contradict each other in ways that seem to void the given information of content. The same goes for the utterance "<u>more or less</u> have a <u>somewhat particular</u> spot" (10) – with "more or less" (mere eller mindre) and "somewhat" (nogenlunde) precisely *not* pointing at a particular spot.

When turning to another type of modality, a similar pattern appears. The objects of the speech are invested with an unpredictable and contradictory character of usuality and frequency through expressions such as "some things that are very alike" (noget der er meget ens) followed by "that happen (pause) often" (som sker (pause) ofte). While "very" (meget) in "very alike" (meget ens) indicates that "some things" (noget) are less "alike" (ens) than if "alike" (ens) was used alone, the mood adjunct "often" (ofte) indicates median usuality, meaning not a high degree of usuality. Simultaneously, Jette makes use of adjuncts marking reinforcement and weakening, respectively: "I'd believe that [...] if you [du] <u>just</u> look at one of them you'll [(vil) du] see that they have <u>the same way</u> of doing things" (27). The weakening adjunct "just" (bare) functions as a confirmation of how usual "the same way" is, while the use of a metaphor of modality ("I'd believe that" (jeg vil tro at)) functions as a distance to the truth value of the utterance – it introduces a reservation. A sense of usuality is further established with the utterance "<u>every time</u> you [du] are in (hesitates) the mosque with someone on Fridays (pause) then you [I] <u>actually</u> do the same things" (3-4) by the use of the adjunct "actually" (faktisk) which strengthens the utterance in relation to the circumstantial adjunct "every time" (hver gang).

The speech thus presents 'the things,' 'Friday prayer,' and 'ritual' in terms that point in opposite directions: Things happen usually – and also unusually, or less usually.

7.4.2 They, you, and the good Muslim

The same feature in TRT1 is at play with regard to the mood persons who are ascribed certain actions and sensations, but at the same time are enclosed with the word "maybe" – a word that is attached not only to the relation between the speaker and the utterance, but also must be understood as attached to the described actions as they are carried out by 'you' [du]. This ascribes the mood person a certain flexible unpredictability, indicating choice and taste. This also becomes visible in the ways in which the speech installs a high degree of inclination in relation to the mood person 'you' [du], for instance in utterances such as: "where you [du] prefer-like to sit." The mood adjunct "gerne" (the Danish word translated as "prefer"), supported by "like to" (kan lide), indicates an inclination and a taste of the "you": it is a "you" flavored with choice and positive preferences and thus intentions and a high degree of inclination indicating the willingness of the "you." The intentional inclination of the "you" ('you' being the addressee attached to the pupil) is expressed through the teacher's speech by a deontic modality wrapped in an informative utterance: "You" thus becomes not only the interacting addressee of the speech, but also a (subject-like) object about whom the information concerns.

Deontic modality is also at work when teacher speech attaches modality to "Muslims"/"they"/"many," for instance when "Muslims before they pray must wash face and hands and feet" (23-24) (where deontic modality also appears in informative speech). But unlike the intentional "you" [du] marked by individuality, "Muslims"/"they" are organized in a practice surrounded by a high degree of obligating precept – they "must" do certain things.

When presenting 'Friday prayer' and 'ritual,' Jette thus uses modality to express (low degree of) usuality/probability, (high degree of) inclination, and (high degree of) obligation.

The collective of Muslims are ascribed necessity while the "you" (the specific pupil, the specific Muslim) – simultaneously the object and addressee of the speech – is ascribed with an individual direction, an individuality marked by unpredictability and non-precision.

The young, individual Muslim "you" appears through the teacher speech in the company of, but also as an observer of, the grown-ups "they"/"someone"/ "many"/"some people" – Muslims – and all of these mood persons are situated in the mosque, performing certain rituals that are "the same" and yet "differ." The mood persons – the interactant as well as the non-interactants – are solely articulated within a positive polarity. In other words, the teacher speech exudes goodwill. Being a "good Muslim" is described as something positive as well as something upon which the teacher is entitled to comment.

7.4.3   There are some things you must do

When Meriam enters the conversation (TRT2), it seems that she does so by linking up to what the teacher has just said about 'rituals.' So why, then, does Jette not incorporate and include Meriam's contribution in the teacher speech, as she did with Sulayman's contribution? A closer look at their respective use of modality shows that there is in fact a contradiction at play in Jette's and Meriam's utterances. This contradiction is the primary information in Meriam's utterance and input to the official classroom text. Meriam expresses a high degree of obligation when she says: "Jette it is something you [man] must [skal] do each time you [man] must [skal] begin with."

105

Thus her utterance, on the one hand, is an extension of what the teacher has said about the collective category of Muslims, but Meriam attaches the obligation to an indefinite plural mood person. Likewise, the high degree of obligation (and thus the category of necessity) is contradictory to the inclination- and truth-attachment that Jette installed in the mood person 'you' in TRT1.

The teacher reacts to this contradiction, as described, by excluding Meriam from the conversation, but only after having attached the pupil to a particular Muslimness – the figure of the literal, fundamental Muslim – with which the pupil did not herself utter any affiliation.

7.5 Summing up: the Muslim subjects

The meaning of 'ritual' – in the text book as well as in Jette's paraphrasing and Meriam's utterances – is inscribed with a symbolically obligating usuality. But from the moment that the teacher starts interacting with the two pupils, 'ritual' becomes a relatively unstable figure. When 'ritual' is filled with 'Friday prayer' and Islam, it is simultaneously attributed a certain probable usuality as well as habits attached to a flexible subject. The stable ritual practice in turn becomes attached to the plural Muslim subject and to something written. The latter attachment presupposes another type of Muslimness, connected with literalness and obedience to the scriptures. Through presupposition, this type of Muslimness becomes attached to Meriam, who is then identified in the teacher speech as someone who views Islam and Islamic practices as generated and determined by scripture.

In contrast, Sulayman appears as cooperative and more in line with the teacher speech, while Meriam's utterances appear to be a strategy for opposing the installation of a flexibility attached to subjects and 'Friday prayer.' In other words, there is an opposition to ritual (and thus Islamic practices of prayer and purification) as something that has to do with the habitual. Meriam is thus closer to the teacher speech than it first appeared, before the interaction with Sulayman, where ritual was described in the sense of symbolic actions and organized practice.

During interaction with the pupils, however, the teacher's speech instead starts drawing upon the bodily, intimate, physiological attachment to rituals that also appeared in the utterances about 'the Jewish wedding ritual' and the meaning of salt. Moreover, it attaches this bodily meaning of ritual to an individual as well as a collective Muslim subject, both flavored with an unpredictable individuality, where 'habits' intimately incorporate intentionality.

However, this works in different ways for the collective subject (they, the Muslims) and the individual subject (you, Sulayman): Whereas the plural Muslim subject is both unpredictable and attached to obligation ("must" [skal] is solely attached to "them"), the singular Muslim subject, personified by "you," Sulayman, is characterized by a diverse inclination, where unpredictability becomes an indication of individual choices as well as helplessly wrapped in habits without a choice and a will of its own.

7.5.1 Legitimate and accessible versus unacceptable spaces of Muslimness

While both the (young) Muslim individual subject and the (adult) Muslim collective subject are spaces to which the teacher speech opens a legitimate access, an illegitimate space also appears – a space that should not be occupied. This space is a Muslim figure whose actions are implied to be generated from scripture. No intentionality is attached to this space. The figure is not a subject, grammatically speaking. Indeed, it is barely a subject at all, but rather a deviant figure emphasizing and rendering visible the flexible subjectified Muslim bodies. It is a figure that evokes what one cannot and should not be, as opposed to what is offered as a possible and desirable space for being Muslim; the willing, cooperating and flexible subject.

With this concept of figures, inspired by Foucault (Foucault 2003a: e.g. 55, 61), I would say that the not-possible figure along with the two subjectified figures (the young individual and the old collective subject) are elements, or circles of meaning, constituting a domain of abnormality/non-normality (ibid:56, 59). The three Muslim figures appearing in the text sample constitute 'the Muslim' and Muslimness as a domain of knowledge and being; two of these spaces are occupiable, the third is access-denied. Meriam is tied to the latter and consequently pushed out of the conversation.

What is not only excluded but rather eliminated in this process of subjectifying knowledge, attaching it to bodies, generating spaces for subjects, is knowledge of 'ritual' as symbolic action and as order. In other words, religion is not represented here as a performance in no need of individuality or any emotionally loaded direction, as solely a recurrent and orderly doing: a practice. When recontextualized in the classroom knowledge about 'religion,' religion becomes populated with persons, and the persons, if perceived to be Muslim by the teacher, come to be filled with a differentiated pedagogized Muslimness.

8. Intimization and flexibilization of acknowledged 'Muslimness'

This chapter sums up the analysis of and findings concerning the B-school.

When themed as 'ritual' and 'Islamic activities,' and as such, filled with content created between and attached to the speakers, the knowledge category of religion becomes embodied self-knowledge, a technology of differentiation and individualization increasing its power by projecting the figure of the non-intentional fundamentalist. The regulatory pattern of knowledge formations between 'individual development' and 'cultural embeddedness' – arising from the educational- and professional-political fields as well as the media field – is, in this re-contextualized form, filled with 'Muslimness' and 'Muslim culture' in an ambiguous interplay. The force of intimacy and subjectification of the knowledge formation of relations between 'religion' and 'culture,' as well as 'individuality' and 'collective inscription,' become all the stronger as knowledge and bodies are tied together in the recontextualized production of the classroom.

This points to the fact that the teacher's place in the room as well as the teacher's practice should be seen as part of a much more extensive pattern of discursive regulation. This is a pattern that apparently cannot be altered through multicultural ambitions on the part of the teacher, ambitions which, in this instance, have been articulated by Jette as the motivation behind the planning of the educational module on Religion. What goes on at the practice level, however, is further illuminated when the distribution of recognition in light of the concept of capitals is taken into account in connection with the perspective of discursive regulation.

The analysis of the teacher's practices of categorization and the projection of pupil dispositions – the degree to which they are recognized, and as what – is one way of reading the process of social classification. The analysis of the pupils' practices and strategies in relation to occupying available spaces within the classroom is another.

8.1 Social classification: recognition of dispositions and position

Turning to the relation between turn-taking practices and the hierarchy of teachers' recognition, two pupils especially stand out: Zainab and Leila. The analysis of dispositions showed that Zainab is evaluated, on the one hand, as passable and legitimate, but on the other hand her educational capital is assessed by the teacher to be quite low. She is quiet in a way that irritates the teacher, who also describes her as the 'most Muslim' of the pupils. There are no 'most Muslim' among the boys – even if Bilal is suspected of preaching Islam – and neither are any other pupils described as problematically quiet. Zainab has several more speaking turns than the three almost invisible majority pupils Christina, Catharina, and Marc, but the 'Muslim' – and in particular, the Muslim girl-gendered – quietness is apparently more disturbing for the teacher. In the teacher's description, Zainab is allocated a place as what could be called the orthodox (and school-wise, not very appropriate) Muslim.

Leila, however, appears even more enclosed by the teacher's concern and problematization. Leila's problem is not that she does not attempt to gain speaking turns – she does so more through the explicitly legitimate option than most other pupils in the school class. She is not as successful in this strategy, however, as for instance, Meriam and Hassan, although she does succeed at a rate comparable to that of Sulayman. Nonetheless, her contributions are not valued as positive as such, just as Kira's contributions are not enough to make the teacher ascribe her any school legitimacy. They both have difficulties being seen and recognized as appropriate pupils.

Leila cannot even be taken seriously as a 'Muslim,' which means that she ranks lower than the Islam-correct 'ADHD kid' Bilal, to whom Jette compares Leila. In the teacher descriptions, Leila is not in any way worthy of recognition, something which is connected to the fact that she appears unsuitable as a Muslim.

Something similar is at stake in the case of Gaja, who similarly disappoints as both pupil and Christian when she fails to meet the teacher's expectations of 'surprise' contributions in the educational module on Religion, based on her presumed Christian affiliation. Gaja says nothing on her own initiative, and when Jette asks her explicitly to contribute, Gaja answers with a mumble that is not recognizable on my audio recording. Perhaps the pupil's reluctance could be related to the fact that Jette tries to make her contribute as something from which she explicitly dissociates herself – but is, nevertheless, well aware that she is attributed.

Gaja and Leila appear impossible as pupils not least because it is not possible for the teacher to turn them into knowledge and incorporate them as part of the content. Leila is one of the few pupils in the school class who is reprimanded for movements and squirms, a common practice that otherwise appears to be legitimate conduct in the classroom.

Sulayman is reprimanded as well, but proportionately less, and he also receives recognition. His mal-adjustedness is not only a source of concern but also of acknowledgement: despite and through his maladjustedness, he is highly adjustable. Sulayman's status as "king of the class" is described as his problem but also his strength, particularly when it comes to the ways in which he manages and converts this status in support of the teacher's authority and agenda. Sulayman recognizes the authority of Jette, and Jette recognizes Sulayman.

A number of pupils function as more of a backdrop for the teacher speech: Tülay primarily figures as the object of Zainab's suspected preaching; Xiang appears as the good-humored but inarticulate pupil who is not able to account for his religious affiliation; Andreas appears in several teacher examples, but merely as an example and not in his own right, neither as problematic nor the opposite. The pupils who are most vividly at stake in the foreground of this backdrop are Meriam and Sulayman.

8.2 Pupils in the game of knowledge and experience

Both Meriam and Sulayman are highlighted by the teacher for their high levels of school legitimacy. Thus, two of the most recognized and diligent pupils in terms of turn-taking practices are both attached to the teacher category 'Muslim pupil.' Their legitimacy, however, is differently organized: Sulayman is put in the place of the adjusted-maladjusted, as the gifted maladaptive who is willing to submit to the teacher's authority; Meriam as gifted in her capacity as pupil as well as being Muslim, with a family background attributed reflectivity as well as a high degree of cultural Bildung capital compared to the rest of the school class. In the text sample about 'ritual,' however, the problem becomes exactly the lack of a flexible sensitivity in her speech, as well as her unwillingness to contribute with herself as a figure of experience. Sulayman, in turn, is quite cooperative in this context, adjusting himself to the space of the flexible Muslim subject. The space carved out for Meriam in the speech is that of the wrong Muslim subject, hardly a subject at all. This space is otherwise occupied by Zainab in the teacher descriptions of the pupils, but in the official classroom text the seats shift, with Meriam being the more visible pupil.

When 'the pupil' – and 'the Muslim pupil,' in particular – becomes (and is required to be) part of the curriculum, the teacher's position as knowledge authority is at stake. In a sense, Jette has to put her space of authority on the line in order for the pupils to contribute with themselves to the production of knowledge, but at the same time the teacher has to maintain herself as an authoritative source of knowledge. In this process, Sulayman assists and confirms the authority of the teacher. Meriam does not. When Meriam is then assigned Zainab's customary space as 'wrong Muslim,' it is to be understood as a defense tactic in the teacher's struggle to retain her knowledge authority in the game of experience, an authority which Meriam alone, as the only pupil who possess enough recognized school capital, could challenge.

8.3 Categories of knowledge, production of subjects

In the game of experience, it is not least the production of 'Muslim experience' that attracts teacher investment in the curriculum of the module. This has less to do with the fact that the majority of pupils in the classroom are categorized as Muslims, and more to do with the fact that the steering-group pupils take this Muslimness upon themselves (Sulayman) or are attached to it (Meriam), as well as the fact that other pupils attached to the category 'Islam' also chip in to the speech about 'Islam' and 'Muslims.'

Because they are the most frequently speaking pupils, Sulayman and Meriam become the pupils upon and about whom most of the classroom knowledge is organized. The price of speaking is, one way or another, to contribute to the knowledge production with experience, and thus with oneself; which is to say, in these instances, to contribute with oneself as a Muslim and to be organized as a

Muslim in the teacher speech. Sulayman is generally willing to occupy the figure of experience. Meriam is not. In contrast, Leila is willing, but not qualified. The occupiable space is thus flavored with the school legitimacy (or lack thereof) possessed by each pupil. In the assignment of school capital, connected to the pupil's willingness to adjust and the teacher's valuation of the pupil's cultural Bildung capital, 'Muslimness' becomes one of the differentiating parameters. Consequently, Muslimness is differentiated in capitals, flexed in varying degrees of cultural Bildung: the more choosing and the more cultivated, the more legitimate as 'Muslim,' as 'pupil,' and as 'Muslim pupil.'

The specific system of social classification appearing in relation to the category of 'Muslim pupils' in the school class becomes prominent not least because the pupils who are most legitimate and strongest in capital, school-wise, belong to this category. However, they are simultaneously subjected to a system of valuation which renders them as always potentially problematic and as objects of concern, precisely in their capacity of being 'Muslim.'

When the daughter of a middle-management office worker (Meriam) is ascribed the highest capital in the school class, this must also be seen in relation to the fact that the total possession of capital in this school class is rather low in comparison to the C-school (which will be analyzed in the next part of the book). The most recognized pupils in the B-school class would not necessarily have occupied this position in the social micro-economy of other school classes. But in the social bookkeeping of capitals in the B-school, this means that 'Muslimness' becomes a contributing factor in the calculation of legitimacy and illegitimacy. This landscape turns out to be rather differently shaped in the C-school.

PART 3
SUBJECTIVITY WITHIN THE PERIMETER OF 'MUSLIM TRADITION': MUSLIM AS 'LOW CLASS'

In the following chapters, I unfold the analysis of empirical material from the C-school. The analysis is structured similarly to Part 2, only the order of the two main analytical tracks is reversed: Chapter 10 explores the official text of the classroom: How knowledge is organized in-between speakers and content – how the speech organizes content and speakers. Chapter 11 then takes a closer look at the categorization practice of the teachers: What pupils are cast as objects of empathetic concern, and how are capital and legitimacy distributed?

9. The school and the teachers' articulation of curriculum

This chapter opens up the analysis through the teachers' speech concerning curriculum at the C-school.

As elaborated in Chapter 4, the C-school, although not far geographically from the B-school, has a different socioeconomic base in terms of pupils' backgrounds, and the teaching is organized differently. The educational module in *Kristendomskundskab* is organized as a shared module for two 4th grade school classes, X and Y, and the teachers Tine and Jens – who are organized in a common team across the two classes and consequently often teach together – share the primary teacher role in the Y-class, whereas Jens shares the primary teacher role in the X-class with another teacher.

Both Tine and Jens have graduated from teachers colleges in Copenhagen. Tine has earned an MA in Natural Sciences and then taken a short teachers education (the so-called *meritlærer* education). Thus, she has not received any basic education in *Kristendomskundskab* at teachers college level. Her main subjects are Nature/Technics, Danish, and Geography. Jens' main subjects from the teachers college are Math and Civics. His formal qualification for teaching Religion is based on having completed the (at the time of his education) mandatory common core subject *Kristendomskundskab*.

Tine is in her early 40s and has a social background in the lower part of the technical middle class. Her mother is a trained office worker and her father employed in trade and sales. She is married (to a man) and resides in the northern part of Copenhagen, in a neighborhood known to be inhabited by rather affluent people.

Jens is in his early 30s, and both of his parents have medium-length educations: His mother works in public healthcare, whereas his father is a teacher. Before starting his career as a teacher himself, Jens had worked at an institution for higher education and in the private sector, working in media and information technology.

Both teachers thus have a certain surplus of educational capital in relation to teaching at a Folkeskole, and both match the special profile of the school, namely, giving priority to the natural sciences.

Tine teaches Danish in the Y-class, including teaching the pupils to whom Danish is their second language, and Jens teaches Math to both school classes. Neither of them describes *Kristendomskundskab* as a professional strength. Quite the contrary: They plan the educational module more 'tightly' than they do with other modules because they do not feel professionally confident teaching this particular school subject. Nevertheless, they voice quite pronounced opinions about the school subject, for instance, regarding the ways in which the ministerial curricular guidelines, in their view, assign Christianity an exclusive and primary position within the school subject. Nevertheless, at the same time, they express regret that it is possible to be exempted from this particular school subject as they consider it to be a "school subject of culture," which is to say they think of it as closely connected to universal "ethics."

They both identify themselves as opponents of bringing the pupils to religious ceremonies, such as a Christian service before Christmas, and Tine says she does not understand why the ministerial requirements for *Kristendomskundskab* include the reading of bible texts. In its current shape, she describes the school subject as "ethics, culture, and then knowledge of the Bible."

As *Kristendomskundskab* is something in which neither of them has "super strong" professional grounding, as Jens expresses it, they have constructed a narrow and "very safe" framework, whereby they will "follow this worksheet boom boom boom." This is unusual for them, they say, because most of the time, their teaching is very "open" with a lot of space for the pupils to "frolic." Jens regrets that they cannot do this sort of "frolicking" with *Kristendomskundskab*:

> "... I think you could easily ... get these pupils to work a lot more exploratively and experimentally with *Kristendomskundskab* but ... I wouldn't feel comfortable doing that, I think ... I think that really it's actually us who are a bit locked up in our kind of lacking ... professional skills or I don't know how to put it but ... then I'm just thinking, arh, the less I'm capable of – the less I feel safe letting the children frolic ... right?"

9.1 The educational module and the teacher speech about curriculum

The educational module was completed over the course of two successive weeks, in which nine of the ten schooldays were used for teaching this school subject. The module was organized in two primary parts: one centered on teacher presentations during the first week, and then another focused on group based pupil projects the following week. Group work was a recurring element in both weeks.

In the written agenda produced by the teachers prior to the module, it states that Day 1 has the sub-theme "What are rituals," and that the subsequent four days have one rite of passage per day: "Birth and baptism"; "Confirmation"; "Wedding"; and "Funeral." The starting point for each day is noted as Christianity, from which perspectives can be drawn for the consideration of "rituals in other religions" and in "Islam." It is noted as well that Bible texts should be included in connection with each rite of passage.

In addition to the teacher-instructed lessons, the second week contained a presentation of Chagall's "religious images" by the school librarian during the school class's weekly library hour, as well as excursions to a local church and a local mosque, during which the pupils met a pastor and some men connected to the mosque who possibly functioned as imams. On the last day of the second week, the pupils were given a test.

During the nine days a recurring activity was allocated for individual reading of material produced by the teachers. It contained texts about Christianity and Islam in general, as well as about some of the rites of passage and a glossary of terms. This individual reading was also to be used as the basis for group work alongside the teacher presentations – and with the pupils' involvement of "each other," meaning each other's "experiences (in)" and "experience (of)" [*oplevelser og erfaringer*].

9.1.1 Rituals in "every culture" and "close to oneself"

Rituals and rites of passage within different religions are central pivotal elements in the educational module. The motivation for this is the composition of the school class, and the method of teaching is comparison: What makes rites of passage a useful content is that they "are" to be found "in every culture," and thus they are comparable, says Tine. She elaborates her intention of including "other religions," even if the ministerial instructions do not require her to do so prior to grade six:

> "I think that with the composition of pupils here it would in fact be very obvious to include other religions (MB: yes) and then I think that this here this is kind of a … it's kind of a very … close to oneself … theme … that- that I expect the pupils to engage in and take interest in and that they will be curious about the others because it's so close to each and every one of them."

By describing religion as "close to oneself," the theme is defined by Tine as something connected to the private and personal, and priority is given to the personal and 'personal experience' throughout the educational module – as well as in the teachers' speech about the module. Both Tine and Jens expect that another kind of knowledge will be brought into play by the pupils' investing of themselves in the subject matter. The question, then, is what kind of knowledge the personal represents in the teachers' speech about curriculum, and how this personal knowledge relates to other kinds of knowledge.

The personal element is also used by the teachers to subdivide the pupils into working groups, as these groups should have an "even distribution" and "dispersion" of specific groups of pupils, namely pupils whom the teachers considered to be particularly connected to one or another religion and thus "experts" in relation to this school subject. These "experts," on the one hand, are the "mini-candidates for confirmation" (meaning pupils who attend early confirmation preparation) and the pupils who attend Christian scout activities. These pupils are described by the teachers as possessing a "preconception" of the subject matter.

On the other hand, it is the pupils who "have another- another denomination we would like to disperse them as well so that we don't all of a sudden end up with four Islam groups and the rest of them being Christian groups." It is thus presupposed that "another denomination" refers to Islam. Whereas the relation to Christianity is described in rather specific terms as participation in certain activities, religion is depicted as something you "have" when it comes to Islam. Any kind of relation to Islam, furthermore, seems to grant "expert" status, whereas a designated relation to Christianity requires relations to specific institutional practices. When asked what other criteria for the distribution of pupils and the composition of groups the teachers have in mind, the answers are quite vague, such as Tine saying:

> "... well that would, I mean that would be based on acquaintance with the pupils ... you could call it group composition on intuition."

9.2 Muslims and Christians: experience knowledge and factual knowledge

The teachers both articulate the expectations and objectives for the educational module in highly positive terms. Central words in their descriptions are "tolerance" and "respect," which they hope will be a "result" of the teaching. Tine also speaks about delivering new "factual knowledge" to the pupils and providing them with new "insights":

> "... and then I think that some of them ... hopefully many of them, actually, will begin to reflect on their own kind of attitude or that their conceptions are pushed a bit."

When articulating more specific goals, Tine does so in ways that simultaneously divide and classify the pupils:

> "I think this is a good way of getting ... Christians and Muslims, so to say, to work together on a joint task ... and we don't have how can I put it enough Muslims to do pair-work."

That the pupils are working together on joint tasks, in various kinds of constellations, is nothing new to this school. In fact, that is how most of the teaching is organized. Yet, Tine articulates this as if it was something new. The new in this familiar form of activity must then be that the pupils would be working together now *as* Muslims and Christians. Certain expectations are also attached to certain groups of pupils, namely, to those pupils whom the teachers categorize as Muslims: they are expected to enter the stage more actively than usual. This expectation is articulated in various ways, as, for instance, when Jens says:

> "[...] that the fact that they are working with Islam that might mean that you would catch up on some children who wouldn't otherwise be hanging in there much (MB: yes) all of a sudden we have someone else who are actually the experts on it, we do actually have some Muslim children who for that reason can actually tell a lot about what it means to and ... how you do the different things how you get married as a Muslim so some of them know this they don't have to find out they actually already know."

These "Muslim children" who would not otherwise "be hanging in there much" are also described by Tine as pupils who are "usually not that happening ... right ... or they are very fiercely happening but not that happening as far as school skills are concerned"[37]. Thus, what the teacher imagines could draw these pupils into other things than being "very fiercely happening," referring mainly to some of the boys, is connected to their Muslimness: It is as Muslims that they can or might be expected to contribute with something, not otherwise. And it is with a different type of knowledge than "the really really clever[38] girls." They are expected to be able to contribute in relation to the content, which in this case would shift from "something exact, meaning something knowledge-heavy" into something "more experience-heavy," as Jens puts it. In other words, the minority pupils (explicitly, the boys, whereas girls are more invisible in the teachers' speech) are expected to be able to contribute with a 'non-knowledge' that is evaluated as lower than the exact 'knowledge-knowledge' from the "clever girls," but nonetheless valued. During and after the educational module, Tine and Jens voice different opinions about how their expectations were met. While Jens assesses the course of teaching in positive terms, mentioning "successes" attached to specific minority pupils, Tine is disappointed:

> "... well I did expect that they maybe especially the Muslim children would be a bit more like more grounded in thei- I mean or well grounded in the sense that they knew a lot about Islam and knew a lot about their own (pause) about about the religion that they (pause) anyway that's how I had imagined it to be it was (pause) more (pause) invested I mean but that they would talk about such things at home and know more- some more things."

Simultaneously, Tine also highlights that she now knows more about how different "the school class's Muslims" are, offering as an example that she has had a conversation with the pupil Aya and discovered that they are simply "Iranians," rather than Muslims per se, a self-perception that Tine evaluates positively.

Despite their different assessments of the outcome, however, both Tine and Jens describe the educational module as particularly attached to the 'Muslim experience,' as opposed to the teacher's descriptions prior to the educational module in which Christianity was foregrounded in accord with the priority that was explicitly legitimized by the ministerial requirements. The discrepancy between the two teachers' speech about the course is that Jens recognizes the knowledge (framed as non-knowledge and experience knowledge) contributed by "the Muslim children," while Tine partly recognizes it, but at the same time invalidates it. Nonetheless,

---

37 This is a free translation of Tine's creative and grammatically impossible use of the Danish expression "i vælten." This expression translates to something like "popular," "in the limelight," or "happening," with positive connotations, but in this context and through Tine's self-made inflection of the expression, the meaning is altered, and it is this meaning that the translation seeks to capture [original text: "... ikke altid er sådan vældig meget i vælten.. ikk.. eller de er så i nogle voldsomme vælter (MB: ja) men ikke så meget fagligt i vælten ..."].
38 "Clever" is a translation of the Danish word "dygtig" which bears both the meaning of clever as in intelligent, but also as in skillful or proficient.

they both speak of "the Muslim children" as a particularly exposed object – in terms of the curriculum of the module, and as such as key to the methodological and content-related successes and failures of the module.

To sum up, we can see a pattern in the way the teachers articulate curriculum which combines strong and weak framing in combining the strongly framed teacher-controlled plenary sessions with weakly framed group sessions, during which the control is outsourced to (specific) pupils. The classification of the religions in curriculum is strong and so is the classification of the identities of the pupils which are differentiated in relation to the religions in curriculum.

10. 'Christianity' as 'universal human conditions' versus the predictable 'Muslim tradition'

One of the main findings of the analysis of the classroom speech unfolded in this chapter is that while the relation of the course content to Christianity is something that gradually unfolds in the speech of the teachers, the relation of the content to Islam or Muslimness arrives abruptly, as something strongly demarcated from the outset. The speech regarding Christianity thus begins with what one could term 'universal human conditions' and is then related to 'something Christian,' while the order of things is reversed in the speech regarding Islam: the teacher begins with 'the Muslim tradition,' which only later, to some extent, is re-framed in the perspective of 'universal human conditions.'

The reading strategies employed in this chapter are similar to the ones employed in Chapter 7. Thus, they focus on an analysis of how relations between the content of teaching and the pupils occur in the classroom conversations; how the speech in the classroom produces both the pupils and the content, as well as relations between the two; how topics and themes emerge, and how this is connected to the interplay among different speakers; how relations between subjects and knowledge are produced in light of the Foucauldian concepts of knowledge, subject, and power.

The focus of this chapter is on the teacher speech and also the pupil speech that intercedes: Which pupil contributions are explicitly initiated by the teacher, which are initiated by the pupils, which contributions are overruled and which are incorporated, and with what effects. The two text samples selected[39] for in-depth analysis are excerpted from the same lecture in which the teacher Tine presents what she characterizes as "the fourth ritual," or more specifically, "what happens when you die ... in the rituals."

Pupil speech appears in both text samples. In the first text sample – about the 'universal' (Christian) funeral – the pupils involved are majority pupils. In the second text sample – initiated by a pupil's question: "what about the Muslims?" – Tine responds by addressing "what it's like in the Muslim tradition if you're a Muslim." In this second text sample, the three pupils involved are all what the teachers describe as 'Muslims' and 'not Danish.'

---

39 The samples are selected from material consisting of audio recordings of plenary sessions (with both classes), selected sessions during which the classes were separated, selected group sessions (all of these with the use of table/room microphone), as well as recordings of selected sessions with teachers supervising groups (recorded with a portable microphone placed on the teacher). These recordings have been transcribed selectively and synoptically and compiled with my observation notes.

10.1 The universal human funeral: organization of 'Christianity' and 'funeral'

The first text sample selected for analysis is excerpted from the teacher-directed opening[40] of the overriding theme: "the fourth ritual," which refers to the organization of the classroom curriculum in four rites of passage (as outlined in the previous chapter). Phrases such as "end of life," "funeral," and "what happens when you die" provide content to this fourth ritual.

10.1.1 Selected text sample 1

Note on translation: Danish is a less varied language than English, and thus the two modal verbs 'skal' and 'kan' are used in the place of several English words and phrases. 'Skal,' which expresses a high degree of obligation, thus equals shall/should, must, has/have to, is going to, needs to. Whenever the Danish original says 'skal,' this is thus noted in [ ]. The same goes for 'kan' which is closer to the use of 'can' in English – and thus expresses a low degree of obligation and thus possibility – but would often also be used in places where one would say, for instance, 'might' in English. Whenever the Danish original says 'kan,' this is thus also noted in [ ].

Each "you" is plural indefinite [man] in the original Danish text, except the "you" [du] used by Gülsen to address Tine, which is singular definite.

For original Danish version: see Appendix B

> TRT1-6: What happens when you die
> 1 Tine (teacher): ... the fourth ritual that we've reached today (pause) that's of
> 2 course the one that (pause) is about (pause) the end of life (pause) about
> 3 the funeral (pause) what happens when you die (pause) in the rituals

---

[40] On this particular day, Tine was responsible for the teacher presentation and for handling the turn-taking system, while the other teacher Jens was located in the back of the room. The C-school is quite differently organized than the B-school, spatially as well as in terms of the planning and practice of teaching. At the C-school the teachers' instruction-based plenary sessions are mixed with group work as well as individual work. Furthermore, the group work modules include each group producing a product that will subsequently be presented by the pupils in plenary. The buildings of the C-school are relatively recently built and comprise houses for each 'department' as well as for special functions such as library, administration, laboratory facilities, and a gym. The rooms for instruction are – with a few exceptions – non-closed spaces with half-walls; so-called open-plan architecture. When the two observed school classes are taught separately, the pupils sit according to a table plan in which they are organized in groups of 4-5. When they are taught together, the teaching often takes place in a larger room called 'the auditorium.' This is the case with the plenary sessions in the educational module observed. In the auditorium, the presenter – the teacher or a group presenting their work – is placed by a whiteboard in one end of the room, where the presenter can write on the board and/or show a PowerPoint presentation. From this point of the room the pupils sit in horseshoe formation. The table plan is often open during these cross-school class plenary sessions, and there are not enough chairs for everyone, so some of the pupils sit on the floor. In all the plenary sessions I observed, the pupils were free to sit wherever they wanted, with the single exceptions of pupils who had for some reason been sanctioned by being assigned a particular place to sit.

4   Pupil: // (mumbles)
5   Pupils: (mumble)
6   Tine: before one is buried or interred or whatever is going to [skal] happen
7   (pause) there is of course someone who dies (pause) and when someone
8   in the family dies there are all kinds of things one has to [skal] sort out
9   (pause) one of course has to [skal] (pause) simply just figure out how
10 the funeral should [skal] even take place (pause, hesitates) and the one who
11 died of course has also lived somewhere and what are you going [skal] to do
12 with all the things and all those things (pause) so there's qui- (pause) do I
13 have to [skal], already now where we only just reached image one[41], say
14 the first hush
15 Gülsen: then you [du] would only have two times (pause)
16 Tine: then there are only two times left, yes (pause)
17 Pupil: (mumbles)
18 Tine: well (pause) there's quite a lot of things that have [skal] to be sorted
19 out and in Denmark we've made such a system where there are some people
20 who work with it who are called undertakers (pause) those can [kan] be both
21 men and women (pause) and those (pause) are the ones you see (pause) you
22 can [kan] also take care of everything yourself (pause) but they are experts
23 (pause) so you go see them (pause) and say that now (hesitates) my – usually
24 it's of course when someone's father or mother has died – if for instance
25 (hesitates) Nikoline's (hesitates) grandmother died then it would be your
26 father's mother (pause) and then it would be your father who would
27 have to [skulle] sort it out right?
28 Nikoline: yes (pause)
29 Tine: (hesitates) and then he goes to the undertaker and says that now
30 (hesitates) my mother has died (pause) and (pause) we need to [skal] sort
31 that out so you make a lot of arrangements about how it should [skal] take
32 place (pause) in what church it should [skal] be (pause, hesitates)
33 should [skal] we have this kind of coffin or that one – all those things you go
34 over with the under-
35 Pupil: and tombstone
36 Tine: and tombstone is also something you can [kan] arrange with the
37 undertaker (pause) and you can [kan] arrange with the undertaker about
38 flowers (pause)
39 Pupil: flowers
40 Tine: because many people choose to have flowers on the coffin (pause)
41 these are all things you can [kan] arrange with the undertaker (pause) and the
42 undertaker (pause) he can [kan] also figure out what church the dead person
43 belongs to (pause) because if you're going to [skal] be buried from a church
44 (pause) you need to [skal] make arrangements with the pastor (pause) then
45 I've written here that it's a great grief to lose someone (pause) that you're
46 related to (pause) a person you care about (pause) but sometimes a ritual
47 can [kan] help you (pause) in the sense that at least that is not something you
48 also have to be very uncertain about what to do (pause) because all kinds of
49 thoughts will pop up in your head (pause) but then you have this ritual

---

41 The teacher is referring to the first slide in the PowerPoint presentation she is using.

50 (pause) that stays the same [er helt fast]
51 Pupil: mumbles
52 Tine: and that's what you do (pause) and then you know (pause) if it's
53 a Christian (pause) who dies (pause) you can [kan] be buried in a church
54 (pause) or in a chapel (pause) or a crematorium (pause) a church we've
55 talked about you know what that is (pause) a chapel that's a place that
56 can [kan] also be Christian but it might [kan] also be that it doesn't belong to
57 any particular religion (pause) which is a space [rum][42] (pause) and often it's
58 (pause) a house placed (pause) at a cemetery (pause) so that (pause) instead
59 of doing it in a church placed far away from the cemetery you can [kan]
60 (pause) do it in a house that's simply placed in the cemetery (pause).

In this predominantly teacher-borne speech, four different types of pupil interactions can be identified: Three instances of indistinct speech that seem to have no impact on the teacher's speech; on two occasions, pupils repeat the teachers speech, supplementing it with the words 'flowers' and 'tombstone' respectively; one intervention is made by Gülsen who comments on a disciplinary action from the teacher (Tine has spelled out earlier in the lesson that she does not want to have to say "hush" in the classroom more than three times during a session); and finally, there is a very short but nonetheless very significant utterance from the pupil Nikoline: With the word 'yes' she affirms a proposition for which the teacher seeks affirmation; more specifically, Nikoline accepts being organized as part of the content through a (fictional) example of her grandmother passing away and her father taking care of the arrangements.

10.1.2   Topics and themes and the organizational power of the speech

As the teacher speech progresses, six themes related to the topic "what happens when you die (pause) in the rituals" can be identified. First, a universal human condition is established: someone dies (TRT1) (6–13). Then 'the undertaker system' is introduced (TRT2) (18–22), and subsequently, a situation where the undertaker is described (TRT3) (23–34). Then the range of possibilities connected to the undertaker is presented (TRT4) (34–44), followed by the claim that rituals are a source of relief when people are grieving (TRT5) (45–52). By the end of the speech, the funeral is spatially fixed (TRT6) (52–60).

It is during the last TRT that the expression "a Christian" appears for the first time. However, this must be understood as the culmination of something that has been gradually projected throughout the entire text sample. Whereas only TRTs 1 and 5 explicitly point back at the topic – rituals – the text sample in its totality develops a connection between, on the one hand, 'funeral' and 'ritual' and, on the other hand, 'Denmark/church' and 'Christian,' and frames that connection as something rooted

---

42 The word "rum" in Danish may mean "room" as well as "space." Though "space" is the translation I have chosen, it is nonetheless my interpretation that both meanings of the word are at stake in this case.

in, as well as prescribing, something common: the 'universal condition' that 'someone' – more specifically, 'someone in the family' – dies, and how this 'can' or 'must' be handled. How this structuring is inflected in persons, relations, and degrees becomes clear by taking a closer look at the use of deictic markers and modality.

10.1.3   Designating persons and places

Turning to the deictic markers attached to persons who are not always but often also interpersonal subjects, there are two types of speech at play in the teacher presentation, namely speech about the content attached to the overall topic and speech about what one could call meta-discursive elements: a speech about the speech, which refers to the specific context, namely the teaching situation. The first type is characterized by the use of non-interactants (particularly the plural indefinite "you" [man]), while the second type points at those present in the classroom; for instance, "we" referring to the pupils as well as the teacher herself and her co-teacher, and "I" referring to the speaker herself and what she has "written" in her PowerPoint presentation. The latter type situates the speech in the teaching context.

The rest of the speech, however, refers to contexts outside of the classroom and is projected in various informing utterances and described situations, bringing these outside contexts into the classroom. In these cases, the carrier is the plural indefinite "you," a position 'anyone' could inhabit. There are two exceptions, however.

The first exception appears in the second TRT: "in Denmark we've made such a system" of undertakers. The "we" in this context includes the speaker. Simultaneously, it could include those who are addressed (the pupils), or could precisely separate itself from them – or both. In either case, the universal condition becomes spatially fixed through the use of 'we' and 'Denmark.' "All those things" that the deceased left behind must be sorted out, and this can be done by utilizing a system, the origins of which are connected to Denmark. 'The Danish' thus provides content to the common and universal 'you' who either sort things out themselves or ask undertakers to do it. Even if the speech uses the plural indefinite 'you,' the funeral practices are no longer entirely universal inasmuch as they have become flavored by Denmark.

The second exception occurs in immediate extension of this, namely in the third TRT: the situation with the undertaker. A 'you' is approaching 'them' (implicitly, the undertakers), but then the teacher interrupts herself and transforms the situation from a non-specific 'you' in the process of burying a non-specific deceased into a situation in which "Nikoline's father" is sorting out the funeral of "Nikoline's grandmother." While installing "Nikoline's father" in the speech, the deictic marker now points directly at a conversational interactant, namely Nikoline. Tine asks Nikoline to affirm her installation in the content with the requesting word "right?," to which Nikoline responds positively ("yes"). The agent in the speech now becomes a 'he,' referring to Nikoline's father. With the exception of a single 'we' – as if quoting 'Nikoline's father' ("should [skal] we have this kind of coffin or that one") – the speech then shifts back to the indefinite plural 'you' with which this 'we' is surrounded and connected. This 'you' is used throughout the sequence.

The example also shows how the 'you' that becomes "Nikoline's father" is attached to 'church,' as the speech is concerned with which church the funeral should take place in, not whether the funeral should take place in a church or not ("in what church it should [skal] be"). Only at a later point in the text sample a proviso is introduced: "*if* you're going to be buried from a church."

What we see is then how the teacher's speech gradually projects ties to specific places, persons, and religions: initially, to "Denmark" (and undertakers), then to "church." In the course of this, the teacher's speech involves Nikoline and her (not really dead) grandmother and her father, who is transformed into an interpersonal subject. As a deictic marker, this interpersonal subject is placed in the position that, before and after, is inhabited by the indefinite plural 'you.' The generalized place, filled out by 'you,' is thus flavored by person as well as the projected context and becomes attached to the specific context (the classroom conversation) and a specific interactant, the pupil Nikoline.

10.1.4   Modality: How 'should' and 'can' install inevitability and choice

The teacher's speech is characterized by the use of the modal verbs 'can' [kan] and has/have to, need to, must, is going to – which, as explained previously, are solely expressed in Danish by the word 'skal' (expressing a high degree of obligation), as opposed to 'can'/'kan' (expressing a possibility). The two modal verbs thus attach the utterances to degrees of necessity and inflect them with high or low degree of obligation respectively. 'Skal' is attached to the organization of the funeral and the sorting out of things related to this.

> "one of course has to [skal] (pause) simply just figure out how the funeral should [skal] even take place (pause, hesitates) and the one who died of course has also lived somewhere and what are you going [skal] to do with all the things and all those things." (9–12)

The factual character inscribed in these statements organizes what the teacher presents as an effectively indisputable condition. The use of 'skal' expresses a lower degree of certainty than a categorical statement would have (for instance, 'then you sort out a lot of things'). The modal verb 'skal' and the subsequent installation of a high degree of obligation, nevertheless, provide a prescriptive character to the statement.

While the plural indefinite 'you' in some statements thus 'has to' sort things out, a range of possibilities is simultaneously presented through the use of the modal verb 'can.' As with 'skal,' the verb 'can' is also linked to obligation and thus necessity, but of a low degree – 'can' prescribes possibility. In the teacher's speech, however, it is the high degree of obligation that becomes the basis by which the possible is installed in an inferior position. As when Nikoline's father 'needs to' sort out the death of his mother and 'you' therefore make a 'lot of arrangements' about how things 'should take place' and in 'what church' it 'should be.' That this has to happen, and that this – regardless of how – has to happen in a church is expressed with a high degree of obligation. So is the fact the 'we have to' have a coffin. However, which church and which coffin are open to choice and 'can' be arranged – the same goes for the tombstone and flowers.

A high degree of obligation and prescribed necessity is thus attached in the teacher's speech to the fact that death is sorted out within a framework of actions – some things must take place in some particular settings – while choices are linked to the use of undertaker, the options of church, tombstone, flowers, and thus, the choice of specific artifacts.

In the teacher's speech, deontic modality is attached to the use of the third person. The utterances must then be understood as propositions, and thus, the prescribing statements attain an informative character, linked to the category of truth (Andersen et al. 2001:79, Frimann 2004:153). In terms of genre, this is no surprise: The utterances are part of a teacher presentation, the aim of which is exactly of an informative, knowledge-oriented – and thus truth-attached – character. What is remarkable, however, is that this informative speech is organized through the use of deontic modality, adding a prescriptive character to the informative level. What is prescribed is, then, that the unavoidable eventuality of death leads to unavoidable practices that 'must' take place – in certain ways and, within these certain ways, with a range of possible variations to choose from.

10.1.5   Choices and limitations set by the ritual

Choice, indicated by 'can,' organizes possibility and thus flexibility and intentionality connected to artifacts: flowers and tombstone, the 'things' of the funeral. The ritual is summarized as a kind of deal/bargain, something that can reduce the amount of doubt related to all 'those things' that must be 'sorted out' when someone dies. As such ritual is measured with a low degree of obligation: It "can help" (but does not necessarily do so), and only "sometimes." However, it offers a meaning that represents an allegedly adequate answer to a situation of doubt. Perhaps one is 'uncertain,' but one does not have to be "very uncertain" when one has "this ritual (pause) that stays the same [er helt fast]." Hereby, the axis of the speech is completed: from installation of a high degree of obligation (['skal']) to a low degree of obligation (can) to a reference to the initiating topic of the speech, 'the fourth ritual,' which is then content-filled with "ritual … that stays the same," attached to 'the Danish' and 'Christian.'

Finally, the teacher adds a concluding "and that's what you do" and "then you know," attaching the practices – presented as a prescriptive manual – to knowledge: a knowledge about the system of undertakers and a knowledge about ritual assume the form of an offer of something stable.

By the time 'Christian' is explicated in TRT6, it is done in a way that does not open up to anything else that might be explicitly non-Christian. The "chapel" "can [kan] also be Christian but it might [kan] also be that it doesn't belong to any particular religion." In other words, the implicit alternative to 'Danish' as Christian here is not another religion, but rather no religion (in particular).

10.1.6 Installation of pupil experience in Danish Christianness – between 'stable' and 'choosing'

The two analytical nodes described above – prescribing obligation and spatial fixing, on the one hand, and possibilities and flexibility connected to choice, on the other hand – can be identified elsewhere in the official classroom text in ways that serve to broaden the perspective of the analysis. After presenting the range of choices connected to the transportation of the body of the deceased – burial or cremation, place of ceremony (chapel or church, and what church) – the teacher draws another pupil into the conversation by referring to this pupil's mother:

> Tine: ... if it's then a Christian funeral (pause) then I've written some keywords there and Niels he simply asked his mother because she's a pastor [præst][43] that is something she works with and making funeral (pause) over at the church (pause) and we've simply written- the first sentence is the same I've written the coffin is in front of the alter (pause) and (hesitates) what's your mother's name again Niels
> Niels: Anne
> Tine: Anne she wrote the coffin is in the church (pause) and that is- that is in fact the same.

Niels' mother functions in the teacher speech as an object of knowledge production and is simultaneously assigned the status of knowledge authority. As such, she provides legitimacy to the teacher's knowledge authority. As was the case with 'the undertakers,' Niels' mother is placed in the role of professional, an expert – being a pastor and "making funeral" it is "something she works with." As such she is deployed to provide solidity to the teacher's speech – what the 'expert' and the teacher wrote about "making funeral" in the church are "in fact the same."

Being Niels' mother, the pastor also functions as a conveyor between the content and the pupils. This is a function that is emphasized by the fact that the teacher, as in the case of Nikoline, asks Niels to confirm this attachment, specifically confirming it by uttering his mother's name.

Pulling in Nikoline and Niels by installing their parents and a (not really) dead grandparent in the speech ties the content to the pupils' bodies and private spheres, thereby personifying the content material and also materializing the pupils. The pulling in of Niels' mother as 'expert' helps to underscore the question of how knowledge is assigned status in the classroom and how the teacher – as the intermediary of knowledge as well as authority of knowledge – is organized in the

---

[43] "Præst" in Danish refers to Protestant pastors and ministers and priests in other Christian denominations and is also used for other religions, though not often in relation to Islam.

interplay with the organizing of pupil experience. How, then, does this relation between the teacher's organization of pupil experience and authorization of knowledge play out when the theme shifts to 'Islam' and 'the Muslim'?

10.2 The 'Muslim' tradition: organizing 'Islam' and 'funeral'

The introduction of Islam as theme is initiated by a pupil intervention, namely by Lamine who wants to know: "what about the Muslims?" Tine replies:

> "yes, I will get to that in the very end because you can exactly be buried in other ways just as you can be married in other ways."

Lamine uses the personified designation "Muslim" (as opposed to the non-personified 'Islam') in a definite sense ("the Muslims"), and the teacher speech then situates knowledge about "the Muslims" as something which, in the order of content, is placed at the "very end." Furthermore, she characterizes this with the phrase "other ways," thus allocating 'Islam'/'the Muslims' the status of appendix to the speech about Christianity, as well as organizing it as otherness. In the following text sample, centering on "the Muslims," which take place during the same lesson, but approximately 20 minutes after the text sample on the 'universal Christian funeral,' it is the practical level – how things are done and take place – that is pivotal in the speech. Contrary to the preceding text sample, the following text sample is primarily driven by pupil initiations, of which some are rejected as irrelevant (Hazem) and some as non-valid (Lamine) knowledge, whereas others are incorporated by the teacher as valid and relevant knowledge (Gülsen).

10.2.1   Text sample 2

For original Danish version: see Appendix B

> TRT1 Teacher presentation (Tine): The Muslim tradition and Muslims
> Tine: Now we're going to talk about what it's like in the Muslim tradition if you're a Muslim (pause) and- and like I wrote in the beginning it's really a- a grief for all people to lose someone they know (hesitates) and so it is for Muslims (pause) so you [man] might say in the Muslim tradition (pause) maybe you [man] also have a greater respect for old people (hesitates) because (pause) it's a (hesitates) way of thanking them for taking care (pause) of you [én] when you [man] were small (pause) and that there's also a tradition of children taking care of their parents when they get old (pause) in Denmark nowadays it's common that most old people (pause) go to an old people's home
> Pupil: old people's home
> Tine: and they have a home carer because we're all so busy (pause).
>
> TRT2 Hazem's contribution – dismissed as non-relevant
> Tine: ... Hazem, did you [du] want to say something? (pause)

Hazem (pupil): [mumbles, quietly] What was it I wanted to say (pause) some Muslims (mumbles) Muhammed[44], you [du] know, that commercial that he (pause) I mean not that Muhammed
Tine: ... OK... so you [du] mean Muhammed Muhammed
Hazem: Not that one [referring to another pupil]
Tine: No (pause)
Hazem: The Prophet
Tine: The Prophet Muhammed (pause) yes
Hazem: Yeah... where they had just put like a star on his hand and said that he was stupid and wrote that he was dead
Tine: But that's not really the issue right now

TRT3 Teacher presentation: "When a Christian dies" vs. "The Muslim tradition"
Tine: well (pause) when a Christian dies it will often be up to four days before you [man] have finished arranging the funeral and all so it will be a few days before you [man] (hesitates) are buried (pause) in the Muslim tradition (pause) you [man] should [skal] preferably [helst] become (blive) buried on the day you [man] die (pause)
Voices of pupils: whoa woooh
Tine: and it's a tradition that it is that way (pause) it's also a tradition that you [man] wash the dead you [man] do that with Christians as well but here (pause) in the Muslim tradition you (man) wash the same way as you [man] wash before // prayer //

TRT4 Lamine's contribution – dismissed as non-valid
Lamine: // you [man]// wash your heart (pause)
Tine: you [man] actually wash the hands (pause) and the feet and the face first (pause)
Pupil: // and the asshole //
Lamine: // and the heart //
Tine: and then afterwards you [man] wash the body (pause)
Lamine: // the heart too // the heart too //
Tine: do you [man] do that? (pause)
Lamine: yes // (mumbles)
Tine: that's not // what it said in the book I read (hesitates) and then you're wrapped in a white cloth and put in a coffin
Gülsen: yes
Jens (ass. teacher): Sami (reprimanding).

TRT5 Teacher presentation: Funeral and Muslims
Tine: at the actual funeral (pause) then the imam reads a prayer (pause) the funeral prayer- that's the pastor [præst] you [man] could say (pause) the one who's in charge of the ceremony (pause) in the mosque (pause) he reads a prayer (pause) and gives a speech to the bereaved (pause) and that's actually also like when the pastor [præst] gives a speech to the bereaved (pause) then I've read (pause) that in

---

44 The Danish spelling of Mohammad (Muhammed) is kept here, as this is closest to the way the speakers pronounce it.

the pay- prayer (pause) or the speech that the imam gives (pause) he reminds the family of the three great things that (hesitates) the deceased has given them (pause) a good life the memory of what happens (pause) and that's actually nice (pause) and then it's very important that Muslims-
Lubna: Tine
Tine: Muslims are not cremated they are all buried (pause)

TRT6 Gülsen's contribution – incorporated
Gülsen: but they are buried into the- their homeland some of them-
Tine: some- Gülsen has an information
Gülsen: some they are buried in their homeland and some they bury in the cemetery
Tine: some are buried here and some are flown back to where they come from- and are buried there and then there is a very important thing (pause) that you [man] should be buried so that the face is directed towards [vender mod] Mekka like when you [man] pray (pause) then you [man] have your head towards Mekka

10.2.2 TRTs between teacher speech and pupil speech

The teacher speech, now filling 'funeral' with the content "what it's like in the Muslim tradition if you're a Muslim" - TRT1 – appears uninterrupted until Hazem is assigned the right to speak (except for one pupil repeating something from the teacher speech – "old people's home" – but the teacher does not take notice of it). Starting from "some Muslims" and thus referring to the topic, Hazem in TRT2 starts speaking about a certain "commercial" connected to "Mohammad" (the Prophet). The teacher's first response is a positive one; she assists Hazem in articulating what or who it is to which he is referring. However, once Hazem has elaborated his point about how "they" put "like a star on his hand and said that he was stupid and wrote that he was dead," the teacher evaluates his contribution negatively: She rejects it as irrelevant. Hazem is most likely referring to something of which neither the teacher nor I was aware at that point in time, but which later became an extraordinarily well-known issue: the so-called Jyllands-Posten cartoons, also known as the Mohammad caricatures, which instigated international political tension. At the moment of this school lesson, however, the cartoons/caricatures had not yet become (in)famous. Hazem is thus referring to a specific text outside of the text – something which is not heard and not explored, as Tine instead moves on to another (longer) teacher presentation in which she compares what happens "when a Christian dies" with "the Muslim tradition." The pupil interventions in this part, TRT3, are a collectively made sound that apparently does not affect Tine's presentation.

In TRT4, the pupil Lamine tries to gain a speaking turn without prior approval from the teacher. This is overruled twice, and thus implicitly evaluated negatively, before Lamine succeeds in getting Tine to respond explicitly to his intervention. This happens when Lamine reinforces his utterance by repeating: "the heart too // the heart too //." The teacher responds with a question – "do you [man] do that" – which can be interpreted both as a questioning of veracity of the utterance, but also as an opening towards the speech of Lamine. When the pupil confirms his utterance, the teacher states that this is not what is written in the book that she has read, thus trumping his utterance with her own and the book's authority – a book only she has access to.

The pupil contribution in TRT5 is Lubna's uttering of the teacher's name. However, Tine overrules this and continues to speak about "the funeral" as such, a speech in which "the imam"/"he" is central and set in relation to "the pastor" (præst). Only when Gülsen enters (in TRT6) with what the teacher characterizes as "an information,"[45] thus assigning legitimacy to the speech, is the pupil contribution evaluated positively by the teacher.

10.2.3 The respectful 'Muslims' and the busy 'we'
Contrary to the way in which Christianity was gradually projected and not named until the end of text sample 1, a specific religious universe is identified in text sample 2 as the framework of the content from the very beginning. This religious framework is not designated by its name ("Islam"), but through personified entities attached to this religion ("Muslim" and "Muslims"). This was also the case with Christianity which was identified through "Christian" and "Christians," but the difference is that these types of markers appear from the beginning in text sample 2, and thus become the point of departure for the teacher speech.

The complex of "the Muslim tradition" and "Muslims" is measured up in third person (the imam/he, Muslims/they) while its opposite – 'the Danish' and 'the Christian' (in the context of text sample 2) – is measured in first person ("we") when 'the Danish' is at the forefront, but third person when 'the Christian' is at the forefront. "The Muslim tradition" is thus not solely set in contrast to something 'other' in a religious sense, but also to 'Denmark,' and thus becomes something framed by the national Danish.

The Muslim plural 'you' [man] is a non-interactant in the speech and, like "Muslims," is indefinite, while "the Muslim tradition" (to which "you" and "Muslims" are attached) appears as definite. "The Muslim tradition" appears seven times throughout TRTs 1 and 3 in the shape of circumstantial information. The indefinite and non-specific is thus framed by definite and demarcated circumstances.

A similar double movement is at play when "the Muslim tradition" is described in the teacher speech: It is something flexible, something less stable than laws or scriptures, for instance, inasmuch as words such as "maybe" and "preferably" [helst] weaken the degree of obligation and add a subjective flavor to the described practices. At the same time, this subjectively flavored inflection of necessity and

---

45 "Information" is actually countable in Danish, unlike in English. The reason I have chosen to translate it literally (and thus grammatically incorrect), is that the correct translation: "information/some information," would misleadingly suggest that Tine in Danish had said "noget information" (indefinite, neither singular nor plural). This would have ascribed a lesser degree of factuality to Gülsens utterance. Instead, Tine's speech suggests that it is not just "(some) information" in the abstract uncountable sense, but *an* information, with the definite, singular form adding a specificity, and thus stability or factuality, to it.

prescription – even though expressed as categorical – evaporates in utterances such as "it's a tradition that it is that way" (referring to specific practices of washing the dead).

When comparing the descriptions of how death is handled in "the Muslim tradition" and what is gradually identified as Christian, the similarity is that the managing of death is unfolded through practical activities. A decisive difference, then, is that the element of choice is absent in the speech about "the Muslim tradition"/"Muslims." The prescriptions are also weaker: When they are used, they are attenuated. "The Muslim tradition," however, appears as something that generates the practices – what "Muslims" do – sometimes with certain modally organized reservations, but nonetheless persistently. When "Muslims" do something, the origins of that practice can be found in "the Muslim tradition."

In these utterances, "Muslims" are set in opposition to a "we" attached to Denmark, where most people are sent to old people's homes because "we're all so busy." "Muslims" instead are purported to take care of their elders, out of "respect" and "tradition." An opposition is set in motion, attaching the "we" in "Denmark" to something that is associated with modernity and working life, whereas the "Muslims" are attached to the old (people); thus, the Muslim "you" points backward in time. This space-time fixing of "Muslims" in an exceptional past (tradition) – as opposed to a universal present – reverberates in the speech which refers to the overall topic of the lesson, dealing with death and funerals: "like I wrote in the beginning it's really a- a grief for all people to lose someone they know (hesitates) and so it is for Muslims." On the one hand, Muslims are included in this universal condition – "for all people"; on the other hand, by specifying that this is *also* the case for Muslims, it is presupposed that Muslims are not, from the outset, counted as part of "all people."

10.2.4   Differentiating comparisons

In the speech about the universal/Danish/Christian, a plural indefinite 'you' pointing at general conditions, and as such a universal 'you,' appeared along with the figure "Nikoline's father": A personification tied to a definite person, expressed in the grammatical singular: an individual. In contrast, in the speech about "the Muslim tradition," "Muslims"/"the Muslims" is a figure that appears personified and plural, and which from the outset is organized as corresponding to a particular "tradition." Whereas the speech about the universal/Danish/Christian plays out between the individual (choice) and the collective, anchored by individuals, the inscribed and collective character of Islam is presupposed from the outset and functions as a consistent structure of the entire speech about Islam.

While Christianness is gradually generated throughout the speech, Muslimness is not generated – rather, it is the point of departure as such. This, in turn, has consequences for the ways in which the universal/Danish/Christian appears in the context of the speech about Islam: a non-inflected speech now appears in which "we," "in Denmark," as well as the definite plural "Christian" and the indefinite single and plural "Christian/s" appear as an expressed and stable entity without the degree of attachment to flexibility and individuality at play in the speech about the universal/Danish/Christian as such. The speech about "the Muslim tradition" and "Muslims" rubs off, so to speak; not in terms of the antique and backward-looking, which is confined to 'Muslims,' but in terms of the stable and collective. The professional and laboring feature of "the pastor" also disappears when set in relation to 'the imam.' Comparisons with "the Muslim tradition"/"Muslims" thus also produce meanings and knowledge in relation to Christianity.

The comparisons come in three variations: The religion-focused sameness-oriented comparison; the religion-focused difference-oriented comparison; and the culturalist, contrasting comparison.

In the religion-focused, sameness-oriented form, comparisons attached to religious authority and institutions as well as ritual practice are made with an emphasis on similarities. The difference established in this variation is attached to ritual practice and framed as difference of a primarily practical character. The religion-focused, difference-oriented variation is exemplified by the teacher's comparison of the time interval between death and funeral. In relation to Christianity, the interval is described as a practicality, whereas it is framed as a prescribed obligation in Islam. To the Christian time interval, "a Christian," a singular indefinite person, is attached; to the Islamic tradition, a collective is attached. In Christianity, ritual practice concentrates on actors and actions directed towards choices, such as the selection of particular commodities or services (flowers, tombstones, church/chapel/crematorium), whereas ritual practice in Islam appears to be dictated by the collective and the traditional.

The third variation – the culturalist, contrasting form of comparison – frames a difference between "The Muslim tradition"/"Muslims" and "we" "in Denmark." The difference is established by attaching "Muslims" to grief as a universal condition but at the same time separating Muslims from "all people." This is emphasized by the framing of a "Muslim tradition" for taking care of elders as opposed to the busy Danish "we." What is compared is tied to culture/sociality, or more specifically, the relation between the institution of the family and the bustle associated with individuals' professional working lives. This type of comparison simultaneously produces the most explicit difference while, in the most value-loaded way, projects "the Muslim tradition" as something positive and sympathetic. More sympathetic than the Danish, at least.

The recurring pattern through these three types of comparison is that Islam is projected with Christianity as the point of departure, and in comparison with Christianity and the Danish. In other words, it is the imam who is 'like' the pastor, not the other way around, whereas Christianity, when introduced at the beginning of the lesson, is projected through a 'universal' frame. However, something happens to Christianity/the Danish when used to project Islam: Christianity/the Danish becomes something more stable and demarcated.

10.2.5   Pupils' speech: the relevant and valid experience

In context of the 'universal' Christian (text sample 1), the interaction with pupils is limited to the teacher's construction of pupil experience, something the pupils were simply asked to confirm. When the speech shifts to Islam, the teacher speech does not make use of the bodies of pupils and pupils' parents. However, the selected text sample shows that more extensive pupils' speech now arises in comparison with the speech about the Christian funeral, with which the lesson began. Apart from the extent of pupils' speech, in text sample 2, every pupil contribution is on the pupils' own initiative. But with the exception of the case of Gülsen, these contributions do not become the object of recognition and inclusion in the speech.

When Hazem enters the conversation in TRT2, Tine ends up excluding his contribution as irrelevant: "that's not really the issue right now." Looking at the teacher speech from which Hazem's speech departs, in fact, Tine herself has strayed from the topic. She is not speaking about "what happens when you die (pause) in the rituals" (the opening, text sample 1), but about busy Danish people sending their parents to old people's homes and traditional Muslims taking care of their elders. Nonetheless, Tine's argument for closing down Hazem's speaking turn concerns its putative irrelevance, and she seems to use the occasion to get back on track as she picks up with a "well (pause) when a Christian dies."

Hazem is what I call a minority pupil, meaning that he is one of the pupils whom the teachers describe as characterized by their relation to something non-Danish, something Islam-connected, and something related to being categorized as bilingual. He is among the 12 out of 47 pupils[46] who receive reprimands from the teachers, and is more often than any other pupil assigned a speaking turn on the teacher's initiative without himself having indicated a wish to speak (7 out of the total of 25 such designations). Hazem is, together with Lamine, the most speaking pupil in the plenary session of the school class, but most of Hazem and Lamine's

---

46 Compared to the B-school, the C-school was a much more complicated setting: There were 50 pupils from two school classes participating in the same educational module, compared to 17 pupils organized in one school class at the B-school. Instead of just one teacher at the B-school, there were two teachers at the C-school as well as a third adult present, who functioned as a support person for one of the pupils. In addition, the educational module was organized as partly plenary sessions, partly group work, making it impossible for me to register speaking turns, movements, and reprimands for the entire educational module systematically (as was done for the B-school). What was calculated when I registered the turn-taking practices was thus what took place within the registered 328 minutes of total 355 minutes that the plenary sessions of the module comprised. These plenary sessions were, however, organized quite similarly to their parallel sessions at the B-school – managed from the teacher's desk with a large part of the speech being teacher presentation.

At the B-school it was possible to take into account the different degrees of absence among the pupils when calculating the distribution of speaking turns, whereas at the C-school I have chosen to simply eliminate the three pupils who were absent from more than 50% of the educational module. Thus, the analysis only includes 47 of 50 pupils.

speaking turns are without prior teacher approval – something for which they both receive reprimands. When they do raise their hands, which they do quite often, they are successful approximately every other time.

Lamine is the other pupil who, without prior approval, intervenes in the teacher speech. As with Hazem, he picks up on the teacher speech (in this case, by addressing the theme 'washing the dead'). The language in the pupil's speech is close to the teacher's speech: Both use the plural indefinite "you" [man], and both relate it to a practical activity, articulated as categorically positive. The word "too" in the pupil speech furthermore indicates that this is a supplement to, and not a contestation of, the teacher's presentation. However, the teacher's lack of response and Lamine's repetition of his utterance point to a situation of struggle.

The teacher refers to the fact that Lamine's point about washing "the heart" is not mentioned in the book she has read – something which should be understood as a rejection of Lamine's speech rather than an admission on the teacher's part that her knowledge is limited to the contents of the book. This dismissal is further confirmed by the fact that the teacher's speech immediately picks up where it left off before Lamine's intervention. Lamine's status as knowledge authority on "the Muslim tradition" is thus trumped by the teacher and "the book" that only she has access to. The pupil's contribution now appears as a challenge to the teacher's authority, precisely because it is rejected as such.

In contrast to this, Gülsen's contribution – even though it starts off with a "but," indicating a discrepancy or opposition to the teacher speech – is not only included but explicitly assigned the status of "information" that Gülsen possesses. Gülsen is also one of the most speaking pupils, but she has even more difficulties than Hazem and Lamine in gaining a speaking turn by raising her hand. In four out of five attempts, this strategy fails, and Gülsen instead has a lot of speaking turns without prior approval from the teacher – as it is the case in the above text sample.

A third type of pupil intervention is Lubna's trying to catch the teacher's attention by uttering Tine's name, apparently with no reaction from the teacher. This is not the only time Lubna's strategy fails. She is one of the more frequently speaking pupils of the school class, but her rate of success is 12 to 30 when raising her hand – which means that she is less successful than Lamine and Hazem, who are themselves not among the most successful in using the officially approved turn-taking system. In other words, Lubna in general has more to say than she is allowed to communicate. In my field notes, I recorded several instances of Lubna taking down her hand when she got tired of waiting, only to make another attempt soon thereafter.

10.2.6   Orchestrating pupil experience (text sample 3)

Whereas Hazem's contribution about "the commercial" is dismissed as irrelevant – both in terms of theme and in terms of valid pupil experience – he is later asked to contribute, precisely with experience:

For original Danish version: Appendix B

> Tine: Now I can tell that this is something I've also read and I remember that (hesitates) then all of a sudden I understood it- Lubna I remember (hesitates) that last year you th- then you went to a (hesitates) to a (hesitates) a- (hesitates) a sort of get-together (pause) forty days after someone had died
> Hazem: that was me
> Tine: and you also went- it was you who went to Sweden (pause)
> Hazem: yes
> Tine: yes (pause) and who was it that had died
> Hazem: (hesitates) my grandmother [farmor] or grandfather [morfar] I don't remember (pause)
> Tine: yes (pause) and then you (I) went to Sweden because it was someone who had been buried in Sweden (pause) and then-
> Hazem: no (pause) she was buried in Iran (pause)
> Tine: Iran but you gathered in Sweden then
> Hazem: //yes//
> Tine: //yes// (pause) because it was someone living in Sweden (pause)
> Hazem: no
> Tine: no then why did you go to Sweden
> Hazem: that's because (hesitates)
> Lamine: that's where she was
> Hazem: (hesitates, long pause) my aunt [moster]
> Tine: your aunt was over there (pause) but you- [man]
> Hazem: and she was going to- [skulle]
> Tine: I've read that the first three days after someone in the family has died (pause) then you don't cook at home but then friends and family bring you [én] food (pause).

Here, it is the teacher who is telling the story of Hazem and his family's gathering, and thus, she is the one to suggest what the pupil experience signifies. Hazem is merely asked to contribute by confirming with documentation. The pupil hesitates and partly invalidates the teacher speech. When Hazem then attempts to begin explaining what actually happened during the gathering and why, the teacher shuts down his speaking turn and returns to what she has "read."

What goes on in this sample is similar to the examples of Niels and Nikoline during the 'universal Christian funeral': The teacher speech organizes the pupil experience. Only this time, it does not seem to work out. The pupil does not deliver the demanded confirmation, and/or the teacher's orchestration of the pupil's experience is not recognizable to the pupil.

Viewed as a whole, the ways in which the teacher speech manages pupil speech – including pupil speech explicitly requested by the teacher – appears to be ambiguous. On the one hand, the pupils are expected to contribute and are allowed to do so. Their experiences are apparently a valid part of curriculum in the classroom text. On the other hand, the pupil experience is managed by the teacher who shapes it to fit the teacher speech – something that often results in having to dismiss the pupil speech. The valid pupil experience becomes one that is able to exemplify the teacher's points: A pupil experience that appears to be self-experienced, even though it is organized and staged by the teacher speech.

10.3 Producing subjects, generating pupil experience

The teacher speech handles pupil experience in a number of ways, as the analysis of the text samples shows. In relation to the universal/Danish/Christian, the teacher generates individual figures connected to pupils. More specifically, "Nikoline's father," for instance, is orchestrated as someone who is going to bury his mother, 'Nikoline's 'grandmother.' Then, later in the speech, "Niels' mother"/"Anne"/ "pastor" appears. These figures provide body, individuality, and experience proximity to the content, as well as tie the content to the pupils' bodies. The fact that this content is attached to Danishness/Christianity stages the two pupils in question as connected to these larger entities. With these two pupils being majority pupils, the Danishness of the content is emphasized by being tied to their bodies. Two parallel motions are thus at work – one that projects the pupils in connection to Danishness and church, and one that strengthens the connection between the content and majority/the Danish.

No individuals are projected in relation to "the Muslim tradition"/"Muslims." On the contrary, this speech evolves around collective entities available from the outset. When the singular figure "the imam" is projected, it is without any attachment to bodies and individuality. The personification rests solely with the collective person "Muslims"/"the Muslims," a collective person that Lamine projects as well and which becomes the point of departure for the teacher's introduction of the theme about "Muslims."

Whereas the pupil contributions in the text sample about the universal/ Danish/Christian take place as reaction to the teacher's direct request, the three pupil speeches, and the subsequent exchanges in connection with Islam, are of a different character. They do not occur at the teacher's request, and two of them apparently occur without prior approval from the teacher. One contribution is dismissed as irrelevant, without struggle.

Furthermore, another one – following a struggle – is dismissed as non-valid with reference to a book the teacher has read. Only a single contribution receives recognition inasmuch as it is labeled "information" and subsequently re-articulated and incorporated into the teacher's speech.

10.3.1 Managing knowledge between 'the book' and the 'self-experienced'

The difference between the pupil experience organized by the teacher and that which the pupils organize themselves is that none of the pupils organizes their contributions as self-experienced, whereas the teacher organizes pupil experience as tied to lived life. The non-successful organizing by the teacher of an experience tied to Hazem, which the pupil himself neither recognizes nor acknowledges in the shape presented by the teacher, points to a schism connected to the assignment of knowledge status. This is the disjuncture between pupil-experience and 'the book,' between pupils as knowledge-delivering and the teacher as the interpreting authority.

The ways in which the teacher generates pupil experience – even when these attempts fail – indicate that it is as experiencing subjects that the pupils can occupy a knowledge-delivering space. The teacher, on her part, is the one who possesses the formal knowledge – which the pupils are then required to apply to private life. Valid pupil experience is then the pupil experience that serves as illustration, as the private and self-experienced image of formal knowledge. The good pupil is the pupil that speaks of her/himself, acting as a subject, or who, by confirming the teacher's organizing of her/himself, accepts being made into an object upon which knowledge can be generated.

In this framework, the space for the universal/Danish/Christian pupil subject appears as a wider and more supple space for lived life inasmuch as discrepancies and deviations would only confirm the range of choice, possibility, and flexibility that characterizes this space. In contrast, the space for Muslim subjects must reflect 'tradition,' and this must serve as the generative foundation from which all subjects emerge. Here, the incorporation of pupil experience is an ongoing potential source of conflict: What if the 'tradition'-generated subject represented by the pupil speech contradicts the 'tradition' as it appears in the teacher's 'book'? Whereas discrepancies seem to not only be possible within but can in fact nurture the representation of the universal/Danish/Christian, discrepancies connected to 'the Muslim tradition' (as it is projected by the teacher) opens up conflict.

Within the setting of "Islam" and "the Muslims," the organizing of pupil experience turns into struggle – a struggle to get pupils to contribute, and to contribute in the required manner, as well as a struggle against the ensuing pupil contributions. It appears that a schism is at stake between including pupils and sustaining the authority of the teacher as the guarantor of school-proper subject matter-content.

The pupil speech also appears schismatic. The uninvited pupil speech seems to be alert: alert to possible incorrect elements that might pop up in the teacher speech. At the same time, the invited pupil speech seems to be reluctant or hesitant. The speaking pupils appear to be placed in a schism between wanting to contest the space that both they and "Islam" are assigned, and at the same time having to sustain this space as well as its monolithic character, inasmuch as it is the only space available to them.

This points to the fact that pupil experience can enter as valid knowledge in the official text of the classroom only in very specific forms. The moments of conflict and the level of struggle to include or exclude pupil contributions thus also indicate that minority and majority pupils operate under different conditions.

10.3.2 Organizing pupil experiences and contributions

The patterns of the speaking turns at the C-school can serve to further illuminate the relations between the content and the speakers, namely the question of which pupils contribute or are expected to contribute to the official text of the classroom – and who are not – and in what ways.

When looking at the turn-taking system at the C-school, the most uncommon type of speaking turn is – as was the case at the B-school – the teacher designation without prior hand-raising (7.76%), while the most common speaking turn is pupil speech without prior approval (51.55%). The distribution pattern of these uncommon and common types of speaking turns, respectively, is noticeable in relation to how the teacher speech relates in different ways to pupil experience. Whereas the pupil contributions that appear in connection to the universal/ Danish/Christian occur on the initiative of the teacher – who asks specific (majority) pupils for confirmation of the content she projects (Nikoline and Niels) – the pupil contributions connected to Islam occurs, in several ways, in another way and has another character. They are not teacher-initiated, and two of them apparently occur without prior teacher approval of the right to speak. One of these contributions is, without struggle, dismissed as irrelevant; one is, following struggle, dismissed as non-valid with reference to the teacher's text book, accessible only to the teacher. A third contribution is recognized, inasmuch as it is denoted "information" and then rearticulated by and included in the teacher speech.

10.3.3 The designated and the invisible

Gaining a speaking turn upon hand-raising is much more common at the C-school than at the B-school (40.68% of the total speaking turns, as opposed to 12.41%). Hand-raising is, however, only a successful strategy in just about half the instances, as opposed to a success rate at around two-thirds when speaking without prior approval. The most successful in the former strategy are the majority boys (62.12% of the instances, as opposed to minority boys who succeed less than half the time). Girls, majority as well as minority, are not as successful as the boys when it comes to using the formal, legitimate turn-taking system. However, both majority and minority girls succeed more than 80% of their attempts to speak without prior approval. In this strategy the minority boys succeed in 64.41% of their attempt, against 51.02% for majority boys.

A broad view of the speaking turn registrations shows that while minority girls and majority boys have a number of speaking turns more or less equaling their share of the school class, majority girls speak significantly less, and minority boys significantly more than their share. The most invisible pupils in the turn-taking system are those whom I have chosen to call 'half minority' regardless of gender category, meaning those about whom the teachers highlight that one of their parents is non-Danish.[47]

---

[47] As with the B-school, I base these categories of minority and majority on the teachers' descriptions of the pupils: Those who were not categorized through a non-Danish national

The teacher-initiated designations of speaking turns are never aimed at pupils in the half-minority category, whereas more than half of the – otherwise relatively rare – designations are aimed at minority boys. Apart from half-minority pupils, majority girls receive the fewest teacher-initiated designations of speaking turns compared to their share of the school class. One could say that minority boys receive most teacher attention at the expense of majority girls, whereas half-minority pupils receive no attention at all. But is it meaningful to frame teacher attention this way? The relatively higher number of designated speaking turns aimed at minority boys could also indicate that they fill a specific function in this particular educational module: They are the ones who are particularly expected and required to contribute with 'themselves.' The fact that this type of designation is significantly more often aimed at pupils with an expected affiliation with Islam (with Hazem receiving the highest number (7) of designations) – and the fact that none of the half-minority pupils fits this teacher categorization – operates in favor of this interpretation. In this case, it seems that minority girls do not serve the same function as 'contributing Muslims' as the minority boys do.

10.4 Summing up: constructing the objects Christianity and Islam

In the analysis of the samples from the official text of the classroom, 'Christianity' is projected through 'the universal,' namely the event that someone dies and a number of obligations that then arise in connection to this. Simultaneously, 'Christianity' is organized by means of a range of choices. These choices relate to things that must be sorted out: the belongings of the deceased, the events that must take place in order to complete the funeral, the choice of flowers, coffin, etc., as well as the choice of transportation of the deceased and the choice between cremation and burial. The undertaker system is projected as the intermediator of these choices, and through this projection the content of the speech becomes identified with the Danish.

---

affiliation, 34 pupils, and those who were described through a non-Danish national affiliation and as Muslims, 9 pupils. There is a third group at the C-school who were described as having one Danish parent and one or more non-Danish parents: Rebecca – "Danish mother and … African father," of whom the latter was no longer present but instead there was "another African man who appears entirely as a father to her." Paula – "Who has a mother from Chile," and was mentioned as one of those pupils who were "half-bilingual, so to speak."
Anders – described as "Thai," something which was further elaborated with the information that his mother was Thai and his father was either "dead" or "non-existent." Benjamin – "half-American," with an "American father" and a "mother who's an academic." In the total counts, the first three are calculated as minority pupils, as their partly non-Danish affiliation appeared primary in the teachers' descriptions, whereas the fourth, Benjamin, is calculated as majority, as the Danishness of his mother appears to be strong enough for the teachers to describe her by another feature, namely, her level of education. Benjamin appeared to be considered more half-majority than half-minority, so to speak.
These four pupils, however, were also counted separately in order to detect possible particularities in the ways in which they were included in or contributed to the classroom conversation.

The figures populating this projection of universal Danish Christianity are individuals: "Nikoline's father," "Niels' mother/pastor" and "the undertaker"; the latter a less private or personalized individual than the other two, but nonetheless it appears in the speech in singular and definite form. Furthermore, "Niels' mother/pastor" and "the undertaker" are emphasized as professional individuals, as individuals at work. Christianity and the practices connected to this are thus characterized as caused by universal conditions as well as something that offers to satisfy the needs generated by these universal conditions; Christianity and Christian practices become strongly flavored by choice and attached to things and artefacts that can be chosen through professional institutions, particularly the undertaker system. Not least Christianity and Christian practices are represented by individuals with a stable affiliation to a collective ritual and institutional framework – the church – and two out of these three individuals are explicitly attached to selected majority pupils in the classroom. Thus Christianity is projected as a frame offering choices as well as a convenient limitation of choices, managed by individual professionals who are themselves part of a limiting and yet flexible framework. The knowledge about Christianity is organized as prescription of possibilities for practices.

The collectivity of Christianity is more strongly emphasized when projected in contrast to "Muslims," but as this collectivity is attached to labor market and bustle, Christian practices become the practical and flexible yet stable framework, that makes the decisions that arise from universal conditions manageable. Islam, on the other hand, is projected as an a priori particular and demarcated tradition, generating practice for a particular collective of persons: "Muslims"/"the Muslims."

The figures populating the projection of Islam and Islamic practices are not individuals, but rather the collective of "Muslims," "the Muslim tradition," and "the imam." The latter appears, as the only figure, in definite singular, but is not described as professional, as was the case with the pastor and the undertaker. Rather, the imam is projected as the extension of "the Muslim tradition." Islam and the practices connected to this are thus, in the classroom speech, characterized by being a particular and demarcated tradition as well as being populated by a collective of Muslims which appear as in opposition to Denmark and the Danish "we." "Muslims" are projected as a collective whose actions are an extension of and can be derived from "the Muslim tradition," and these actions are tied to "old people" and to "respect" in contrast to the busy, labor market-oriented Danish. Islam appears as a kind of non-Danish nationality marked by a – sympathetically described – retrospectivity, and not by relation to labor, profession, and things and services that must be sorted out and among which one can choose.

"The Muslim tradition" in this context becomes the primary figure and an enunciation modality (a subject) in and of itself, unlike the different individuals populating the projection of Christianity. This means that the conditions for incorporating and organizing pupil experience in relation to the two religions – and for being a pupil who is attached to either of these religions – are different.

10.4.1 Formal knowledge and experience knowledge

Whereas the teacher speech organizes pupil experience as attached to lived life – particularly when designating specific contributions – none of the pupils, however, organizes their contributions as something self-experienced. When the teacher attempts to explicitly attach such a lived life experience to a pupil, as is the case with Hazem, this is unsuccessful: Tine suggests a content to which Hazem is asked to confirm his attachment to, he hesitates, disconfirms and is then excluded from the speech. Even when unsuccessful, however, the teacher projection of pupil experience suggests that it is as experiencing subjects that the pupils have a place as knowledge suppliers. The teacher possesses formal knowledge, whereas pupils are included in order to tie the formal knowledge to the private. Valid pupil experiences are thus those that serve to illustrate the formal knowledge through something experienced and private.

The good pupil is then, as this analysis suggests, a pupil who speaks out of him/herself, and thus acts as a subject, or who, by confirming the teacher's organizing of him/herself as a subject, accepts being the object of knowledge construction. When the by tradition derived Muslim subject then says something else than what Muslim tradition – as projected in the teacher speech – says, conflict emerges. Not so for the by choice- and labor market-flavored Christian subject: Here discrepancies between teacher utterances and potential pupil utterances are not only manageable within but can also nourish the representations of the universal/Danish/Christian. Within this frame things can be done in many different ways, and this only serves to affirm the universal-ness/Danishness/Christianness.

That the projection of Islam takes its point of departure in pre-given, collective figures means that the organization of pupil speech becomes a latent struggle: a struggle to make the pupils contribute, to deliver themselves, in the desired way, and a struggle against pupil contributions. There seems to be a schism between incorporating pupils and preserving teacher authority. The pupil speech appears schismatic as well: Alert to un-correctness that might appear in the teacher speech, as well as hesitant and reluctant. The pupils organized as Muslim pupils appear to be placed in a schism between wanting to contest the space allocated to them and to Islam, and at the same time, inasmuch as this is the only space available to them in the speech, they have to maintain this space and its monolithic character.

To sum up, the strongly classified religions and pupils related to these religions, which appeared in the teacher speech about curriculum, appears when recontextualized into practiced classroom text, as subjects with different qualities attached to them.

The by tradition derived Muslim is projected as antique and timeless, and without any relation to labor and consumption, whereas the universal Danish Christian subject is flavored with choice, especially consumers' choice and connected to professionalism and labor market. This is worked up through a teacher-controlled category of experience knowledge which is contested but nevertheless produced in a socioeconomically flavored landscape of knowledge and identities.

At the C-school, however, the official text of the classroom in the plenary sessions is not the only frame of teaching, and as presented in the school and teacher speech about curriculum, neither is plenary what the teachers regard as the primary frame. The next chapter will dig deeper into the school economy of 'the group' in relation to the socioeconomy of the school classes. What does the classroom as social space look like when we analyze teacher categorizations of pupils? In what follows, hierarchies of recognition are analyzed in relation to another type of focus, namely on individual pupils and specific groups of pupils that appear in the teachers' descriptions as well as in relation to one of the groups organized by the teacher. In this group, the pupils have been distributed according the teacher criteria framing them as for instance 'religious experts' and socially and school-wise talented pupils.

11. The hierarchy of problematization: teachers' interest and teachers' concern

Chapter 10 dealt with the relations between content and speakers in the landscape generated through the plenary classroom speech. At the C-school, however – unlike at the B-school which was more 'traditionally' organized in terms of educational methods – group work forms an equally central part of the educational module at the C-school as the plenary sessions do. This chapter thus zooms in on the pupils in a working group composed by the teachers for the group work part of the educational module in *Kristendomskundskab*.

11.1 The empirical material

The analysis will focus on the five pupils in a teacher organized group as they are described by the teachers in relation to other pupils, contrasted with the pupils' self-descriptions. In particular the two pupils Gülsen and Niels will serve as a point of departure. The empirical material is similar to that which was analyzed in Chapter 6 from the B-school, namely interviews with teachers before, during and after the educational module, as well as interviews with pupils. In this chapter, however, observations from the registrations of the turn-taking practices are also incorporated when it serves to elaborate or support the analysis, with particular attention to the Bourdieu-inspired analysis of the pupil strategies and positionings.

Furthermore, the examination of the degrees to which the pupils are the object of teacher recognition (in relation to their respective social backgrounds) is expanded to also include a third type of material that was only produced in relation to the C-school: namely information about the pupils' social background variables collected through questionnaires distributed among the parents of the pupils.[48]

Through a reading of all these types of material, I analyze the forms of teacher categorization and the forms of capital that are recognized or unrecognized. I draw up a socioeconomic landscape of the selected group and, when it serves to expand the analysis, relate these five pupils to other pupils in the school classes.

One of the general patterns that appears when we shift the focus from the official classroom text to the teacher descriptions, pupil self-descriptions, and parental accounts of social backgrounds is that the bottom of the school group landscape is populated by girls – both majority girls possessing a low level of capital and minority girls (regardless of disposition) – whereas the top end is populated by majority pupils (including majority girls) whose cultural Bildung capital is valued highly.

---

[48] Not all parents filled out these questionnaires, and not all of the pupils were interviewed. There were a total of 50, among whom 47 were present for more than half of the educational module. When one or more of the three types of material is missing in relation to a specific pupil this is explicated as well as factored into the analysis.

11.1.1   The group composition

The five pupils – Gülsen, Niels, Clara, Daniella, and Janus – included in the group in focus were assembled from the criteria of the teachers (as described in Chapter 9). These criteria are strongly explicated, on the one hand, centering on the 'spreading out' of 'experts' represented by 'Muslims' (related to 'other religions') and 'Scouts' and 'mini-candidates for confirmation' (related to 'Christianity') as well as "others with pre-understanding" (as was articulated in the written plan for the educational module). On the other hand, the criteria are vague when articulated in terms of social skills and the ability to cooperate and work collaboratively.

Gülsen – who in the plenary sessions, as one of the few pupils, is more than once asked to contribute without prior hand-raising – appears here as the pupil who is selected to represent the 'Muslim expert,' whereas the mini-candidate for confirmation Clara and the pastor's son Niels represent Christianity. Gülsen is one of the most frequently speaking pupils and uses both formally approved and not explicitly approved speaking turns, though she is not very successful in the former. She has difficulties gaining access the legitimate way, but is rarely reprimanded for speaking out of turn. There is, in other words, not entirely accordance between what Gülsen aims for and what she can achieve, but if she is persistent, she can usually occupy the desired position.

Niels speaks less than Gülsen – though still quite a lot. He attempts to gain access to both formally and informally approved speaking turns, but neither option seems very open, and the risk of being dismissed and reprimanded is a permanent condition. In Niels' case, his attempts to use formally approved turn-taking are successful in half the instances, but he is reprimanded every time he tries to speak without prior approval. He is, however, along with Gülsen, among the few pupils to whom the teacher designates speaking turns without them having asked for it.

Daniella and Janus, two other pupils in the teacher-composed working group – both majority – have between no and low rate of success with their hand-raising in the plenary sessions. However, Janus often speaks without prior approval and thus belongs to the one third of the pupils who occupy two thirds of the speaking turns. In the teacher's descriptions neither Daniella nor Janus are highlighted for their contributions to the school content. Instead, both are described as socially problematic: Janus as "noisy" and "mean" to the other children, something the teacher explains by the fact that he has a history of illness (Juvenile Rheumatoid Arthritis), and Daniella as someone who generally overreacts and who does not reflect on the potential "consequences" of her actions. Janus' school proficiency is not described at all, whereas Daniella's is estimated to be "below average."

The fifth pupil in the group is the majority pupil Clara. In terms of her function in the teacher-composed working group, she is – apart from, as a mini-candidate for confirmation, representing Christianity – selected to fit a specific element of another more vague type of teacher criteria, namely an idea that Tine has about good and bad leaders:

> "There are some groups in which the strong clever group leader ... right ... step in and says don't you worry about ... say 'I'll fix that'-kind of, right ... or at least that becomes the outcome ... and it might not be exactly the intention but then bub and prrrr (making sounds) and then they just work and work and the others become sort of extras and then there are those who really try."

The good group leader is thus not the kind of leader that renders the other members redundant by doing all the work – in Tine's view, the good group leader is someone who could incorporate the others, organize them, and manage their skills, or at least would try to do so. As an example of this type Tine mentions Clara:

> "I mean Clara she's just sitting there and she could have done everything a hundred times faster by herself right but she just patiently sits there by the computer and lets someone like okay now I'm writing one sentence and then you write a sentence and then you write a sentence I mean really trying to turn it into group work."

In the plenary sessions, Clara was one of the eight pupils who said nothing at all; she neither attempted to speak nor was she asked to do so. But silence is not necessarily interpreted and valued negatively by the teachers. As the teacher Jens remarked during the descriptions of the pupils: "Who says that everything revolves around speaking in plenary?" There is problematic silence – the sort that indicates a lack of interest or skills to contribute – and there is productive silence. In the educational module in *Kristendomskundskab*, some of "the girls that are actually really really clever and and ... would usually raise their hand all of the time" have been standing in the background, something which in itself can be useful, according to Tine. She adds: "You can also contribute by not saying anything." In such cases, silence is interpreted by the teacher as an ability to step back and not having to "constantly draw attention to yourself." This is the kind of silence that is attributed to the 'good leader' Clara.

11.1.2 Organizing the material and the analysis

All three types of research material exist in the case of Gülsen, whereas Niels' parents did not fill out the questionnaire; however, the interviews with him provided quite detailed information about their socioeconomic background, which was the primary objective of the questionnaire. I seek to make use of the different conditions for analyzing the different pupils – including those in relation to whom Gülsen and Niels are set – by analyzing socioeconomic background as something that is seen, and seen differently by different agents; for instance, the degree of detail provided, including in the questionnaires, varies quite a lot.

In other words, dispositions are analyzed as relational, and the emphasis is put on the practices of categorization in relation to forms of capitals, whereas the concept of habitus, as was the case with the B-school, serves more as a backdrop. At the same time, however, the analysis situates the pupils as precisely sociological occurrences and, by juxtaposing the concept of capital with the practices of categorization, I seek to sustain an analysis of the classroom and its agents as occurrences in the social space rather than to ascribe power to the categories as such.

A pivotal lever of the analysis is to analyze the teachers' ways of projecting pupils by relating utterances about one specific pupil to utterances about other pupils, whenever this technique can serve to expand upon the analytical findings. The basis of these comparisons are the categorizations that the teachers use to describe the individual pupils, and in some cases the teachers themselves make explicit comparisons between particular pupils.

11.2 Gülsen and Amalie: "A kind of girl that ... lacks some social filters" and "The most social and diplomatic child"

Gülsen and Amalie are not explicitly related to one another by the teachers. However, there are striking similarities in their ways of conducting their gender, something which makes the lack of relation between them in the teachers' descriptions remarkable. They also show a similar pattern in the turn-taking system: Both speak often without prior teacher approval, and most of the time they do so successfully. Amalie, however, is more successful than Gülsen when it comes to using the explicitly legitimate turn-taking system. She raises her hand 16 times, of which she gains 6 speaking turns. For Gülsen, in contrast, the rate of success is 3 to 15.

In the teachers' descriptions, Gülsen and Amalie are both first and foremost categorized by their social skills, albeit in different ways: respectively, as socially deviant in a problematic way, and as socially capable as well as deviant, but in an interesting way.

11.2.1   Gülsen about Gülsen, and the teacher about "that kind of girl"

Gülsen is one of the tallest pupils in the school class. She wears sports clothing and often plays soccer in the schoolyard during the period of my observations. She seems attentive and interested during the interview and is very curious to know if she will be part of a book. She does not hesitate when asked to present herself:

> MB: Gülsen would you talk a little about yourself?
> G: Yes, sure I will [...] my name is Gülsen and I'm 10 years old (pause, hesitation) and my last name is [...] and live in Copenhagen and I live up at [...] and my birthday is [...] then I'll be 11 ... and I'm in the 4th grade at the [...] school.

Gülsen is also the only of the 15 interviewed pupils from the C-school who, on her own initiative, starts talking about the educational module in *Kristendomskundskab*. She does so while elaborating on her answer to which school subjects she likes best (Danish, English, and Math):

> G: ... but Christianity and religion they're also great actually that's what we're doing this week
> MB: yes ... do you like that?
> G: yes, I like it
> MB: what about it do you like?
> G: I liked that I got to know a lot exciting it's very exciting to hear Christianity and ... it's also quite- a little about Muslim cause I'm also Muslims[49] myself (MB: yes yes) and I got to know things from a Muslims because I kne- didn't know that much about Muslim
> MB: no ... so you also got to know about Mu- about being Muslim
> G: yes (MB: yes yes) and then we went to the mosque and got to know something about that ... then we went to the church and got to know something about that ... but then I saw those ... then I asked the lady in the church ... the lady ... the pastor can we see that thing you're baptized in ... (MB: yes yes) ... that ... and then she said yes and we were allowed to touch the water.

Gülsen both indicates that she herself is Muslim and that she previously did not know much about this – she does not give the impression that she has much experience with this. Nonetheless, she is one of those pupils whom the teacher Jens highlights for "suddenly" being able to "contribute with something," precisely in her capacity as one of the "Muslim children." Tine, who is generally disappointed that "the Muslim children" did not "know more," highlights Gülsen for the opposite – for being non-knowledgeable – for instance, stating that Gülsen "keeps asking where Mekka is and those kind of things, really," which Tine finds "really difficult to stand."

Gülsen herself highlights concrete undertakings such as visiting the mosque and the church, as well at touching the font, as the exciting part of the module. As a whole it seems that Gülsen mentions everything that she can think of, related to the themes about which I ask her. For instance, when I try to conclude the interview, she continues on her own initiative:

> MB: Okay ... that was it, Gülsen
> G: I also have a friend who comes from Hindu (MB: yes okay) ... but she has one at home she has ... her God it is all kinds of things about animals ... giraffes horses all kinds of things
> MB: okay ... you mean that there are Gods?
> G: yes (MB: yes yes) and then I was just like one day do animals as well- do we also have animals ... then my mother said no we don't have any animals
> MB: no ... well that's interesting ... what's her name?
> G: yes ... her name is [...] she comes from India ... I was at someone's place ... she has a closet ... and then there were all kinds of Gods and all those I know what Gods what they're called

---

49 Cf. chapter 1: The words Muslim and Islam are the same in Danish as in English, but many Copenhagen area school children, regardless of relation to migration history, use the wording 'en muslimer': a Muslims (singular plural, so to speak) about a person, and 'Muslim' about Islam.

MB: what's it called
G: [mumbling to herself] … shivi (MB: yes yes) shivin (MB: yes yes) he's called shivin.

Among the pupils interviewed Gülsen is the one who speaks most extensively about the school content of the educational module. She is also the one who most explicitly emphasizes an outcome of the module, and who – as this excerpt shows – relates it to what she assumes to be knowledge relevant to the theme, namely, observations from the home of a friend and what this tells about that friend's religion.

Gülsen says she generally likes school, but that the homework can be difficult – she does not always understand the tasks because sometimes she cannot hear properly what the teachers say:

> "because we have some classes that are open … and then you can't at all hear what for instance my teacher he's called Jens […] if you can't hear anything then you can't understand either."

By open classes, the pupil is referring to the particular spatial organization of the C-school (as explained earlier) in which plenary sessions as well as group work often takes place in open rooms, meaning rooms only partly secluded by walls (a so-called open plan architecture); sometimes the pupils work in small groups, sometimes two school classes (50 pupils) sit in the same lesson. Furthermore, when speaking of her difficulties, Gülsen presents herself as a dedicated pupil.

The teacher descriptions of her are remarkably different. The first categorization by the teacher Jens highlighted that Gülsen is "from Turkey." Whereas both of her parents are born in Turkey and indicate in the questionnaire that "Turkish/Kurdish" is their mother tongue, Gülsen herself is in fact born in Denmark. The pupil expresses it this way: She is "also from Turkey," but born in Denmark. The teacher's second categorization of Gülsen concerned her gender ("that kind of girl"), in relation to her having "great difficulties in … that she wants- she- she lacks some filters some social filters." For Jens, these missing "filters" are exemplified as follows: "when you enter the school class she'll instantly be all over you and … and- and say things that and … even very personal stuff right away" upon which he mentions that "she also receives some special needs education."

The teacher mentions nothing about Gülsen's background (other than her being "from Turkey"). Gülsen herself describes, however, her parents' occupations, and the parents have also filled out the questionnaire quite thoroughly. The family (two adults and four children) live in the social housing neighborhood in which the rental apartments recently have been sold as cooperative apartments. Both parents state that they have primary and lower secondary education from Turkey, and that the mother is home-based, whereas the father "works at restaurant." From the interview with Gülsen it seems that her father in fact owns a store, a pizza parlor, and is thus self-employed. About her mother, Gülsen says that she is on maternity leave and otherwise works in the kitchen at an old people's home.

The teacher's information about Gülsen receiving special needs education is also the only direct mention of her school skills. As this information is given as a direct extension of her lacking "social filters," it appears that Gülsen's social and school skills are interwoven in the teacher's projection of her as a pupil. The same pattern appears in the description of Daniella who is projected as a socially inappropriate pupil, a description that is directly linked to the valuation of her school skills as low.

The teacher described Gülsen's problem with behaving in school culture as a problem with maintaining the appropriate boundaries between public and private: problems controlling herself and being intimate in the right places at the right ways. For the other 'sports girl' in the school class, the majority pupil Amalie, in contrast, the teacher descriptions are diametrically opposite: Amalie lacks no "social filters"; rather, she is "the most social and diplomatic child ever." In the plenary sessions Amalie speaks without prior approval 12 times, and only twice does she receive a reprimand for this.

11.2.2 The teacher regarding "a real kind of sports girl"

Gülsen's way of doing her gender (both in terms of appearances and practices) seems to attract neither interest nor problematization from the teachers; rather, her gender is only emphasized in relation to the projection of her as socially problematic ("that kind of girl").

In contrast, the gender aspects of Amalie – who, like Gülsen, wears sports clothing and plays soccer – is central to the teacher descriptions of her. In the following excerpt, Tine leads the conversation, while the other teacher Jens listens and comments:

> Tine: Amalie she must be the most social and diplomatic child ever … clever and sweet and … and- and under pressure … because she's interested in soccer and not in nail polish and I mean not nail polish but girls' stuff, right (MB: yes yes) she doesn't collect [incomprehensible] and [incomprehensible] and they also don't have a lot of money and then they also have some … principles so … it's not just a matter of money it's also about that you … don't have to buy everything (MB: yes yes) and things like that right … and they sometimes feel that- sometimes she's a little under pressure by that
> MB: and that's Amalie?
> Tine: that's Amalie (MB: yes yes) dark-haired Amalie who also wears soccer clothing (MB: yes yes) and physically she is really great she's really great at playing ball and those kinds of things actually
> Jens: Yes, yes
> Tine: Actually she's in fact not just I mean she's a real kind of sports girl … runs as well … and mother works with … at the technical aids center and father … studies and work at the postal service (MB: yes yes) History I think.

As with Gülsen, the first categorization of Amalie is aimed at her social skills. She is described as "clever," but this is supplemented with the added characteristic "sweet." Then, Tine voices what she depicts as partly an effect of the parents' priorities, partly as a matter of fact: That Amalie is "under pressure" by not being like the other girls, by having no interest in "girls stuff," as well as not being able – or allowed – to consume certain things that other girls collect. The teacher thus expresses a sympathetic concern about the pupil's difficulties with fitting into what both teachers call "the girl group" of the school classes. In other words, she expresses sensitivity towards the pupil's problems with adjusting to her gender, a gender that is framed by something and someone other than the teacher – probably the other pupils, as well as the companies, for instance, that produce the collectable items marketed to girls in this age group. In contrast, Gülsen's gender is not subject to this kind of sensitivity. Amalie is described as 'pressured' (by the pupil culture), whereas Gülsen is described as 'pressuring.'

It is Gülsen's other deviations – her Turkishness, her social deficiencies – that are highlighted. Gülsen's gender appears naturalized, and related to the problematic kind of pupil she is, whereas someone else or some other social forces, outside of the teachers themselves, are pressuring Amalie and thereby narrowing the space for her to be the good pupil who she truly is.

Considering what kinds of dispositions the teachers attached to Amalie, an explicated valuation is at work, which may be understood in the light of the concepts of economic and cultural Bildung capital. "They" (referring to Amalie and her parents), have no money – something which is sidelined by their having "principles" that involve a critical attitude towards consumerism. Tine concludes that the reason Amalie cannot collect the girls' items is not only money but also the expression of a deliberate choice: "you don't have to buy everything." The parents' lack of economic capital is thus ascribed a certain cultural capital value.

The teacher describes the professional and educational backgrounds of Amalie's parents with a degree of detail that matches the degree of detail with which these parents themselves have filled out the questionnaire; they have both graduated from high school, and the mother is an occupational therapist, while the father has two bachelor degrees and works at the post office. The parents also state that their mother tongue is Danish and that they own a cooperative apartment. In the teacher's description, the father's lower-status job, working at the post office, is encircled by the words "studies" and the specification of those studies: "History." In other words, Amalie's parents are projected as temporary and classy poor: Their lack of opportunities for consumption is ascribed cultural value by explaining it as a choice based on informed attitudes, and the father's university studies indicate a potential for acquiring a certain future economic capital. Thus, this family appears in the teacher's categorization practices as belonging to the cultural middle class.

In contrast, Gülsen's background is not ascribed any kind of economic or cultural Bildung capital or potential, whatsoever. In this framework, Gülsen is described as a defective pupil, socially and vocationally (the only indication of her school skills being the mention of her receiving special needs education), whereas

Amalie is described as a clever and socially functional pupil whose functionality is constrained by the pupil hierarchy. Thus, the minority pupil with low passable capital becomes problematic ("that kind of girl"), while the majority pupil with a high degree of passable capital becomes the object of emphathetic teacher efforts to defend the pupil's right to negotiate her gender.

11.3 The girl group hierarchy: the academics' daughter, a girl who thinks she's clever, and one who's out of proportion

Gülsen's gender-bending does not become the object of sensitive interest from the teachers, neither is she projected in the teacher speech as belonging to what is called "the girl group." Two prominent figures in this hierarchical configuration are the majority pupils Clara and Caroline. Partly due to her status as a "mini-candidate for confirmation" and partly due to Tine's identification of her as exemplary of a 'good leader' (whose lack of contributions in the plenary sessions was evaluated positively by the teacher), Clara is placed in the same working group as Gülsen.

Clara is described by the teacher with expressions such as "she maintains a perfect order, I mean she's just completely on top of everything." In contrast, her counterpart, Caroline – presented as such in the teacher speech – is described as "also vocationally very very competent but not at all with the same discipline as Clara, I mean self-discipline and she doesn't challenge herself like Clara does." The teachers describe Clara's parents as "academics," although in fact only one of them has a degree at the Master's level.[50] This discrepancy between fact and description can be understood in light of the function that the "academic" designation might have in the categorization practices of the teachers: namely, as a way of projecting parents' skills as qualified school parents. They represent a "sensible family that's supportive ... and that reacts on things when you talk with them about it," a characteristic that is emphasized in relation to Clara's ability to be 'completely on top of things.'

It is not school discipline, however, that Clara herself highlights in the interview. She says she enjoys school and, when asked why, she replies:

> "because it's not like you have to stay in your seat all of the time ... you're allowed to be with your friends as well and then ... it's also just ... fun."

Unlike Gülsen, Clara expresses appreciation for the social and variable physical environment of school, emphasizing the various types of group work where you can "be together with who you want." Although group work in Clara's speech is framed as entirely positive, she nevertheless pays more attention to what the teachers say than what the other pupils say, "because you know that it's correct

---

50 Being an 'academic' in Denmark has customarily been associated with having a degree on at least the kandidat level (similar to the Master level) from the classical universities and similar institutions of higher education.

because the teachers say it and of course because they are educated to do so and things like that." In other words, the recognition of Clara's school skills that the teacher expresses when describing her as "on top of things" is reciprocated by the pupil, who articulates a trust in the teacher's knowledge authority.

11.3.1   The wrong kind of dominance

Among her specific friends, Clara mentions the majority girls Emma and Caroline. The teacher Tine often compares Clara and Caroline explicitly. While Clara is described as the epitome of a 'good leader,' Caroline is described as "very dominating in relation to the girl group ... and not always in the most diplomatic and charming way." Further, Tine adds:

> "but that- they've also started to stand up against that and so on but- but ... I mean she- she- she her she self-confidence is just way up there (MB: yes yes) I mean I don't think *she* [strong intonation] knows that there are some who do not- actually think she's wonderful so ... she's ... yes."

Later, in relation to another pupil, Frederikke, Tine adds that Caroline "has lots of competitors" in terms of being "number one" in class, and that she is "actually not at all the most clever ... she just thinks she is." While Clara is primarily described in extension of other pupils, even as she was distinguished from them, Caroline is only described in contrast to other pupils, primarily with various negative evaluations. In the teacher's speech, a pupil hierarchy appears which the teacher not only describes but also takes sides in. Hence, number one in class is not actually the most clever one. Such a seemingly contradictory utterance nevertheless becomes intelligible in light of the interweaving of the vocational, the self-managing, the personal, and the social, which were all variously projected in the teacher speech about Clara and Caroline.

A specific type of school knowledge, taking the form of skills that ought to be achieved, namely self-management skills, becomes visible.

According to Tine, with agreement from Jens, both girls are described as "really really clever," but with regard to the latter, a "but" is attached, and Caroline's cleverness is negated by her lesser degree of "discipline" – understood here as self-discipline – and her lack of ambition to "challenge herself," and thus her lesser ability to exercise self-management. She is also dominant in the wrong way, unlike the 'good leader' Clara.

In the pupil hierarchy, it is not dominance per se that the teacher describes as problematic, but rather the ways in which dominance is exercised. Furthermore, the teacher enters into a debate on the girls' hierarchy: Tine does not question the fact that something and someone is recognized by the girl group while other things/others are not; she simply questions the particular judgments as such. Thus, for the teacher, Caroline is not worthy of the status that she enjoys, and Tine applauds what she interprets as indications that Caroline's status as "number one" might come to be challenged.

11.3.2   Below the hierarchy

Of the female pupils not described in relation to a 'girl group' or a 'girl hierarchy' we find Gülsen – as well as the other minority girls – and for instance the majority girl Daniella. The description of Daniella widely follows the same pattern as that of Gülsen. First, a social problematic-ness is elaborated, closely followed by a concluding comment on her vocational skills: "she's … just below average."

In contrast to Gülsen, though, Daniella's parents constituted a part of the teacher's description of her, not least her social deficiencies and socially inappropriate reactions, such as an "exaggerated sense of justice," which means that if someone is "cheated" or "treated unfairly," Daniella "get's so outraged that she starts to cry herself." Different versions of this 'sense of justice' categorization are used to describe several pupils as being socially problematic (to varying degrees). Moreover, this categorization is exclusively used to describe girls. In Daniella's case, it is emphasized with the word "exaggerated," indicating that it is the pupil's sense of proportion that is fundamentally wrong: She tends to overreact – her reactions lack socially appropriate proportions. She also appears to be illegitimate, or at least unsuccessful, in the turn-taking system. Apart from the single speaking turn she gains by speaking out of turn – something for which she is not reprimanded, however – she attempts to gain an explicitly legitimate speaking turn by raising her hand four times, but with no results.

With regard to Daniella's parents, the first information supplied in the teacher speech is that they are divorced, that Daniella lives with her father and has "very little contact" with the mother. Notably, this does not correspond with the ways in which Daniella describes the relationship. The mother is a recurring figure in Daniella's speech, among other things, as one of the people with whom she has discussed the educational module in *Kristendomskundskab*. Daniella, like Gülsen, speaks extensively about the content of the module – not so much about "the Christian things," but about how it was "quite fun" to learn about "how Muslims are doing" and how Muslims do things. Daniella explains this interest with the fact that her mother has a lot of Muslim friends whom the mother knows from her own school days. Her mother works as a cleaner, and according to Daniella, this is the reason that she cannot always stay with her every other weekend, as planned – because the mother has to work odd hours and during the weekends.

Daniella is preoccupied with the social relations in the school class and describes friends and relations as the primary factors affecting whether or not she enjoys school, and whether or not she is able to learn things. In the positive sense, she describes how (girl)friends during group work can help her understand the things that she did not understand from the teachers. In the negative sense, group work could sometimes turn into a struggle that she is always able to navigate: When the teachers do the matching and she ends up with someone she does not know well, she sometimes ends up being "pressured to choose something" (for instance, a theme on which she did not want to work).

Whereas Daniella describes herself and her schooling as closely interwoven with her social relations (particularly with other girls), she is not described by the teachers as part of the 'girl group' or pupil hierarchy. A pattern seems to be that the girl group hierarchy in the teachers' descriptions includes only those girls with some level of recognized economic and cultural capital, as well as the skills to convert this capital into status in the school context.

Neither Daniella's father, who works as a painter (craftsman), nor Daniella's cleaning worker mother (depicted by the teacher as absent) is ascribed much economic capital and no cultural Bildung capital in the teacher speech. As such, Daniella, like Gülsen, in the teacher categorization practice ends up not at the bottom of the girl group hierarchy, but rather outside and beneath it. In the teacher speech, the majority girls with no recognized capitals and the minority girls, in general, populate the bottom of the classroom economy.

11.4 Those that bring bad influences from other institutions and those that bring it from home

There are several pupils – boys – who are described in terms of 'obstructive' school behavior, such as "naughty"/"cheeky," "back-talking," "trouble-making," etc. However, their behavior is explained by the teachers in various ways: The 'origins' of the problem are be identified differently; the problematic behavior is described with different degrees of emphasis and different degrees of prospective progress, and it is set in relation to different issues and contexts.

11.4.1 The one who picked it up

One of the pupils whom the teachers describe as "cheeky" is Niels. His parents both have relatively high levels of education: the mother a Master's degree in academic Theology and the father an MA in Medicine. As already mentioned in the previous chapter, the mother is a pastor, and the father is a doctor who "travels a lot" and therefore is not very present in the home, according to Niels. The professions and educational backgrounds of his parents are not part of the teacher descriptions of Niels – though the fact that his mother is a pastor is a recurring theme both in the interviews and the teaching. Nevertheless, the parents do appear as figures in the teacher descriptions, namely as allies in the project of moderating Niels' socially problematic behavior:

> Jens: then there's Niels ... who's relatively new he came along with someone named Rasmus ... last year and [...] he's that kind of ... cheeky little boy ... he's ... he attends- there is- at another club than our own[51] ... and this means that he has some big role models who are nothing like those the others have here ... so for instance he's one of those who had porn photos on his cell phone that he showed to the others (MB: yes yes) ... that's also ... he also has some blossoming linguistic images that he introduced in ... in the school class that are definitely not very appropriate ...

---

51 "our own" refers to a pedagogical institution in which the pupils can spend their spare time, physically located at the school.

MB: for instance?
Jens: yes for instance saying whore and (MB: yes yes) things like that
Tine: He's gonna die, I'll pop him
Jens: yes (MB: yes yes) … so he he- there are also some things that (MB: yes yes) he- but we're very alert to that and the parents as well
Tine: but he attends that same club where- where Johannes and- and Sif, attend also, right?
Jens: yes but
Tine: that have not at all- I mean [they /MB] have not at all picked this up
Jens: yes but
Tine: actually he also went to [...]⁵² school (MB: yes yes)
Jens: so-
Tine: probably he also … picked up some things there.

In this description, in which both teachers participate at the same time, Niels' problematic behavior is identified as something he brought with him to this particular school and school class, something from 'outside,' and more specifically, from other institutions. These were depicted as places, in contrast to the C-school, where one could 'pick up' things such as pornography, inappropriate language, and cheeky attitudes.

That Niels' improper conduct is not something that the teachers attach to his social background appears in the fact that the parents are projected as allies in straightening out Niels' behavior: "we're very alert to that and the parents as well." Niels himself is also somewhat exonerated: He is not described as the source of his socially unacceptable conduct; rather he is projected as the mere medium of bad influences derived from other institutions. Niels' inappropriateness, attached to inappropriate institutions, can thus be remedied with attention from appropriate teachers and appropriate parents. About Niels' school capacities, vocationally speaking, Jens adds that "he's not … vocationally he's sort of fairly sort of fairly good … and hanging in there."

The socially problematic behavior associated with Niels is thus described as something isolated, that neither 'rubs off' on his ability to 'hang in there' in relation to his education, nor is it projected as something attached to his social background.

The other majority boy in the group, Janus, is likewise projected as socially problematic in a way that is as external to his background. "I was just thinking, where does that come from … he's just not like that," the teacher Tine says about Janus being "mean" to others. His parents' professional backgrounds are not the object of detailed descriptions by the teachers, but in the questionnaire Janus' parents themselves state that the mother has several therapist educations on college level and works as a senior professional in family counseling. The father is an artisan within a high-income craft, and they live in an owned apartment. They both state Danish as their mother tongue. While they do not fall directly in the category

---

52 The teacher names a specific school in the Copenhagen area.

of 'academics,' they nonetheless possess a relatively high level of educational as well as economic capital.

Janus' parents are not in the same way as Niels' projected by the teachers as allies in handling his inappropriate behavior, but they are, however, projected as someone with whom the teachers can communicate, as well as they are described as having a certain level of insight into Janus' situation, and a certain authority with regards to being able to correctly diagnose the source of his problems. Thus, in the cases of both Niels and Janus, their social problematicness is described as something coming from the 'outside,' and as something that can, potentially, be remedied.

Social inappropriateness is framed differently by the teachers, however, when it comes to minority boys.

11.4.2 *The one who brought it from home, and the one who brought nothing*

In the case of Lamine, the boy's home becomes the main explanation of his problematicness, as well as the most explicitly articulated problem as such. Like Gülsen, Lamine is highlighted by the teacher Jens as a success in relation to the teacher ambition of 'catching up' on "the Muslim children," who are not otherwise expected to be able to contribute adequately. About Lamine, Jens says:

> "[he] has not just been sitting there, copying what others have written, he has once in a while also been able to say well it's like this and that as Muslims we do so and so and then of course it's all of a sudden a new experience to some of the children who are used to … only being able to take actually being able to give something."

Lamine is relatively successful in his attempts to gain speaking turns, but his contributions are not always evaluated as valid by the teacher. For instance in the text sample previously analyzed, Tine initially tried to overrule Lamine's contribution about 'washing the heart' by not reacting to it, and eventually ended up closing his speaking turn by trumping his input with 'the book' that she had read. In the teacher descriptions of Lamine, he is not first and foremost categorized by trouble-making; rather, he is characterized as a "truly lovely boy" with a "magnificent sense of humor." Lamine is described as "much more clever than what he gains from it," immediately followed by the addition: "it's also really difficult attending school in Denmark if you don't have … the support from home." For this reason, Tine calls him "someone … that I could … be a little concerned about." Something else about Lamine that is also the object of discrete problematization is his physique, and his way of utilizing it.

> Jens: he can also be like very physical in his behavior when- when he gets angry right
> Tine: is also strong big and // like that //
> Jens: //but it's// but it is though something where he's really improved.

Lamine is thus described as having more school potential than his actual achievements verified, and as someone who does not altogether manage his physical size and strength appropriately. However, his ability to improve is recognized by the teachers. Unlike Niels, the cause of Lamine's problems is framed as precisely a problem of home and family. Lamine is "alone with his mother and his younger brother who's ill and his father is … dead," and that is "a dramatic history," explained Tine, further elaborating:

> " … in relation to that fam- that family structure he's somewhat trapped because mother does have to take care of little brother a lot and- and maybe there's not all that much … space left for him and mother does not speak Danish well and they are from … Se- Senegal she very bad at- or very bad but- you can speak with her but- but … she can't read a weekly newsletter I mean and- and she doesn't follow up on that weekly newsletter either and supporting him in doing his homework, well that's … "

The mother is described with positive terms such as "lovely and sweet and all that" but also as someone who not only did not help and support Lamine in the right ways, but also as someone who, in effect, obstructs the efforts made by the school: Lamine was once offered the chance to see the school psychologist, but "then mother doesn't think they have a problem." Lamine's home is described as a place where there is "lots of love," and yet the teacher's conclusion is that Lamine does not have the support of the home when it comes to schooling – and that this is his biggest problem. In contrast to Niels, whose parents are framed as allies in the moderation of the boy's behavior, and whose school skills are not problematized, Lamine's mother is framed as a hindrance rather than as a possible ally in the enhancement of Lamine's school suitability. Lamine's home is primarily framed as a problem for his schooling: a single West African mother whose education and profession are not even mentioned by the teachers, and who does not contribute any kind of capital to Lamine – indeed, quite the contrary.

The other minority pupil who, like Lamine, is successful in using the informal access to speaking turns, Hazem, is described in a similar scheme, although his family is more invisible in the teacher descriptions. In the questionnaire Hazem's parents state that they are born in Iraq, both have high school education and the mother also has a university education equaling teachers college. She works as a pedagogic assistant, and the father works as a taxi driver. Even though they do belong to the explicitly visible part of the minority parent group in the teacher descriptions, their educational background and profession receive no attention.

Hazem is categorized as "doing quite well" in terms of school skills, but the main part of the description revolves around his behavioral problems: "he is socially … not very smooth and has no sense of the fact that other people exist." Hazem is undergoing a "psychological assessment," and as the only minority pupil he is in fact not categorized in the teacher descriptions by his non-Danish national relation (his parents were born in Iraq, they stated in the questionnaire): As was the case at the B-school, 'social illnesses' trumped the category of 'migrant'-ness. His parents are included as among those "that you see" (meaning that they participate in school/parents meetings, for instance), and as such they belong to the legitimate group of minority parents – but they are not described as partners in relation to working to remedy Hazem's problems, and their professional and educational backgrounds receive no attention from the teachers.

While Lamine is thus described as "doing quite well" despite his mother's lack of skills as a school parent, Hazem's parents are described as legitimate school parents. However, their educational and professional backgrounds do not translate into *Bildung* capital, but instead entirely slip out of the descriptions. Consequently, Hazem's parents are not projected as school allies in relation to remedying his social problematicness. With Niels, however, the opposite is the case. His socially problematic behavior is described as external to his background, and his parents – whom the teacher indirectly, through the emphasis on his mother's position as a priest, ascribes a certain amount of *Bildung* capital – are precisely projected as a counterweight that can and eventually will balance Niels' improper school behavior. This points to a general pattern which is also at stake in for instance the case of Gülsen, namely that the educational resources of minority parents are of no interest to the teachers. Thus minority pupils are seen as either bringing problems from home or bringing nothing at all.

11.5 The categorization practices of the teachers in descriptions of pupils

In the teacher-articulated curriculum (Chapter 9), the pupils appear as religiously defined: as 'Muslim pupils' and 'Christian pupils,' respectively, with the former being framed as those who are expected to particularly gain from the educational module in *Kristendomskundskab*. These 'Muslim pupils' are presumed to be able to contribute to this particular school content, contrary to what they were presupposed to be or to be capable of doing, otherwise. This distinction between the pupils recurs in relation to the composition of groups for group work, where 'religious experts' are to be dispersed evenly.

The previous chapter has shown, however, that the 'pupils with a preconception of Christianity' and 'pupils with another religion,' who are placed in the groups on a religious basis, are however not first and foremost categorized religiously in the teacher descriptions. Rather, those descriptions are marked by characterizations of behavior and distinguished by psychologizing phraseology or designations attached to personal skills – and then, followed by value judgments: 'that kind of girl who lacks some social filters,' 'a cheeky little boy,' 'the most sweet and diplomatic child' and so on. What this chapter also showed, though, is that nation-state affiliation is only projected in relation to minority pupils – unless these pupils have explicit 'social illnesses,' in which case national otherness is relegated to a less prominent position; otherwise, no mention of nation-state affiliation implies a presumptive Danishness, as was equally the case at the B-school.

Finally, there are also categorizations related to school skills at play, such as, for instance, when Niels is described as "sort of fairly good," or Gülsen's skills are indirectly referenced by mentioning that she is receiving "special needs education," or when Hazem, who is "doing quite well" in terms of educational content skills, is nevertheless characterized as psychologically problematic. Indeed, it was just such commentary related to school performance and achievement that took up most space in the teachers' descriptions.

11.5.1 Pupils through parents

The inclusion of the parents as part of the teachers' descriptions of the pupils, or alternatively, the precise absence of parents from the descriptions, are the two overarching ways of projecting pupils through their parents. An example of the former arose in the detailed descriptions of Amalie's parents, and the particular emphasis put on her father's university-level studies as something that was deployed to re-frame his job at the post office. Moreover, a general tendency – based on the entire range of interview material, including the portions not explicitly discussed in the previous chapters – is that the more highly educated the parents are, the more likely the teachers will mention their specific educational background and professions.

To the educationally legitimate parents, furthermore, personal skills or qualities would also be assigned, such as "nice and sensible," "sensible supporting family," or, as in Amalie's case, parents "with some principles." Less demarcated but nevertheless effective subcategories are attached to parents who are described as allied in the project of socially moderating the pupil, as in the case of Niels.

Another categorization of parents involves those who are projected as 'socially problematic,' who come to form a constitutive part of the social problematic-ness of the pupil. In many cases, this is attached to divorced parents, where the teachers' speech notably distinguishes between 'ugly' divorces and less problematic ones. Similarly, there seems to be a correlation between divorces projected as problematic and the attribution to the pupil of relatively useless or no cultural Bildung capital or a lack of school skills. A related categorization is an emphasis on parents being single, something which is attached in the teacher speech to social problems or the installation of the 'home as an obstructing influence,' as in the case of Lamine.

Finally, there are pupils who are not at all projected through their parents, as was the case with Gülsen. Her parents are projected as neither a hindrance nor a resource to her appropriateness and suitability as a pupil. They are not entirely without background in the teacher speech, though. When the Danish-born Gülsen with the Turkish-born Kurdish parents is projected as being "from Turkey," the parents, and the absence of 'handed down' educational capital that seems to be at play in the teacher descriptions, become an implied element. They are not school parents in a way that enables the school logic to project them as either problematic or supportive.

Either way, mentioning Gülsen's 'Turkishness' appears as a sufficient indication, in and of itself, in the teacher descriptions. Minority parents are not always mentioned explicitly, but often implicitly by nation-state reference (as with

Gülsen), or as part of such a nation-state reference, as with the pupil Amir who is presented in the teacher descriptions as: "Amir, he's Iranian ... his parents are Iranian and they are divorced." When minority parents are mentioned, their education and profession are not. The only exceptions from this pattern are the pupil Lubna, who "is Moroccan" and whose father is a city hall janitor, and Aya ("Iranian"), in whose case the mother is presented rather imprecisely by the teacher Jens:

> "the mother is employed at the hospital I- I think she's a nurse I'm not sure (MB: yes) if she's a nurse or maybe something else then something technical- technical medical personnel right (MB: yes) she's not a doctor but she is- she could be bio-analyst as well I don't know."

In both Lubna and Aya's cases, the professions of the father and mother, respectively, are each in their own way attached to legitimacy: In Lubna's father's case because he works at a parliamentary institution, indicating a measure of 'integration' with institutional Denmark. Despite her father's credibility, however, it is emphasized that Lubna's mother "speaks very bad Danish."

11.5.2   Pupils through the pupil hierarchy

Another way of reading the pupils is through the pupil hierarchy. One version of this is Tine's attention and concern regarding how a wrongly placed pupil (Caroline) has apparently cornered the truly clever pupil's space and occupied the position which more properly belongs to someone else in what both teachers call 'the social hierarchy of the school class.' In her descriptions of how this hierarchy plays out, Tine appears as an engaged spectator to the struggles that take place in the 'girl group' of the Y-class. The teacher's doubts or reservations about Caroline's position are connected to her perceived lack of intelligence at the level of her own real skills, something which is assessed in the teacher speech as a low degree of cultural Bildung capital.

The classroom hierarchy is described by the teachers in two ways: partly as a fact, partly in its capacity to judge – particularly, when it establishes what the teachers deem to be a wrong order. The first usage is applied to pupils who are not projected as remarkable, whereas the latter is used as a way to project some pupils as vocationally and socially clever, attached to the broader area of self-management skills. Thus, in the teacher's estimation, Clara really ought to have been placed at the top of the hierarchy, higher than Caroline. Likewise, the sports girl Amalie is "under pressure," despite her being both clever and sweet as well as the "most social and diplomatic child ever."

This 'social hierarchy of the school class' – which in both teachers' speech appears as something taken for granted, and moreover as something toward which Tine is a highly engaged and side-taking spectator – appears as homologous to (recognized) educational as well as cultural Bildung capital, which in most pupils' cases is also attached to their respective amounts of economic capital. The pupils whom the teachers describe as socially incompetent or problematic, such as Daniella and Gülsen, in general, are not situated in relation to this social hierarchy. In Gülsen's case, this is also connected to the fact that no minority girls whatsoever are interpreted as having any substantive relation to the 'social hierarchy,' just as no boys – minority or majority – are described through this. 'The social hierarchy of the school class' thus appears in the teacher speech as gendered, and gendered with 'girl' as well as reserved for the majority.

Being 'girl' is thus attached to being majority and to not being (significantly) socially problematic as well as associated with a certain amount of Bildung capital – more, for instance, than Daniella possesses. As the analysis of Amalie and Gülsen's soccer-playing athletic clothing-wearing practices showed, minority girls are not counted as girls in the teacher speech. They are Turkish girls or Iranian girls and otherwise problematic girls, but not 'girls' in the sense that they are counted in as part of the hierarchical struggle that the teachers observe and – as long as it ranks the pupils more or less adequately – also approve. The pupil hierarchy thus appears, through the teachers' interpretations of the pupils, as not only a mode of categorization flavored by class and gender; rather, it also renders gender visible as it is projected, flavored, and shaped by class, and minority girls in this context are situated in the same outside space as the capital-weak majority girls. They are not girls, and since they are not boys either – and also not projected through categories of 'trouble,' 'back-talking,' etc., like the boys – the gender assigned to them must then be understood as an un-girled one.

11.5.3 *The structure of social classification and the group*

Turning now to the category 'boys,' they are not measured in the same way as a group. Whereas both teachers use the 'girl hierarchy' as an almost descriptive reference, in a way that extends far into the categories of vocational and not least self-managing skills, the sociality of the boys is not the object of specific problematization and attention in the teacher speech. Whereas Lamine and Hazem are both described as problematic and with emphathetic concern, the majority boys – who in different ways are attached to trouble-making and cheekiness – are not the object of profound concern. While the boys are not subject in the teacher speech to internal hierarchization similar to that which organizes the 'girl group,' there was nonetheless a differentiation at play in the categorization and projections of the different kinds of problematic-ness among boys, whether this problematic-ness is emphathetically described or not. Lamine and Hazem are projected as determined and pathological in their social deviancy, whereas Niels and other majority boys are not attached in any determining or conclusive way to their trouble-making.

This kind of teacher categorization can be understood as a recontextualized form of the speech about various types of pupils in relation to 'many kinds of intelligence,' which is strongly emphasized in the institutional self-understanding of the school (cf. Chapter 4), as well as a recontextualization of knowledge about the influence of social conditions.

Simultaneously, this sort of categorization tells something about the nature of the teaching profession (as it has developed in Denmark): Teachers are not only meant to enhance the subject-related skills of the pupils – skills that can be measured in 'above,' 'below' and 'average' – but also to enhance the pupils' social self-managing skills which the teachers cannot control and discipline in quite the same ways, exactly because the pupils are supposed to exercise them by themselves.

What the analysis also shows is that the composition of the teacher-composed groups is socially differentiated in a way that appears as a micro-version of the social structure of classification in the school class. In the hierarchy of capitals, the 'good group leader' Clara is placed in the top, followed by the unstable but capital-strong Niels with the trustworthy parents, followed by the unremarkable, occasionally socially problematic majority pupil Janus. At the bottom of the structure of social classification, the majority pupil Daniella with the low degree of Bildung capital shares a space with the low-capital (or rather, not capital-assigned) minority pupil Gülsen.

11.6 Summing up: pupil disposition and -positioning, teacher recognition and the opposite

The theme of this chapter has been how agents, in this case pupils, are recognized within a social space in which they are to assert themselves, as well as for what they are recognized – or unrecognized. The teachers have been maintained as being 'those who see' and potentially recognize the pupil dispositions as relevant and legitimate; the teachers as those who manage the institutional recognizing bodies when valuing pupils and their achievements, when distributing speaking turns and attention among the pupils, when judging in their internal conflicts, when discussing the pupils among themselves, etc. I have contrasted this with utterances from pupils who position themselves in relation to the positions made available in the educational module.

This reading includes how these positions appear in context of the turn-taking system as well as when the pupils position themselves – and are positioned through distribution in and composition in groups – in the context of group work, and the ways in which the pupils speak of themselves as pupils. Finally, I have included parents, who, in the official self-articulation of the C-school, are projected as an object, in and of itself, of the school enterprise. I have paid attention to how parents are projected by the teachers and the pupils as well as how they project themselves through the data they have chosen to state in the questionnaires, and the degree to which they choose elaborate on this data. Which pupils prioritize to explain their parents' education and professions, and which parents do? Which parents are visible or invisible in the teachers' descriptions of the pupils, in which ways and to which extent?

In Gülsen's case, for instance, the parents state about her father that he "works at restaurant," whereas Gülsen herself prioritizes to mention the specific job function of her father and indicates a status of him as being his own boss. In this context it becomes noticeable that the teachers describe nothing at all about Gülsen's parents' education and professions.

A central incision in this analysis has been the question of how such socio-economic histories are projected differently by different agent groups and with which consequences for the school-wise and social categorizations along which the teachers 'arrange' the pupils, as well as how the pupils 'arrange' their own school situation. This has been read particularly from the relations among pupils, primarily as these relations are projected in the teachers' speech about the pupils: Sometimes because the teachers explicitly compare and relate pupils to one another, as with Caroline and Clara, sometimes because it is remarkable that they don't, as with the two 'sports girls' Amalie and Gülsen. Whereas the former is described with sensitivity to the potential problems she might face for her football, sports clothes-wearing behavior, Gülsen is not the object of such sensitivity. Rather, Gülsen is described as 'lacking social filters,' and instead placed, in the teachers' descriptions, at the bottom of the school class social economy along with the majority girl Daniella, described as lacking social as well as school skills and carrying little or no capital with her.

11.6.1 The practices of teacher categorizations of pupils

In the teacher-articulated curriculum (Chapter 9) pupils appeared religiously defined as 'Muslim pupils' and 'Christian pupils,' respectively, and the module was articulated as something that particularly would accommodate 'some of the Muslim pupils' who where otherwise not perceived as able to contribute. As seen in this chapter, these religiously defined pupils where distributed as 'experts' in the working groups during the module, but did not appear religiously defined in the teachers' descriptions of them in relation to other pupils. Gülsen, being the only minority pupil in the group, is, however, described in relation to nationality – as the only one of the five pupils. In other words: Nothing mentioned means Danishness, or non-migrant-ness.

The teacher descriptions are on the one hand focused on characterizations of the pupils' behavior, psychologizing use of language, and designations attached to personal skills. On the other hand, the category of school skills appears central. The pupils are thus valuated as good, average, or below average in this context, and some descriptions of pupils are characterized by an implicit or a non-categorization of their school skills.

In the descriptions of pupils through parents, the teacher speech also delineates a landscape of those who either bring nothing (Gülsen) or something problematic from home (Daniella) in contrast to those who bring something useful from home (Clara) or whose parents can be relevant conversation partners in relation to problems (Janus), and finally those who, if displaying socially problematic behavior, are interpreted as having picked it up somewhere outside of the home (Niels). In contrast to the latter are the minority boys, who bring either nothing or something problematic from home, and whose parents are not projected as relevant conversation partners, but rather become invisible (Hazem) or are described as obstacles (Lamine).

In the descriptions of pupils through pupil or girl hierarchy, it is noticeable that this hierarchy in both the teachers' descriptions appears as something they take for granted, and of which Tine is even an engaged and judging spectator. What is also noticeable is that the girl hierarchy appears as homologous with educational capitals as well as cultural Bildung capital, which, in most cases (though not for Amalie, for instance) are connected to economic capital. The pupils described as socially problematic are generally not projected in relation to this hierarchy.

One of these pupils is Gülsen who also, due to her minority categorization, could not have accessed the girl hierarchy anyway, as no minority pupils are described in relation to this hierarchy by the teachers. Neither are the boys, majority or minority. The social hierarchy among pupils thus seems to be gendered, and gendered by 'girl,' which points to the fact that minority girls are not girls in the teachers' descriptions. They might be Turkish girls or problematic girls, but not girls in the girl hierarchy sense. Being a girl in the two school classes of the C-school thus seems to be attached to being majority, and to not being (overtly) socially problematic, as well as to a certain amount of Bildung capital. The minority girls thus share the space outside this hierarchy with the capital-weak majority girls.

The boys are in contrast more explicitly projected in relation to the school skills-related categorization and, in the cases of them being described as socially problematic, this problematization appears to be delivered with much more enthusiastic interest than with the girls. Whereas the problematic behavior of majority boys, such as Niels, appears not to worry the teachers much – they are for instance certain that Niels' parents are handling it – the problematic behavior of the minority boys appears as the object of concern as well as of sensitive empathy.

When zooming in on the particular five pupil group, we can see that the composition, arranged by the teachers, is socially differentiated in a way that appears as a micro-version of the social classification structure of the school classes. In the top end of the hierarchy of capital we find the 'good group leader' Clara, daughter of academics, followed by the more volatile Niels with the reliable school parents. In the not that noticeable middle we find the, sometimes problematic, Janus, who also has reliable middle-class parents. At the bottom of the social classification structure are the majority pupil Daniella with low amount of Bildung capital and the low-valuated or rather not capital-valuated minority pupil Gülsen.

12. Assembling knowledge production and social classification

Summing up the analysis in the previous three chapters, at the C School, 'Muslim boys' are generally cast as objects of empathetic concern. This was shown in the previous chapter and will be elaborated in the following. They stand as currently or potentially school-illegitimate even if they are also assigned a certain amount of school capital in the form of intelligence, mathematical skills, congeniality and a desire to adapt after all.

The minority girls, on the other hand, hardly stand out as objects of concern at all. They are assigned from medium through low to no school capital, and the latter is associated with social problems. Nor are these girls included by the sensitive interest in 'girl hierarchy' dynamics voiced by the teachers: an interest which teachers direct towards majority girls with medium to high school capital exclusively. The interest in the 'girl hierarchy' is part of dividing pupils into specific types that come to the fore in the teachers' descriptions of pupils: a division of pupils according to capabilities and knowledge pertaining to self-administration. As far as their self-administrative skills are concerned, the minority girls are at the bottom of the school's social economy – regardless of their parents' education and profession. They are accompanied by the capital-lacking majority pupils, particularly the capital-lacking majority girls.

Simultaneously with the differentiated allocation of concern-driven interest – and of school capital in relation to self-administration – 'the Muslim pupils' are also discursively produced as a coherent and particularly low-performing underclass at school. When teachers discuss the curriculum, these pupils make up a special object for the educational module, i.e. as particularly and by definition tied to 'their religion' and as potential subjects of 'experience knowledge,' as elaborated in Chapter 9 about the teachers' articulation of the curriculum. But 'their religion' and the demand for their contribution in the form of 'experience knowledge' are tied to them and directed towards them as particularly under-achieving pupils when it comes to 'real school knowledge.'

The official self-presentation of the C-school involves a focus on "natural science" as well as a distinction between "everyday knowledge" and "school knowledge" (Chapter 4). "Experiments," it says, are supposed to depart from the "the pupils' backgrounds and everyday knowledge," thereby creating an "overlap" between these forms of knowledge. In the speech about the pedagogical targets of the school, emphasis is put on 'individualities' as key to communities characterized by "diversity" and by "room for" 'backgrounds' and differences in 'backgrounds.' These distinctions can be seen as recontextualized in the expectations of how the different pupils can and will contribute to the content in the educational module, as well as in the composition of the group. 'Muslim pupils' are expected to both particularly gain from the educational module and particularly contribute as 'experts' along with 'Christian experts.' The difference is, however, that the knowledge that the 'Muslims' are expected to contribute with is projected as being of a specific everyday kind, in contrast to factual or formal knowledge.

Another difference is that the conditions for contributing, by attaching one's own experience to the content of teaching, appear to be quite different for pupils whom the teacher connects with Islam and those who are connected to Christianity respectively. Whereas the former are tied to a collective and stable 'Muslim tradition' and thus create conflict if they do not serve to unambiguously support the content of the teacher presentation, the latter are tied to individual and choosing universal Christian practices, and are thus received as potentially enriching, even when they deviate from the content of the teacher presentation.

The underclass space in school is primarily made available to the minority pupils that are categorized as 'Muslim' – both as a special problem and as individuals in need of particularly sensitive attention. Non-Muslim minority pupils and capital-lacking majority pupils, on the other hand, vanish from conversations about and during the module.

12.1 Speech about types of pupils and forms of knowledge

The official self-articulation of the C-school is characterized by vague speech and thus weak classification when it comes to 'backgrounds' connected to minority/majority and strong classification when it comes to technologies related to the recontextualization of natural science as well concepts such as 'styles of learning' and 'multiple intelligences.'

In the teacher speech about curriculum, however, differences between Muslims/school-weak pupils and Christian/to Christian practices-attached pupils appear strongly classified, and the 'Muslim pupils' are projected as a particularly school under-achieving group, that might, though, be able to contribute to the school content with a particular type of experience knowledge to the module on religion, not counting as 'real' and factual school knowledge.

The teachers similarly project this particular module as completely different from the natural science focus of the school. The educational module on religion is thus projected as a form of non-school related subject matter, but the module is nonetheless simultaneously described by means of a distinction that parallels the school's customary speech, in which a distinction between everyday knowledge and school knowledge is made, but in relation to religion, the teachers reconfigure this distinction as a difference between the personal and the factual.

In other words, when the teachers speak about the curriculum of the module, including how 'pupils' are part of this curriculum, 'experience' and 'backgrounds' become a way of operating with another kind of school-knowledge which is not really a school-knowledge as such. At the same time, 'experience' and 'back-grounds' become a method, a strategy, to enable pupils who are not otherwise counted as individuals but who can potentially contribute to and assert themselves in terms of school performance, to now contribute with something 'other.' This 'other' type of knowledge is focused on 'the personal' and is particularly attached to Muslimness. Simultaneously, 'rituals' and how these ought to be practiced as content in the instruction are measured in two ways in the teacher speech about curriculum: as a factual track and, additionally, as an experience-oriented track aimed at all pupils.

When school knowledge is described in relation to descriptions of pupils and pupils' achievements, however, school knowledge and school skills appear in the teacher speech as something so consensually self-obvious that there is no need to define them: the pupils are described with valuations such as 'hanging in there quite well,' 'below/above average,' etc.

Although 'background' and 'Muslim' and 'Christian' pupils become strongly demarcated in the speech about curriculum, this demarcation is, however, subdued when the individual pupils are described as pupils (independently as well as in comparisons with one another). In this context they are not projected through their Muslimness or their experiences with Christianity-related practices. Rather, apart from 'above-/below-average' school skills or self-management skills, the pupils in this context are attached to parents, to national reference, to social skills versus social problems or illnesses, and to pupil hierarchy in a way that can be viewed as homologous to a distribution of (recognized) capital. But these categorizations, however, seem to be what is filling out the category of Muslimness as an underachieving category of pupils to whom contributing with experience knowledge can be part of the cure.

12.2 Remaining an under-achiever; winning a space, but not legitimacy

There is a remarkable amount of discrepancy between the ways in which the teachers project some pupils as under-achieving (Daniella) and some as generally not school-skilled, but with potential as experience-contributing "Muslims" (Gülsen), and the ways in which these pupils appear through their self-descriptions. In the interviews, the only two pupils who explicitly expressed an interest in the educational module in *Kristendomskundskab*, and who spoke most extensively about the content of the module, are the two pupils who – in different ways – are not recognized as contributing to the 'real' school content: Daniella and Gülsen. The former is almost invisible in the plenary sessions; the latter has to struggle for most of her speaking turns by using the not-explicitly approved access to the official classroom text, and thus she can be seen as a pupil who tries to win legitimacy.

Whereas Daniella is merely categorized as 'below average' in terms of school skills, the teacher speech frames Gülsen's questions during teaching as annoying because they indicate a disappointing lack of experience knowledge. Gülsen is projected differently in the teacher speech than she presents herself: In the teacher speech, she is not an engaged pupil with a general interest in religion, but a pupil whose only possible contribution is as a 'Muslim expert' contributing with herself. When Gülsen does not meet this specific teacher expectation, her school skills go unrecognized. However, when her contributions are recognized – by the teacher Jens, who assesses the outcome more positively than Tine – they are recognized in a way that is connected to the space which is deemed to be not-usually recognition-worthy; a space that in this particular module is asscribed a special purpose, as one from which the non-school legitimate pupils can elevate themselves as 'religious experts' in an experience-knowledge – opposed to factual knowledge – sense.

While Daniella remains in the under-achieving school underclass, Gülsen wins a space to which she does not usually enjoy access as a pupil, but which, in this particular module, she can occupy as a 'Muslim pupil.' It does not necessarily provide her traditional school recognition, but it can provide her with a certain recognition related to self-management skills, and it can provide her with the possibility to speak in plenary.

12.3 Knowledge and speakers in an agent-, practice-, and capital perspective

As shown in Chapters 10 and 11, Gülsen's contributions are recognized, also by Tine, inasmuch as they are recognized as a form of experience knowledge. In contrast, Hazem and Lamine's contributions are difficult to organize as experience. Lamine's contribution about 'Muslim practices' is dismissed as non-valid; it is neither valid as factual knowledge nor as experience knowledge. Hazem's first contribution, where he brings in something from outside of the classroom context, is recognized by the teacher neither as relevant nor as 'experience' ('close to one-self'), and when the teacher later on her own initiative seeks to foreground a specific pupil experience, which turns out to be Hazem's, his attempt to articulate the experience himself is then abruptly excluded by the teacher speech. It does not fulfill the assigned function: to simply serve as an example of what the teacher had just said.

The incorporation of Nikoline and Niels in the teacher speech (Chapter 10), in contrast, represents the successful version of teacher-organized and pupil-confirmed pupil experience. In Nikoline's case, it was a hypothetical experience in which she did not object to being installed; on the contrary, she answered the teacher with a confirming "yes" (this was also one of her very few speaking turns). In the case of Niels, the pupil is also merely asked to confirm being installed in the experience, which he does. Common for both Niels and Nikoline is the fact that the type of experience figure with which they become involved – albeit in different ways – is attached to professionalism. 'Nikoline's father' as a customer at an undertaker business represents a phenomenon in the teacher speech that is explicitly connected to Denmark and a 'we.' In the case of 'Niels' mother,' the example revolves around a legitimate job function; an odd one, perhaps, but nevertheless something you can 'be' just as you can 'be' a teacher. It is a profession, and as such, connected to knowledge and authority.

The two pupils are thus attached to figures that appear as legitimate and distinctly Danish institutions, and thus, attached to a Danish and professional 'we,' while the signs on their bodies – and their non-'migrant'-ness, in itself – contribute to the projection of the phenomenon 'funeral' as universal conditions concerning loss and death; universal conditions that gradually become filled with the content 'Denmark,' 'Christians,' and 'church.' It is two relatively school-legitimate pupils who are attached to this content, a legitimacy connected with a recognition that they repay by 'letting themselves assist' in the personification.

Opposed to this projection is the way in which Islam is installed in the teacher speech: as a universe unto itself, given from the outset. The theme 'Islam' is initiated by Lamine as something attached to 'the Muslims.' In the teacher speech this becomes 'the Muslim tradition' which appears as a generating subject in extension of which 'Muslims' act. It is therefore – as produced by a framing subject – that one can play out the required personification, as a 'with-experience-contributing Muslim pupil.' The subjectivity is then not only framed by 'personal experiences'; these experiences must also correspond to 'the Muslim tradition' as it is projected in the teacher speech.

The teacher speech figure – 'the imam' – works in extension of this: appearing as a figure generated by 'the Muslim tradition' and as such as something ancient. 'The imam' becomes the answer to the universal condition of 'loss' and 'sorrow' as they play out between 'the Muslims.' In this way, 'the Muslim tradition' is maintained as a possible comparative to 'the universal Danish Christian.' But whereas the answer to 'the universal Danish Christians and not-so-Christians' is continuously flavored by options of choice – as in terms of chapel (not-so-Christian) and church (more-Christian), and in terms of the range of products and services offered by the undertaker – 'the Muslim tradition' is not measured in terms of choice. Rather, it arrives in the shape of an already completed frame. Consequently, the imam does not appear as a 'professional.' This occupation is not projected as a legitimate future option, as a job attached to education and income (even if it is an unusual one). As such, the teacher speech contains an uneven basis of distribution between the ways in which knowledge about Islam and knowledge about Christianity is produced.

In this framework, the pupil speech and the teachers' attempts at staging pupil speech both fail. The pupils who are expected to contribute do seek to make their contributions. But only Gülsen manages to navigate in such a way that she, without actually delivering personal experiences 'close to oneself,' has her speech incorporated in the teacher speech, and as such, attains legitimacy as a part of the classroom's knowledge production which at the same time differentiates the projected Muslim practices. Nevertheless, by attempting to speak at all, even if the speech is rejected, the pupils contribute with their bodies to the flavoring of the content: With their partly recognized, partly not-recognized minority pupil bodies they emphasize and co-produce the Muslimness that is attached to themselves, which has already been allocated to them. Simultaneously, their dubious and questionable school legitimacy flavors the produced content.

As an area of knowledge 'Islam' becomes flavored with 'underclass.' This is further emphasized by the general rejection of their attempts to occupy the space for experience knowledge – the only space available to them. They thus become even more unsuited as pupils, even more unable to contribute. The alternative, however, is the silence that some minority pupils choose in the plenary sessions.

'The Muslim pupils' thus become a highly projected minority with a dubious legitimacy and dubious abilities to assert themselves. The societal minority status of these pupils, which (unlike at the B-school) is also a minority status in the socioeconomy of the school classes at the C-school, thus comes to be reproduced – on the occasion of the module – as a heavily exposed qualitative minority status that is, on the one hand, in demand, but on the other hand emphasizes their condition as a school underclass even more, even when these pupils actually do succeed with experience contributions. In an arena where 'Muslims' are outnumbered, these are the conditions for being a pupil identified with 'Muslimness.'

The consequences of contributing as well as not contributing are an intensified production of 'Muslim pupils' tied to 'their religion': A religion that is highlighted as either the prerequisite for these pupils to become able to contribute with (a lower-ranking type of) subject matter content or as yet another example of an area in which these pupils lack knowledge. The distinction between experience knowledge and formal/factual knowledge that was articulated in the teacher speech about curriculum thus, when played out in the official text of the classroom, appears as a particularly exposed social classification of a Muslim school underclass attached to a Muslim parent underclass. This is a parent underclass that is not recognized as labor- and education-flavored subjects, paralleled by the space for Muslim subjectivity that is made available in classroom speech: a timeless, by tradition derived subjectivity with no relation to labor market and future, generated in the knowledge formation about Islam that emerges through the practiced curriculum of the classroom.

In contrast, 'being busy' and 'professionalism' are attached to a universal Danish Christianness; a knowledge formation to which pupils, who in various ways receive recognition from the teacher, are attached. This knowledge formation of the Danish is further populated by the not-primarily-religiously exposed school upper class comprised of girls and boys who contribute to group work and plenary sessions. These pupils – whose parents are ascribed medium to high economic and cultural Bildung capital – are not over-exposed, like the contributing minority pupils are, but are rather projected as appropriately and legitimately speaking and restrained respectively. In the teacher descriptions they appear not as (potential) 'religious experts' but rather as school legitimate in appropriately contributing or appropriately non-contributing ways. The capital-weak majority pupils appear as the under-exposed ordinary school underclass to whom no knowledge of religion is attached. A group that – along with half-minority pupils in absentia – accompanies 'the Muslim school underclass' at the bottom of the hierarchy of recognition.

PART 4
RELIGION AND CULTURE AS KNOWLEDGE AND SOCIAL CLASSIFICATION

13. Pedagogizing religion. Concluding remarks

In the analysis presented in the previous chapters, categories such as 'Muslim' and 'Danish'/'Christian' have been analyzed in relation to knowledge production and the production of social difference. When summarizing and putting into discussion the findings from the B-school and the C-school classrooms, especially three questions are important to focus on: What knowledge of religion is produced? What spaces for subjects? What ways to be a pupil? And in what ways do 'Muslimness' and 'Danishness'/'Christianness' appear in the social economy of the school class? The study of the classroom suggests – across the Foucault- and the Bourdieu-inspired analysis and across the two schools studied – that 'religion'/'culture' can be seen partly as knowledge clusters, partly as subject-producing technologies coloring and shaping bodies.

These knowledge clusters, in turn, are colored by the social economy associated with the agents' bodies, making it a productive and potent part of social classification. To sum up, this means that categories such as 'Muslim' and 'Danish'/'Christian' are in themselves to be understood as processes of social classification and distribution, and hence that 'religion' may be understood as a class-producing practice when the latter is transformed and produced in the pedagogical field of practice. In this recontextualized form of 'religion' the pedagogical aim of including the pupils' 'background' and 'experiences' and hence also pupil personality in education policy initiatives and as doxa among e.g. teachers plays an important part. The demand for pupils to contribute with 'their experience' plays a crucial role in how categories such as 'Muslim' and 'non-Muslim' or 'Danish-Christian' are produced while pedagogized in the classroom and hence in social classifications of pupils and in what becomes the possible ways to 'be a pupil.' This will be elaborated and discussed in the following.

13.1 Religion as race and class

In this book the category religion is analyzed as overlapping with the category of culture as it, in effect, becomes an identity political technology that distinguishes/secretes 'Muslims' from the majority population, in this case more specifically the pupils populating the classroom. The sociologist of education Sherene Razack unfolds similar perspectives in her analysis of the ways in which the category of 'Muslim' as 'culture' operates in various social arenas such as the educational system, in which it plays out as a new form of racialization (e.g.

Razack 1998, 2004a,b, 2007a,b, 2008), thus drawing on and adding new perspectives to previous studies of institutionalized racism in schooling such as Troyna & Williams (1986).

Etienne Balibar diagnoses a culturalized metaracism: the category of 'culture' has taken over the semantic space from the concept of race which drew its legitimation from Biology (Balibar 1991). The category of Muslim may thus, by extension, be seen as a culturalization of the category of race. On the other hand, the colonial historian Ann Laura Stoler points to the historically complex relation between the category of culture and the category of race, and suggests that it could also be possible to understand the matter the other way around, namely that the category of culture that took over the space of race is to be understood as a re-emergence, rather than as a new formation (Stoler 2002, see also 1995).

This points to a complicated history of culture as a social category and as social distinction, also at play in the field of pedagogy and education. As a pedagogical category culture has been used to differentiate pupils with regard to levels of civilization and their relation to the division of labor (Buchardt 2013b). Based on the analysis in this book I will suggest that this is also the case with the culturalized and pedagogized category of religion as it emerges in the classroom. Not least through the analysis of the classroom as *social space* (Bourdieu 1998e), I seek to pave the way for discussing religion-related categorizations and forms of knowledge in a perspective of social classification, hence intelligible in relation to social economy and questions of social and economic distribution. The fact that this is deeply embedded in the knowledge production of the school is elucidated through the analysis of the relation between subject and knowledge production.

Sociologists of education (especially in the Bernstein-inspired tradition) have pointed to the neglect of the category of knowledge in education research, and pointed to the necessity of a sociology of knowledge in relation education (e.g. Goodson, Young et al.). Recently e.g. Karl Maton points to the fact that on the one hand learning and on the other hand power, society, and social structure often overshadow the question of knowledge on educational research (e.g. Maton 2014, see also 2000).

The analysis in this book takes its point of departure in an analytical separation of the study of social structure and the study of forms of knowledge, paving the way for studying knowledge production as a powerful part of what takes place in the classroom, but also in order to study how the classroom curriculum and its forms of knowledge contribute to social classification and the other way around. My study of forms of knowledge is thus based on an understanding of knowledge production as embedded with power, and as related to the production of subjects, with a special impact on pupil subjects. In that sense one could say that I explore, not what is learned, but what becomes possible to learn in school, in consequence of, if not the hidden, then the practiced curriculum of the classroom (drawing on Jackson 1968, as well as on the critique of the implied distinction between hidden and non-hidden, Callewaert 1998).

Also, the study of the relations between forms of knowledge and the spaces for subjects that are produced brings to the fore the impact of the pedagogical focus on pupil experience and pupil personality, as this plays out when Muslimness and Danishness/Christianness are produced in the classroom.

13.2 Religion as 'experience knowledge'

In a Nordic context, several important studies have dealt with the complex character of what it means to be Muslim for young people with a migrant history and thus with a minority status in the Nordic welfare states (e.g. Østberg 1998, Otterbeck 2000, 2010, von Brömssen 2003). The strength of these studies is that they bring to the fore the experience and lived life of young people who identify as Muslims. When studying 'Muslim pupils' within schooling and in light of the school institution, not least Laura Gilliam's analytical findings on how the category Muslim becomes a counter-cultural category and identified with 'trouble-making' – also by the agents who identify with the category – is of significance. Gilliam points to the fact that school as such is part of creating Muslim communities and identification through schooling, through the school's exercise of cultural hegemony and thus marginalization of minority pupils (Gilliam 2010, see also 2009).

This study, however, employs a different take by studying how pupil experience is organized through schooling, how it is made into knowledge, and what spaces for being subjects that are produced in this process. Here it is my point that a certain form of experience knowledge, what with Bernstein can be called "everyday common knowledge," which is (or should perform to be) specifically related to daily life – as opposed to principal educational knowledge, which is general and abstract – is produced with the pupils as the material (cp. Bernstein 1971, see also Goodson 1992). My point is also that school demands such a form of knowledge.

School and its individualized pedagogy demand pupils to contribute with 'experience,' but in a pedagogized form, reshaped for curriculum, to the extent that the pupil does not even necessarily have to say anything, if only he/she willingly lets the teacher organize her/his life as curricular material. In later research conducted together with Liv Fabrin, we have shown how this is not only a pattern that occurs in relation to the teaching of religion, but spreads across the practiced school subjects in general, albeit with different results depending on which forms of knowledge the concrete teaching is allegedly obliged to deal with: religion, physics, social studies, etc. (Buchardt & Fabrin 2010).

The question which I will point to in the following is in particular how experience knowledge related to religion can be seen as part of social classification in the classroom; how pedagogical interest in pupil personality and background is an important part of how religion as a category becomes a culturalized/racialized class structure in the practiced curriculum of the classroom. As such the research behind this book also inscribes itself in the curriculum history and social epistemology of curriculum which reconsider the impact of religion in schooling, and thus do not take the secularization hypothesis at face value (e.g. Popkewitz 2007, Baker 2009a,b. See also Buchardt 2013b).

For that purpose I will now turn to how this – following the analysis presented in this book – plays out differently in the two classroom and schools studied; how Muslimness and Danishness/Christianness in both classrooms can be understood as class-producing technologies, but in different ways.

13.3 The differentiated Muslim class structure at the B-school: the Muslim subjects

In the analysis of the material from the B-school, the most recognized pupils – both in terms of teacher categorization and their level of success within the turn-taking system – belong to the category categorized by the teacher as 'Muslim.' No majority pupils belong to the very talkative and school-wise recognized portion of the school class.

Here a carefully differentiated hierarchy of recognition and forms of capital emerges in which the kind of Muslimness ascribed to the pupils as well as the level of acceptability versus non-acceptability attributed to this Muslimness appear to be proportionate with the school capital and cultural capital ascribed to the respective pupils. Markers linked to Muslimness are included when cultural capital is ascribed to pupils.

An example of this is when potential use of headscarf enters into the teacher's description of pupils categorized as 'girls' and 'Muslims'; in this instance: Meriam, whom the teacher recognizes as a highly achieving pupil and who is successful in the turn-taking system. Meriam's potential future use of the headscarf – and her headscarf-wearing mid-level manager mother trained as an office clerk – is presented as connected to choice and reflection. In contrast, Zainab's use of the headscarf is projected as predictable and notorious, whereas the pupil Leila's potential use of the headscarf is presented by the teacher as frivolous.

While the presumably reflective and intentional choice to wear the headscarf is associated with a professional future involving education, Zainab's use of the headscarf appears to be related to her 'too quiet' school behavior. Furthermore, she is suspected of preaching "correct Islam" to the pupil sitting next to her.

Leila's poor school capital corresponds to her low capital as a seriously contributing 'Muslim.' She is taken seriously neither as a pupil nor as a 'Muslim pupil.' As far as turn-taking practices are concerned, Leila and Zainab range in the 'middle'-achieving part of the class. However, they range low and at the bottom respectively of the Muslim class structure as well as in the general class structure in the classroom as this structure emerge from the teacher's categorization practices.

The ascription of degrees of Bildung depends – as the analysis suggests – on adaptability, aptitude for, and ability to choose as well as educational capital in the form of parents' education and own potential education. Muslimness may be more or less educated and more or less powerful in terms of capital. The more capital, the more legitimacy.

In classroom conversation on content related to subject matter, the analysis shows that a legitimate and an illegitimate Muslimness are installed through the speech, and become attached to conversational interactants as well as non-interactants. The legitimate Muslim subject is characterized both by predictable cultural habits and by unpredictable flexibility and of being willing: a subject figure appearing as both pathological and obligingly pluralist.

The space for illegitimate Muslimness is produced in and simultaneously excluded from the speech. This undesirable, yet verbally projected, Muslimness appears as inflexible and tied to literalism and fundamentalism.

The space for 'wrong Muslimness' is organized as an object that can or should be either imparted appropriateness or eliminated in that the flexible and unpredictable Muslim subject is cast as its alternative. At the same time, by virtue of its inflexibility, 'wrong Muslimness' contributes to the production of the flexible legitimate Muslim subject.

At the B-school, these 'Muslim figures' are attached to the boy-categorized pupil Sulayman and a girl-categorized pupil Meriam respectively. Both belong to the very talkative and teacher-recognized portion of pupils in the school class. At the same time, these pupils are constructed as part of the curriculum, where Sulayman becomes a key figure in the teacher's speech about 'rituals,' loaded with sensation. Through the teacher speech Sulayman emerges not as a pupil asking a content matter-related question in the classroom, but as a Muslim praying in a mosque, as the teacher 'tells the pupil's personal experience.'

Through a hammering out of spaces for subjects, then, the pupils are tied to knowledge production. At the same time, the precondition for speaking is an attachment to certain forms of subject spaces tinted by Muslimness. To pupils whom the teacher associates with Muslimness, the condition for participation in knowledge production, and hence active and legitimate school activity, is their participation as 'Muslims' rather than as pupils who are more or less well-versed in the subject matter.

While the Muslim subject spaces and various degrees of Muslimness associated with the pupils' school capital appear to be strongly and sophisticatedly differentiated, knowledge of the 'non-Muslim,' 'Christian' and 'Danish' is not nearly as productive in terms of the production of spaces for subjects. The production of these spaces is unsuccessful: The pupils do not respond to the teacher's attempts to include them as 'Christians,' as is the case with Gaja; or they are tinted by non-religiousness and atheism, as is the case with the non-baptized Andreas.

In the space in which not all, yet some minority pupils appear as the most school-legitimate, 'Muslimness' is flexed as a specific form of social differentiation. In this context, the ability to choose and be flexible generates a high level of recognition, while silence, the suspicion of unreflective headscarf usage, etc., lead to an estimated low school capital and cultural capital. At the same time, 'the Muslim pupil' is the object of subjectifying and flexibility-enhancing knowledge measures in the face of which these pupils appear to be special objects – not least the capital high-scoring pupils in the school class setting. Either way it boils down to an intimization and graduation of Muslimness.

13.4 Subjectivity within the perimeter of 'Muslim tradition.' The Muslim underclass at the C-schools highly differentiated class structure

At the C-school where minority pupils, including the portion of minority pupils categorized as 'Muslims,' are a minority also quantitatively speaking, flexibility, choice, and opportunities are not associated with 'Islam,' but with 'Christianity' as a field of knowledge. 'Christianity,' however, is not the immediate point of departure for projecting 'Christianity': Rather, the point of departure is 'universally human conditions' that gradually and through associations with choice, commodity, and work/profession become projected as linked to 'Christianity.' This field of knowledge is associated with majority pupils with a certain amount of school legitimacy and possession of capital. It is the 'experience' of such pupils that is installed in speech about 'Christianity' and that intimizes knowledge of 'Christianity.'

As was the case at the B-school, it seems that for pupils whom the teacher identifies as Muslim the condition for entering the official text of the classroom is that they participate in the speech as Muslims. Also this seems to be the light in which pupil speech is interpreted by the teacher when this speech originates in pupils categorized as Muslims.

However, the space for contributing with oneself 'as Muslim' is more delimited at the C-school than at the B-school as a consequence of the ways in which the teacher speech organizes knowledge of 'Islam.' A central and recurring figure in the teacher's speech, 'the Muslim tradition,' here defines the boundaries of the personal experience in demand. 'The Muslim tradition' poses as timeless with a touch of the antique. And the space demanding to be filled by personal experience is generated by it: a Muslim subject formed by tradition.

As is the case at the B-school, 'Muslim boys' are cast as objects of empathic concern. They stand out as currently or potentially school-illegitimate – even those who are also assigned a certain amount of school capital in the form of for instance intelligence, mathematical skills, congeniality, and a desire to adapt after all. The 'Muslim girls,' however, hardly stand out as objects of any concern. They are assigned from medium through low to no school capital, and the latter is associated with social problems. Nor are these girls included by the sensitive interest in 'girl hierarchy' dynamics that appears in the teachers' descriptions of the pupils: an interest which teachers direct towards majority girls with medium to high school capital exclusively.

The interest in the 'girl hierarchy' is part of the teachers' measurement of pupils in relation to a specific form of knowledge that comes to the fore in the teachers' descriptions of pupils: a measurement of pupils according to capabilities and knowledge pertaining to self-administration as well as capabilities of administrating others (such as 'being the good group leader').

As far as their self-administrative skills are concerned, the minority girls are at the bottom of the school's social economy – regardless of their parents' education and profession. They are accompanied by the capital-lacking majority pupils, particularly the capital-lacking majority girls. Simultaneously with the differentiated allocation of concerned interest – and of school capital in relation to self-administration – 'the Muslim pupils' are projected in the teacher speech as a coherent and particularly low-performing school underclass. When teachers speak about curriculum, these pupils make up a special object for the teaching in the particular educational module, i.e. as particularly and by default tied to 'their religion,' as well as they are projected as potential everyday experience knowledge-contributing subjects. However, in the demand for and expectation of their participation as 'religious experts,' contributing with 'something close to themselves,' they are simultaneously cast as particularly under-achieving pupils, who can only be expected to contribute with 'experience knowledge' as opposed to 'real school knowledge.'

The underclass space in school is primarily made available to the minority pupils that are categorized as 'Muslim' – both as a special problem and as individuals in need of particularly sensitive attention. Non-'Muslim' minority pupils and capital-lacking majority pupils, on the other hand, disappear from the teacher speech about the module as well as from the official text of the classroom.

13.5 Recapitulation: production of knowledge and production of social classification as interlinked

The production of social classification in the classrooms of both schools may be seen as connected to the production of the fields of knowledge of 'Islam' and 'Christianity.' It is connected in such a way that knowledge production also contributes to producing and internalizing social classifications, namely as subjectivities that ought to be assumed, occupied, and internalized as a curricular precondition of active participation.

Similarly, flexibility and choice in both instances figure as something that is attached to what appears to be optimum – and potential – pupil legitimacy. In both instances, 'Muslimness' is a specific object of problematization and school civilizing, but it plays out in different ways depending on the type of space that minority pupils occupy as 'Muslim pupils' in the differing social economies of the two school classes respectively.

From the analysis developed in this book, the knowledge cluster 'religion'/'culture' may be understood as practices of power and technologies producing subjects that on the one hand are objects of knowledge generation and on the other are subjected to and subject themselves to self-knowledge. These subjects are produced by the demand for confession of experience related to 'religion'/'culture,' and they are thus intimately attached to different sites in a landscape of identities dispersed along the lines of a social economy. The classroom produces 'religion'/'culture' as something tied to 'background' and 'personality' and thus as in conjunction with the attachment of 'religion'/'culture' to pupils' bodies. This landscape is drawn up differently at the two schools, but in both settings a similar logic of recognition appears: The more flexible subjects – the more legitimate.

The pedagogical doxa of personal experience and identification with the subject matter may then be conceptualized as politics that organizes and differentiates bodies as well as turns bodies into subjects seasoned with 'religion'/'culture.'

Subsequently, when the knowledge category 'religion'/'culture' is analyzed in connection with Bourdieu's graduated concept of capital, 'religion'/'culture' appears as social classification. In this light, differentiation in 'culture' and culturalized religion becomes class differentiation. Populated by subjects, the subject-generating knowledge cluster related to 'religion'/'culture' makes up a productive and potent part of social classification that may be seen as linked to – and having consequences for – social distribution. Hence, the category 'Muslim' should not be understood as *related* to social classification and social distribution processes exclusively; it *is* in itself a social classification – as a socially differentiating and as a social distribution process. Inspired by Razack's so-called interlocking perspective: "The systems are each other" (Razack 2007a:343).

13.6 The school's production and classification of knowledge and bodies. 'Muslimness' and 'universal Danish Christianity' pedagogized

How is this 'system' then produced within the pedagogical field of practice in particular? In the analyses of the classroom, figures of flexibility and choice pose as both professional requirements and method and as something coloring knowledge clusters and hence generating subjects and their social differentiation. What has been analyzed is the school institution's own special coloring and shaping of categories such as 'Muslimness' and 'Danishness'/'Christianness' – its pedagogizing of the categories – both with regard to knowledge production and with regard to the associated production and differentiation of subjects.

The fact that flexible subjectivity in the school context poses both as a general requirement – and hence also a requirement associated with 'Christian'/'non-Christian' pupils – and, when associated with 'Muslims,' as a special parameter of legitimacy, points to a feature of pedagogic discourse (to sum up with Bernstein): a recontextualizing of that which in ministerial and education-political texts plays out as an orientation towards individuality and competence (Hermann 2003, Krejsler 2004a,b. See also Saugstad 2004, 2011, Hultquist 2004, Frykman 2005).

By extension, the production of 'Muslimness' and 'Danishness'/'Christianness' may also be explained as a recontextualizing of the potent and vital production of knowledge of and about 'Muslimness' and 'Danishness'/'Christianness' in other societal fields and in other subfields of practice within the educational system. But the school's production of 'Muslimness' and 'Danishness'/'Christianness' is to be seen as homologous and *not* identical to productions in other fields. Seemingly, they appear to be parallel structurings, but the school's production of 'Muslimness' is colored and shaped in a particular way by the school's own special knowledge-shaping framework and requirements and, not least, by the focus on the personal.

The culture-focused formation of knowledge in the debate on *Kristendomskundskab* that has taken place in a Danish context during the last decades may also be rediscovered in the classroom, but again: in a particularly pedagogized form. 'Culture' here becomes a specific causally-oriented interpretative key explaining the pupils as culturally 'Muslim' and hence as culturally different from the 'universal Danes.' In this sense, multiculturalism – the discursive production of, sensitivity towards, and appreciation of differences as cultural – may be seen as something that forms part of social differentiation in conjunction with the classroom. The convergence of 'religion' and 'culture,' as it appears when the emphasis on minority pupils' 'Muslimness' turns into specific pedagogical strategies aiming to 'reach' these pupils, may be seen as recontextualized multiculturalism.

It can be argued, then, that the mutual shaping of knowledge and social classification not only *stabilises through institutions*, to phrase it with Foucault (1997:169). Knowledge and social classification are also *produced on the school institution's own terms*. At the same time, it becomes clear that the two studied classrooms may be said to color curriculum – the curriculum populated by pupils – in dissimilar ways.

Keeping this in mind, if we now turn to the main theme 'religion'/'culture' as this plays out in the classroom where it stands out as a potent form of categorization linked to minority and majority groups and persons, I would argue that religion in this light must be understood as something that is (also) produced in the school institution: as intimately related to the identities produced, as a prescription of practices, and as something associated with different types of bodies in different ways (Foucault 1992). Religion, then, is attached to 'the Muslim body' and 'the universal Danish body,' both of which again are attached to the socially hierarchized bodies of minority and majority pupils respectively. In this sense, the culturalized category of 'religion' – *culturalized* in Razack's and Balibar's meaning of the term – not only functions as a metaform of the concept of race. Based on the analyses presented in this book, the culturalized category of 'religion' may be explained as micro-identity politics (Foucault 1997, Deleuze & Guattari 2004) internalizing social classification and social distribution. This micro-identity politics plays out in other social fields as well – but, as we have seen, also within the state educational institution. 'To be Muslim' and 'to be Universal-Christian-Danish' are indeed things you can learn in school.

References

Ahrenkiel, A. 2004: *Kontrol og dynamik i pædagogiske processer. Et diskurs-analytisk studie af kommunikation i en "usynlig" pædagogisk læringskontekst med daghøjskolen som eksempel*, Roskilde/Frederiksberg: Roskilde Universitetsforlag.

Andersen, T. et al. 2001: *Sproget som ressource. Dansk systemisk funktionel grammatik i teori og praksis*, Odense: Odense Universitetsforlag.

Apple, M. 1979: *Ideology and Curriculum*, Boston: Routledge & Kegan Paul.

Baker, B. M. 2001: *In perpetual motion: Theories of power, educational history, and the child*, New York: Peter Lang.

Baker, B. M. 2009a: "Borders, Belonging, Beyond: New Curriculum History," B. Baker (ed.): *New Curriculum History*, Rotterdam/Boston/Taipei: Sense Publishers, pp. ix-xxxv.

Baker, B. M. 2009b: "Western Worldforming? Animal Magnetism, Curriculum History, and the Social Projects of Modernity," B. Baker (ed.): *New Curriculum History*, Rotterdam/Boston/Taipei: Sense Publishers, pp. 25-68.

Balibar, E. 1991 [1988]: "Is there a 'Neo-Racism'?," Balibar, E. & Wallerstein, I.: *Race, Class and Nation. Ambiguous Identities*, London/New York: Verso, pp. 17-28.

Banks, J. A. 1986: "Multicultural Education and its critics," Banks, J. A. & Lynch, J. (eds.): *Multicultural Education in Western Societies*, London: Holt, Rinehart & Winston, pp. 196-203.

Baumann, G. 2004: "Introduction. Nation-state, Schools and Civil Enculturation," Schiffauer, W., Baumann, G., Kastoryano, R. & Vertovec, S. (eds.): *Civil enculturation. Nation-state, School and Ethnic Difference in four European Countries*, Oxford: Berghahn Books, pp. 1-18.

Baumann, G. & Sunier, T. 2004: "The School as a Place in its Social Space," Schiffauer, W., Baumann, G., Kastoryano, R. & Vertovec, S. (eds.): *Civil enculturation. Nation-state, School and Ethnic Difference in four European Countries*, Oxford: Berghahn Books, pp. 22-36.

Berglund, J. 2010: *Teaching Islam. Islamic Religious Education in Sweden*, Münster: Waxmann.

Bernstein, B. 1971: "On Classification and Framing of Educational Knowledge," Young, M. F. D (ed.): *Knowledge and Control: New Directions for the Sociology of Education*, London: Collier-Macmillan, pp. 47-69.

Bernstein, B. 1990: "Social construction of pedagogic discourse," *Class, codes and control, vol. IV: The structuring of pedagogic discourse*, London/New York: Routledge 1990, pp. 165-218.

Bernstein, B. 1997 [1978]: "Class and Pedagogies: Visible and Invisible," Halsey, A. H. et al. (eds.): *Education. Culture, Economy, and Society*, Oxford/New York: Oxford University Press, pp. 59-79.

Bernstein, B. 2000a: "Pedagogic Codes and Their Modalities of Practice," *Pedagogy, Symbolic Control and Identity. Theory, Research, Critique*, Lanham: Rowman & Littlefield, pp. 3-24.

Bernstein, B. 2000b: "The Pedagogic Device," *Pedagogy, Symbolic Control and Identity. Theory, Research, Critique*, Lanham: Rowman & Littlefield, pp. 25-39.

Bernstein, B. 2000c: "Pedagogising Knowledge: Studies in Recontextualising," *Pedagogy, Symbolic Control and Identity. Theory, Research, Critique*, Lanham: Rowman & Littlefield, pp. 41-63.

Bernstein, B. 2009 [1965]: "A socio-linguistic approach to social learning," *Class, codes and control, vol. I: Theoretical studies towards a sociology of language*, London: Routledge & Kegan Paul, pp. 118-139.

Bjerke, F. 2005: "7. lektion. Foucaults diskursanalyse: Tankens Analytik," downloaded from www.diskurs.dk, January 29.

Börjesson, M. 2005: *Transnationella utbildningsstrategier vid svenska lärosäten och bland svenska studenter i Paris och New York*, Dissertation, Sociology of Education and Culture (SEC), ILU, Uppsala University.

Böwadt, P. R. 2007: *Livets pædagogik? En kritik af livsfilosofiens pædagogisering*, Copenhagen: Gyldendal.

Böwadt, P. R. 2009: "The courage to be: the impact of Lebensphilosophie on Danish RE," *British Journal of Religious Education* 31 (1):29-39.

Bourdieu, P. 1971: "Systems of Education and Systems of Thought," Young, M. F. D (ed.): *Knowledge and Control: New Directions for the Sociology of Education*, London: Collier-Macmillan, pp. 189-2007.

Bourdieu, P. 1975 [1975]: "The specificity of the scientific field and the social conditions of the progress of reason," *Social Science Information* 14 (6):19-47.

Bourdieu, P. 1993 [1968-1987]: *The Field of Cultural Production. Essays on Art and Literature*, New York: Columbia University Press.

Bourdieu, P. 1997 [1986]: "The Forms of Capital," Halsey, A. H. et al. (eds.): *Education. Culture, Economy, and Society*, Oxford/New York: Oxford University Press, pp. 46-58.

Bourdieu, P. 1998a [1989]: *The State Nobility. Elite Schools in the Field of Power*, Cambridge: Polity Press.

Bourdieu, P. 1998b [1994]: *Practical Reason. On the Theory of Action*, Oxfordshire: Polity Press.

Bourdieu, P. 1998c [1994/Lecture, Tokyo 1989]: "The New Capital," *Practical Reason. On the Theory of Action*, Oxfordshire: Polity Press, pp. 19-30.

Bourdieu, P. 1998d [1994/Lecture, Wisconsin 1989]: "Appendix: Social Space and Field of Power," *Practical Reason. On the Theory of Action*, Oxfordshire: Polity Press, pp. 31-34.

Bourdieu, P. 1998e [1994/Lecture, Tokyo 1989]: "Social Space and Symbolic Space," *Practical Reason. On the Theory of Action*, Oxfordshire: Polity Press, pp. 1-13.

Bourdieu, P. 1998f [1994/Lecture, East Berlin 1989]: "Appendix: The "Soviet" Variant and Political Capital," *Practical Reason. On the Theory of Action*, Oxfordshire: Polity Press, pp. 14-18.

Bourdieu, P. 2004a [1979]: *Distinction. A Social Critique of the Judgement of Taste*, New York/London: Routledge.

Bourdieu, P. 2004b [2001]: *Science of Science and Reflexivity*, Cambridge: Polity Press.

Bourdieu, P. 2005 [1992]: *The Rules of Art. Genesis and Structure of the Literary Field*, Cambridge/Oxford: Polity Press.

Bourdieu, P., Chamboredon, J.-C. & Passeron, J.-C. 1991 [1968]: *The Craft of Sociology. Epistemological Preliminaries*, Berlin/New York: Walter de Gruyter.

Bourdieu, P. & Passeron, J.-C. 2000 [1970]: *Reproduction in education, society and culture*, London: Sage.

Broady, D. 2002 [1998/2000]: "Kapitalbegrebet som uddannelsessociologisk værktøj," Bjerg, J. (ed.): *Pædagogik – en grundbog til et fag*, Copenhagen: Hans Reitzels Forlag, pp. 453-490.

von Brömssen, K. 2003: *Tolkningar, Förhandlingar och Tystnader. Elevers Tal om Religion i det Mångkulturella och Postkoloniala Rummet*, PhD Dissertation, Göteborg Studies in Educational Sciences 201, Gothenburg: Acta Universitatis Gothoburgensis.

Buchardt, M. 2004: "Religious Education in the School: Approaches in School Practice and Research in Denmark," Larsson, R. & Gustavsson, C. (eds.): *Toward a European Perspective on Religious Education*, Stockholm: Artos & Norma bokförlag, pp. 117-26.

Buchardt, M. 2006a: "'Store Forventninger' – Konstruktion af identitet i multikulturalistisk religionsundervisning," Andersen, P. B. et al. (eds.): *Religion, skole og kulturel integration i Danmark og Sverige, Chaos, Dansk-Norsk Tidsskrift for Religionshistoriske Studier*, Copenhagen: Museum Tusculanum, pp. 263-91.

Buchardt, M. 2006b: "Kristendoms status i kristendomskundskab," Buchardt, M. (ed.): *Religionsdidaktik*, Copenhagen: Gyldendal 2006, pp. 216-228.

Buchardt, M. 2007: "Teachers – and Knowledge and Identity Technologies around 'Religion.' Discursive and other Social Practices in the Classroom," Bakker, C. & Heimbrock, H.-G. (eds.): *Researching RE Teachers. RE teachers as Researchers, Religious Diversity and Education in Europe*, vol. IV, Münster: Waxmann, pp. 17-36.

Buchardt, M. 2008: *Identitetspolitik i klasserummet. 'Religion' og 'kultur' som viden og social klassifikation. Studier i et praktiseret skolefag*, PhD dissertation, Faculty of Humanities, University of Copenhagen.

Buchardt, M. 2010: "When Muslimness is pedagogized. 'Religion' and 'culture' as knowledge and social classification," *British Journal of Religious Education* 32 (3):259-273.

Buchardt, M. 2011a: "How did 'the Muslim pupil' become Muslim? Danish state schooling and 'the migrant pupils' since the 1970s," Nielsen, J. S. (ed.): *Islam in Denmark. The challenge of diversity*, New York: Lexington Books, pp. 115-142.

Buchardt, M. 2011b: "Wenn 'Religion' und 'Kultur' im Klassenraum zur 'Erfahrung' werden. Pädagogisch transformiertes 'Muslimsein,'" *Zeitschrift für Pädagogik und Theologie* 63 (4):333-344.

Buchardt, M. 2012: "Undervisningsformer – historisk og aktuelt," Andersen, P.Ø. & Ellegaard, T. (eds.): *Klassisk og moderne pædagogisk teori*, Copenhagen: Hans Reitzels Forlag, pp. 315-336.

Buchardt, M. 2013a: "Religion, education and social cohesion: Transformed and traveling Lutheranism in the emerging Nordic welfare states 1890s-1930s," Buchardt, M., Markkola, P. & Valtonen, H. (eds.): *Education, state and citizenship: A perspective in the Nordic Welfare State History, NordWel Studies in Historical Welfare State Research*, vol. 4, Helsinki: University of Helsinki, pp. 81-113.

Buchardt, M. 2013b:"Pedagogical transformations of 'religion' into 'culture' in Danish state mass schooling 1900s –1937," *Paedagogica Historica* 49 (1):126-138.

Buchardt, M. 2013c: "'The Immigrant Pupil' between 'Cultural Difference' and Division of Labor in Danish Curriculum since the 1970s," paper presented at the American Educational Research Association (AERA), Annual Meeting, San Francisco, USA, April 28-May 1.

Buchardt, M. 2014: "Religious Education in Schools in Denmark," Rothgangel, M., Jäggle, M. & Skeie, G. (eds.): *Religious Education in schools in Europe*, vol. 3, Vienna: Vandenhoeck & Ruprecht (Wiener Forum für Theologie und Religionswissenschaft), Vienna University Press, pp. 45-74.

Buchardt, M. et al. 2006: *Religionsdidaktik*, Copenhagen: Gyldendal 2006.

Buchardt, M. & Fabrin, L. (eds.) 2010: *'Kultur' i 'kulturfagene.' En interkulturel og transnational læreplan i klasserummet? Et aktionsforskningsprojekt*, Copenhagen Municipality & Section of Educational Science, University of Copenhagen, UCC's Forlag: Copenhagen.

Buchardt, M. & Fabrin, L. 2012: *Interkulturel didaktik. Introduktion til teorier og tilgange*, Copenhagen: Gyldendal.

Buchardt, M., Markkola, P. & Valtonen, H. 2013: "Education and the making of the Nordic welfare states," Buchardt, M., Markkola, P. & Valtonen, H. (eds.): *Education, state and citizenship: A perspective in the Nordic Welfare State History, NordWel Studies in Historical Welfare State Research*, vol. 4, Helsinki: University of Helsinki, pp. 7-30.

Bugge, K. E. 1968: "Striden Bentzen – Kaper 1933-34. En episode i dansk kristendomsundervisnings historie," *Årbog for Dansk Skolehistorie 1968*, Odense: Selskabet for Dansk Skolehistorie, pp. 97-126.

Bugge, K. E. 1979: *Vi har rel'gion. Et skolefags historie 1900-1975*, Copenhagen: Nyt Nordisk Forlag Arnold Busck.

Bugge, K. E. 1994: *Vi har stadig Rel'gion*, Frederiksberg: Materialecentralen Religionspædagogisk center.

Callewaert, S. 1997: *Bourdieu-studier*, Copenhagen: Institut for Filosofi, Pædagogik og Retorik, University of Copenhagen.

Callewaert, S. 1998: "Skjult læreplan," *Pædagogisk opslagsbog*, Copenhagen: Chr. Ejlersens Forlag, pp. 258-264.

Callewaert, S. 2002 [1998/2000]: "Uddannelsesfilosofi, Frankfurterskolens kritiske teori og Pierre Bourdieus sociologi," Bjerg, J. (ed.): *Pædagogik – en grundbog til et fag*, Copenhagen: Hans Reitzels Forlag, pp. 491-516.

Callewaert, S. 2003: "Har alle skolefag samme værdi?," Callewaert, S.: *Fra Bourdieu og Foucaults verden*, Copenhagen: Akademisk Forlag, pp. 258-270.

Chouliaraki, L. 1998: "Regulation in 'progressivist' pedagogic discourse: individualized teacher-pupil talk," *Discourse & Society* 9 (1):5-32.

Chouliaraki, L. 2001: "Pædagogikkens sociale logik – en introduktion til Basil Bernsteins uddannelsessociologi," Chouliaraki, L. & Bayer, M. (eds.): *Basil Bernstein. Pædagogik, diskurs og magt*, Akademisk Forlag, pp. 26-67.

Chouliaraki, L. & Fairclough, N. 1999: *Discourse in Late Modernity, Rethinking Critical Discourse Analysis*, Edinburgh: Edinburgh University Press.

Clausen, I. M. 1986: *Den flerkulturelle skole: Om interkulturel, anti-racistisk undervisning*, Copenhagen: Gyldendal.

Dahllöf, U. 1967: *Skoldifferentiering och undervisningsförlopp*, Stockholm: Almqvist & Wiksell.

Deleuze, G. & Guattari, F. 2004 [1980]: *A Thousand Plateaus. Capitalism and Schizophrenia*, London: Continuum.

Dreyfus, H. L. & Rabinow, P. 1986 [1982]: *Michel Foucault. Beyond Structuralism and Hermeneutics*, Sussex: The Harvester Press.

Englund, T. 1990: "Curriculum History Reconsidered," *Scandinavian Journal of Educational Research* 34 (2):91-102.
Fairclough, N. 1992: *Discourse and Social Change*, Cambridge: Polity Press.
Fairclough, N. 1995: *Critical Discourse Analysis: the critical study of Language*, London & New York: Longman.
Fairclough, N. 2001: "The Discourse of New Labour: Critical Discourse Analysis," Wetherell, M. et al. (eds.): *Discourse as Data, A Guide for Analysis*, London: Sage/The Open University.
Fairclough, N. 2003: *Analyzing Discourse, textual analysis for social research*, London: Routledge.
Fairclough, N. No date: *The dialectics of Discourse*, upublished paper.
Fekete, L. 2004: "Anti-Muslim Racism and the European Security State," *Race & Class* 46 (1):3-29.
Fetzer, J. S. & Soper, J. C. 2005: *Muslims and the State in Britain, France and Germany*, Cambridge: Cambridge University Press.
Foucault, M. 1971 [1969]: *L'archéologie du savoir*, Bibliothéque des Science Humaines, Paris: Nrf Edition Gallimard.
Foucault, M. 1984: *L'Usage des plaisirs. Histoire de la sexualité*, vol. 2, Paris: Gallimard.
Foucault, M. 1991 [1975]: *Discipline and Punish. The Birth of the Prison*, London: Penguin Books.
Foucault, M. 1992 [1984]: *The Use of Pleasure. The History of Sexuality,* vol. II, London: Penguin Books.
Foucault, M. 1993 [1971]: "Nietzsche, Genealogy, History," Bouchard, D. F. (ed.): *Language, Counter-Memory, Practice. Selected Essays and Interviews by Michel Foucault*, Ithaca, N. Y: Cornell University Press, pp. 139-164.
Foucault, M. 1994 [1966]: *The Order of Things. An Archaeology of Human Sciences* [Les Mots et les choses], New York: Vintage Books.
Foucault, M. 1997 [1982/1984]: "Sex, Power and the Politics of Identity," *The essential works: Ethics. Subjectivity and Truth*, vol. 1, New York: The New Press, pp. 163-173.
Foucault, M. 1998 [1976]: *The Will to Knowledge. The History of Sexuality*, vol. 1, London: Penguin Books.
Foucault, M. 2000 [1994/1982]: "The Subject and Power," *The essential works: Power*, vol. 3, London: Allen Lane, The Penguin Press, pp. 326-48.
Foucault, M. 2001 [1971]: "Talens Forfatning" [L'ordre du discourse], *Talens Forfatning*, Copenhagen: Hans Reitzels Forlag, pp. 11-50.
Foucault, M. 2003a [1999]: *Abnormal. Lectures at the College de France 1974-75*, New York: Picador.
Foucault, M. 2003b [1969]: *The Archaeology of Knowledge*, London & New York: Routledge.
Foucault, M. 2003c [1963/1972]: *The Birth of the Clinic. An Archeology of Medical Perception*, London & New York: Routledge.
French, P. & MacLure, M. 1981: "Teachers' questions, pupils' answers. An investigation of questions and answers in the infant classroom," Stubbs, M. & Hillier, H. (eds.): *Readings on Language, Schools and Classrooms*, London: Methuen, pp. 193-211.
Frimann, S. 2004: *Kommunikation – tekst i kontekst. Tekstanalyse med Systemisk Funktionel Lingvistik,* Aalborg: Aalborg Universitetsforlag.

Frimann Trads, S. 2000: *Interpersonelle relationer i medarbejdersamtaler*, PhD dissertation, Dept. of Communication, Aalborg University.

Frykmann, J. 2005 [1998]: *En lys fremtid? Skole, social mobilitet og kulturel identitet*, Copenhagen: Unge Pædagoger.

Gilliam, L. 2009: *De umulige børn og det ordentlige menneske: identitet, ballade og muslimske fællesskaber blandt etniske minoritetsbørn*, Århus: Aarhus Universitetsforlag.

Gilliam, L. 2010: "Den utilsigtede integration. Skolens bidrag til etniske minoritetsbørns muslimske identitet og fælleskab", Lippert-Rasmussen, K. & Holtug, N. (eds.): *Kulturel diversitet. Muligheder og begrænsninger*, Odense: Syddansk Universitetsforlag, pp. 123-141.

Gitz-Johansen, T. 2006: *Den multikulturelle skole. Integration og sortering*, Frederiksberg: Roskilde Universitetsforlag.

Goodson, I. F. 1988: *The Making of Curriculum. Collected Essays* (second edition 1995), Oxon: RoutledgeFalmer.

Goodson, I. F. 1990: "The Social History of School Subjects," *Scandinavian Journal of Educational Research* 34 (2):111-121.

Goodson, I. F. 1992: "On Curriculum Form. Notes Towards a Theory of Curriculum," *Sociology of Education* 65 (1):66-75.

Goodson, I. F. 1995: "A genesis and genealogy of British Curriculum Studies," Sadovnik, A. R. (ed.): *Knowledge and pedagogy: the sociology of Basil Bernstein*, Norwood, NJ: Ablex Publishing, pp. 359-369.

Grue-Sørensen, K. 1965: *Pædagogik mellem videnskab og filosofi*, Copenhagen: Gyldendal.

Haaber Ihle, A. 2007: *Magt, Medborgerskab og Muslimske Friskoler i Danmark. Traditioner, idealer og politikker*, Working paper, University of Copenhagen, Department of Cross-cultural and Regional Studies.

Haas, C. 2003: "Nationalisme og/eller multikulturalisme: et centralt identitetspolitisk konfliktfelt i fremtidens flerkulturelle Danmark?," *GRUS* 69: *Identitet, Minoritet, Magt*, pp. 66-83.

Haas, C. 2004: "Demokratididaktik som fagdidaktisk og identitetspolitisk kategori," Schnack, K. (ed.): *Didaktik på kryds og tværs*, Copenhagen: Danmarks Pædagogiske Universitets Forlag, pp. 201-226.

Halliday, M. A. K. & Matthiessen C. M. I. M. 2004: *An Introduction to Functional Grammar*, London: Arnold.

Hermann, S. 2003: "Fra folkeskole til kompetencemiljø – tendenser i vidensamfundets kapitallogik," Borch, C. & Madsen, L. T. (eds.): *Perspektiv, magt og styring. Luhmann og Foucault til diskussion*, Copenhagen: Hans Reitzels Forlag, pp. 231-66.

Hervik, P. 2002: *Mediernes muslimer. En antropologisk undersøgelse af mediernes dækning af religioner i Danmark*, Copenhagen: Nævnet for Etnisk Ligestilling.

Hervik, P. 2004: "Anthropological perspectives on the new racism in Europe," *Ethnos: Journal of Anthropology* 69 (2):149-155.

Hervik, P. 2011: *The Annoying Difference. The Emergence of Danish Neonationalism, Neoracism, and Populism in the Post-1987 World*, Oxford: Berghan Books.

Hestbæk Andersen, T. & Smedegaard, F. 2005: *Hvad er meningen?*, Odense: Syddansk Universitetsforlag.

Hofstetter, R. & Schneuwly, B. 2002: "Institutionalisation of Educational Sciences and the Dynamics of Their Development," *European Educational Research Journal* 1 (1):3-26.

Hopmann, S. & Riquarts, K. 2000: "Starting a Dialogue: A Beginning Conversation Between Didaktik and the Curriculum Traditions," Westbury, I. et al. (eds.): *Teaching as a reflective practice: the German Didaktik tradition*, Mahwah, N. J.: Lawrence Erlbaum, pp. 3-11.

Howarth, D. 2000: *Discourse*, Buckingham & Philadelphia: Open University Press.

Hultquist, K. 2004: ""Fremtiden" som styringsteknologi og det pædagogiske subjekt som konstruktion," Krejsler, J. (ed.): *Pædagogikken og kampen om individet. Kritisk pædagogik, ny inderlighed og selvets teknikker*, Copenhagen: Hans Reitzels Forlag, pp. 159-189.

Huntington, S. P. 1998 [1996]: *The Clash of Civilizations and the making of a new world order*, London/New York: Touchstone Books.

Hussain, M. et al. 1997: *Medierne, minoriteterne og majoriteten: En undersøgelse af nyhedsmedier og den folkelige diskurs i Danmark*, Copenhagen: Nævnet for Etnisk Ligestilling.

Hvenegård-Lassen, K. 2002: *På lige fod: samfundet, ligheden og folketingets debatter om udlændingepolitik 1973-2000*, PhD dissertation, Section of Minority Studies, Dept. of Nordic Philology, University of Copenhagen.

Jackson, P. 1968: *Life in the classrooms*, Chicago: University of Chicago Press.

Jenkins, P. 1998: *Moral Panic, Changing the Concepts of the Child Molester in Modern America*, New Haven: Yale University Press.

Kampmann, J. 2006: "Multikulturalisme, anti-racisme, kritisk multikulturalisme. Overvejelser om en debats fravær," Horst, C. (red.): *Interkulturel Pædagogik. Flere sprog – problem eller resurse*, Vejle: Kroghs Forlag: pp. 127-140.

Kampmann, J. 2012: "Pædagogisk-kritiske og kritisk-pædagogiske traditioner," Andersen, P.Ø. & Ellegaard, T. (eds.): *Klassisk og moderne pædagogisk teori*, Copenhagen: Hans Reitzels Forlag, pp. 462-478.

Klausen, J. 2009: *The Cartoons that Shook the World*, New Haven: Yale University Press.

Kofoed, J. 2003: *Elevpli. Inklusion-eksklusionsprocesser blandt børn i skolen*, PhD dissertation, Copenhagen: Dept. of Educational Psychology, Danish University of Education.

Korsgaard, O. 2004: *Kampen om folket. Et dannelsesperspektiv på dansk historie gennem 500 år*, Copenhagen: Gyldendal.

Krejsler, J. (ed.) 2004: *Pædagogikken og kampen om individet. Kritisk pædagogik, ny inderlighed og selvets teknikker*, Copenhagen: Hans Reitzels Forlag.

Krejsler, J. 2004a: "Introduktion: Når uddannelse rammes af individualisering," Krejsler, J. (ed.): *Pædagogikken og kampen om individet. Kritisk pædagogik, ny inderlighed og selvets teknikker*, Copenhagen: Hans Reitzels Forlag, pp. 7-31.

Krejsler, J. 2004b: "Pædagogiske spil med personligheden som indsats. Om den lærende, selvets teknikker og muligheder for at tænke anderledes," Krejsler, J. (ed.): *Pædagogikken og kampen om individet. Kritisk pædagogik, ny inderlighed og selvets teknikker*, Copenhagen: Hans Reitzels Forlag, pp. 63-88.

Laursen, H. P. & Holm, L. 2010: *Dansk som andetsprog. Pædagogiske og didaktiske perspektiver*, Copenhagen: Dansklærerforeningens Forlag.

Lindblad, S. & Sahlström, F. 2002: "Klasserumsforskning. En oversigt med fokus på interaktion og elever," Bjerg, J. (ed.): *Pædagogik. En grundbog til et fag*, Copenhagen: Hans Reitzels Forlag, pp. 245-278.

Lundgren, U. P. 1972: *Frame factors and the teaching process: a contribution to curriculum theory and theory on teaching*, disputats, Gothenburg 1972, Göteborg studies in educational sciences vol. 8, Stockholm: Almqvist og Wiksell.

Lundgren, U. P. 1981: *At organisere omvärlden, en introduktion til läroplansteori*, Stockholm: LiberFörlag.

Mamdani, M. 2005: *Good Muslims, Bad Muslims. America, the Cold war, and the Roots of Terror*, Lahore: Vanguard Books.

Maton, K. 2000: "Recovering pedagogic discourse: A Bernsteinian approach to the sociology of educational knowledge," *Linguistics and Education* 11 (1): 79-98.

Maton, K. 2014: *Knowledge and Knowers. Towards a realist sociology of education*, London & New York: Routledge.

Mehan, H. 1979: *Learning Lessons. Social organization in the classroom*, Cambridge: Harvard University Press.

Meidahl, C. 1989: *Mennesker og religioner* [Human beings and religions], Temahæfte [theme booklet] 1 & 2 and Lærervejledning [Teacher's Manual], Copenhagen: Aschehoug dansk Forlag.

Mills, S. 1997: *Discourse*, London & New York: Routledge.

Modood, T. & Werbner, P. 1997: *The Politics of Multiculturalism in the New Europe: Racism, Identity, and Community*, London: Zed Books.

Moldenhawer, B. 2001: *En bedre fremtid? Skolens betydning for etniske minoriteter*, Copenhagen: Hans Reitzels Forlag.

Moldenhawer, B. 2007a: "De indefra ekskluderede. En analyse af inklusions- og eksklusionsstrukturer i en gymnasieskole for alle," Alsmark, G. et al. (eds.): *Migration och tillhörighet. Inklusions- och exklusionsprocesser i Skandinavien*, Göteborg/Stockholm: Makadam Förlag, pp. 221-258.

Moldenhawer, B. 2007b: "Lika utbildning för alla? Integration eller exkludering i gymnasieskolan," Dahlstedt, M. et al. (eds.): *Utbildning, arbete, medborgarskap. Strategier för social inkludering i den mångetniska staden*, Umeå: Boréa Bokförlag, pp. 79-110.

Mottelson, M. 2003: *Lærerarbejdets koreografi. En empirisk undersøgelse af læreres praksis, habitus og professionelle stil*, PhD dissertation, Dept. of Philosophy, Educational Science and Rhetorics, Faculty of Humanities, University of Copenhagen.

Muschinsky, L. J. 1991: *Om mellemlagslivet og dets naturalisering*, Working paper, Dept. of Educational Science, University of Copenhagen.

Nielsen, J. S. 2004: *Muslims in Western Europe*, Edinburgh: Edinburgh University Press.

Nielsen, J. S. 2011: "Setting the scene. Muslims in Denmark," Nielsen, J. S. (ed.): *Islam in Denmark. The challenge of diversity*, New York: Lexington Books, pp. 1-12.

Osbeck, C. & Skeie, G. 2014: "Religious Education in Schools in Sweden," Rothgangel, M., Jäggle, M. & Skeie, G. (eds.): *Religious Education in schools in Europe*, vol. 3, Vienna: Vandenhoeck & Ruprecht (Wiener Forum für Theologie und Religionswissenschaft): Vienna University Press, pp. 237-266.

Otterbeck, J. 2000: *Islam, muslimer och den svenska skola*, Lund: Studentlitteratur.

Otterbeck, J. 2010: *Samtidsislam. Unga muslimer i Malmö och Köpenhamn*, Stockholm: Carlssons bokförlag.

Padovan-Özdemir, M. 2012: "Migratoriske dannelsesprocesser. Når indvandrerskolen ikke nødvendigvis fører til antidemokratisk radikalisering," *Dansk pædagogisk Tidsskrift* 2:28-37.

Parekh, B. 1986: "The Concept of Multicultural Education," Modgil, S. (ed.): *Multicultural Education. The Interminable Debate*, London: Falmer, pp. 19-31.

Pedersen, L. 1988: "Islam, muslimer og indvandrere i Dagbladet Information," Dindler, S. & Olsen, A. (eds.): *Islam og muslimer i de danske medier*, Statens Humanistiske Forskningsråd, Århus: Aarhus Universitetsforlag, pp. 120-133.

Pinar W. F. et al. 1995: *Understanding Curriculum*, New York: Peter Lang.

Popkewitz, T. S. 1998: *Struggling for the Soul. The Politics of Schooling and the construction of the Teacher*, NY/London: Teachers College Press, Columbia University.

Popkewitz, T. S. 2001: "The Production of Reason and Power. Curriculum History and Intellectual Traditions," Popkewitz, T. S. et al. (eds.): *Cultural History and Education*, New York, NY: RoutledgeFalmer, pp. 151-183.

Popkewitz, T. S. 2006: "Pædagogik mellem religion og psykologi," Elle, B. et al. (eds.): *Pædagogisk psykologi*, Copenhagen: Roskilde Universitetsforlag, pp. 211-239.

Popkewitz, T. S. 2007: *Cosmopolitanism and the age of school reform. Science, education and making society by making the child*, Boca Raton: Taylor and Francis.

Popkewitz, T. S. & Brennan, M. 1998: *Foucault's Challenge. Discourse, Knowledge and Power in Education*, NY/London: Teachers College Press, Columbia University.

Qureshi, E. & Sells, M. R. (eds.) 2003: *The New Crusades. Constructing the Muslim Enemy*, New York: Columbia University Press.

Rasmussen, J. 1996: *Socialisering og læring i det refleksivt moderne*, Copenhagen: Unge Pædagoger.

Razack, S. H. 1998: *Looking White People in the Eye. Gender, Race, and Culture in Courtrooms and Classrooms*, Toronto: University of Toronto Press.

Razack, S. H. 2004a: *Dark Threats and White Knights. The Somalia Affair, Peacekeeping and the New Imperialism*, Toronto/Buffalo/London: University of Toronto Press.

Razack, S. H. 2004b: "Imperilled Muslim Women, Dangerous Muslim Men and Civilised Europeans: Legal and Social Responses to Forced Marriages," *Feminist Legal Studies* 12:129-174.

Razack, S. H. 2007a: "How is white supremacy embodied? Sexualized racial violence at Abu Graib," *Canadian Journal of Women and the Law* 17 (2):342-363.

Razack, S. H. 2007b: "Stealing the Pain of Others. Reflections on Canadian Humanitarian Responses," *Review of Education, Pedagogy, and Cultural Studies* 29 (4):375-394.

Razack, S. H. 2008: *Casting out. The Eviction of Muslims from Western Law and Politics*, Toronto: University of Toronto Press.

Reeh, N. 2006: *Religion and the state of Denmark. State religious politics in the elementary school system from 1721 to 1975. An alternative approach to secularization*, PhD dissertation, Copenhagen: Faculty of Humanities, University of Copenhagen.

Reeh, N. 2009a: "Ideas and State-Subjectivity in History: the introduction of the equestrian schools in 1720 and the confirmation in 1736," *Ideas in History* 5 (3):83-110.

Reeh, N. 2009b: "Towards a New Approach to Secularization: Religion, Education and the State in Denmark 1721-1900," *Social Compass* 5 (2):179-188.

Rubow, C. 1993: *At sige ordentligt farvel. Om begravelser i Danmark*, Copenhagen: Anis.

Rubow, C. 2000: *Hverdagens teologi. Folkereligiøsitet i danske verdener*, Copenhagen: Forlaget Anis.
Rubow, C. 2008: "Kristendommens ankomst i antropologien, og antropologiens adkomst i teologien," Schjørring, J. H. & Bak, J. T. (eds.): *Fra modernitet til pluralisme: nation, stat, folk, kirke i det 20. århundredes Europa*, Copenhagen: Anis, pp. 267-288.
Sahlström, F. 1999: *Up the Hill Backwards. On Interactional Constraints and Affordances for Equity-Constitution in the Classroom of the Swedish Comprehensive School*, Acta Universitatis Upsaliensis, Uppsala Studies in Education 85, Uppsala/ Stockholm.
Saugstad, T. 2004: "Vejledning og intimitetstyranniet," Krejsler, J. (ed.): *Pædagogikken og kampen om individet. Kritisk pædagogik, ny inderlighed og selvets teknikker*, Copenhagen: Hans Reitzels Forlag, pp. 89-107.
Saugstad, T. 2011: "Livslang læring – mellem det modernistiske og det postmodernistiske læringsunivers," Christensen, G. et al. (eds.): *Pædagogiske perspektiver på arbejdslivet*, Frederiksberg: Frydenlund Academic, pp. 61-86.
Schiffauer, W., Baumann, G., Kastoryano, R. & Vertovec, S. (eds.) 2004: *Civil enculturation. Nation-state, School and Ethnic Difference in four European Countries*, New York/Oxford: Berghahn Books.
Schnack, K. 1999: *Er didaktik og curriculum det samme?* Arbejdspapir, Danmarks Pædagogiske Universitet, http://www.dpu.dk/everest/Publications/Medarbejdere/ schnack/20051005174113/CurrentVersion/Er%20didaktik%20og%20curriculum%2 0det%20samme.pdf, downloaded November 15, 2007.
Schnack, K. 2001: "Curriculum," "Dannelse," "Didaktik," Muschinsky, L. J. & Schnack, K. (eds.): *Pædagogisk Opslagsbog*, Copenhagen: Christian Ejlers Forlag, pp. 34-48 and 66-74 respectively.
Schnack, K. 2004: "Dannelsens indhold som didaktikkens emne," Schnack, K. (ed.): *Didaktik på kryds og tværs*, Danmarks Pædagogiske Universitets Forlag, pp. 9-24.
Sefa Dei, G. J. & Calliste, A. (eds.) 2000: *Power, Knowledge, and Anti-Racism Education. A Critical Reader*, Halifax: Fernwood Publishing.
Selander, S. 1984: *Textum Institutionis: Den pedagogiska väven, en studie av textraduktion utifrån exemplet Freire och dialogpedagogiken i Sverige*, Studies in Education and Psychology 15, Stockholm Institute of Education, Department for Educational Research, Malmö: CWK Gleerup, Liber Förlag.
Sheikh, M. K. & Crone, M. 2011: "Muslims as a Danish security issue," Nielsen, J. S. (ed.): *Islam in Denmark. The challenge of diversity,* New York: Lexington Books, pp. 173-195.
Sinclair, J. McH. & Coulthard, R. M. 1975: *Towards an Analysis of Discourse. The English used by teachers and pupils*, Oxford: Oxford University Press.
Singh, P. 2002: "Pedagogising Knowledge: Bernstein's Theory of the Pedagogic Device," *British Journal of Sociology of Education* 23 (4):571-582.
Skeie, G. 2001: "Citizenship, Identity Politics and Religious Education," Heimbrock, H.-G. et al.: *Towards Religious Competence. Diversity as a Challenge for Education in Europe*, Schriften aus dem Comenius-Institut, vol. 3, Münster: Lit-Verlag, pp. 237-252.

Skeie, G. & Bråten, O. M. H. 2014: "Religious Education in Schools in Norway," Rothgangel, M., Jäggle, M. & Skeie, G. (eds.): *Religious Education in schools in Europe*, vol. 3, Vienna: Vandenhoeck & Ruprecht (Wiener Forum für Theologie und Religionswissenschaft), Vienna University Press, pp. 209-236.

Stoler, A. L. 1995: *Race and the Education of Desire. Foucault's History of Sexuality and the Colonial Order of Things*, Durham/London: Duke University Press.

Stoler, A. L. 2002: *Carnal Knowledge and Imperial Power. Race and the Intimate in Colonial Rule*, Berkeley/Los Angeles/London: University of California Press.

Sunier, T. 2009: "Teaching the Nation. Religious and Ethnic Diversity at State Schools in Britain and the Netherlands," *Teachers College Record* 111 (6):1555-1581.

Troyna, B. & Williams, J. 1986: *Racism, Education and the State: the Racialisation of Education Policy*, London: Croom Helm.

Villadsen, K. 2002: "Michel Foucault og kritiske perspektiver på liberalismen. Governmentality eller genealogi som analysestrategi," *Dansk Sociologi* 3 (13):77-97.

Westbury, I. 2000: "Teaching as a Reflective Practice: What Might Didaktik Teach Curriculum?," Westbury, I. et al. (eds.): *Teaching as a reflective practice: the German Didaktik tradition*, Mahwah, N. J.: Lawrence Erlbaum, pp. 15-39.

Westbury, I. et al. (eds.) 2000: *Teaching as a reflective practice: the German Didaktik tradition*, Mahwah, N. J.: Lawrence Erlbaum.

Würtz Sørensen, J. 1988: "Fjendebilleder. De muslimske fremmedarbejdere i de danske medier i slutningen af 1960'erne," S. Dindler & A. Olsen (eds.): *Islam og muslimer i de danske medier*, Århus: Aarhus Universitetsforlag, pp. 76-93.

Young, M. F. D. 1971: "An Approach to the Study of Curricula as Socially Organized Knowledge," Young, M. F. D. (ed.): *Knowledge and Control: New Directions for the Sociology of Education*, London: Collier-Macmillan, pp. 19-46.

Øland, T. 2007: "Det registrerede og det væsentlige – om former for anerkendelse," *Klassisk og moderne pædagogisk teori*, Copenhagen: Hans Reitzels Forlag, pp. 559-572.

Øland, T. 2010: "A state ethnography of progressivism: Danish school pedagogues and their efforts to emancipate the powers and the child, the people and the culture 1929-1960," *Praktiske Grunde. Tidsskrift for kultur- og samfundsvidenskab* 1-2:57-89.

Østberg, S. 1998: *Pakistani Children in Oslo. Islamic Nurture in a Secular Context*, PhD dissertation, Warwick: Institute of Education, University of Warwick.

Østergaard Andersen, P. 2012: "Pædagogik og pædagogiske teorier i Danmark fra 1960," Andersen, P.Ø. & Ellegaard, T. (eds.): *Klassisk og moderne pædagogisk teori*, Copenhagen: Hans Reitzels Forlag, pp. 58-87.

Legislation and other documents

Act on the Folkeskole of 1993 (The Danish Primary and Lower Secondary School), Copenhagen: Ministry of Education, 1994.

Dupont, K. & Holm-Larsen, S. (eds.): 2004. *Folkeskoleloven 2004: Sammenstilling, bemærkninger og gennemførelsesbestemmelser m.v.* [The Act on Folkeskolen 2004: Synopsis, remarks and rules for implementation], Vejle: Kroghs Forlag.

Fælles mål. Faghæfte 4: Kristendomskundskab [Common objectives. Guide to school subjects 4. Kristendomskundskab], Copenhagen: Ministry of Education, 2004.

Holm Larsen, S. 2010: *Folkeskoleloven 2010-2011. Sammenstilling, bemærkninger og gennemførelsesbestemmelser m.v.* [The Act on Folkeskolen 2010-11: Synopsis, remarks and rules for implementation], Frederikshavn: Dafolo.

Ministry of Education 1970: *Cirkulære om undervisning i folkeskolen af uden-landske børn*, November 30. [Departmental circular on the instruction of foreign children].

Ministry of Education 2006: *Lov om ændring af folkeskolen* [Act on the change of the Folkeskole], www.uvm.dk, retrieved November 9, 2007.

Municipality of Copenhagen 2004a: *Orientering fra Københavns Kommunes Stati-stiske Kontor* [Information from the Municipality of Copenhagen, Statistical Office], "Folketal i bydele [Population in districts], 1. januar 2004" (7).

Municipality of Copenhagen 2004b: *Indvandrere og efterkommere. Faktaoversigt* [Immigrants and their descendants. Facts Summary], Københavns Kommunes Statistiske Kontor [Municipality of Copenhagen, Statistical Office].

The Constitutional Act of Denmark, Copenhagen: The Folketing 2013, http://www.thedanishparliament.dk/Publications/The_Constitutional_Act_of_Denmark.aspx, retrieved April 16, 2014.

Appendix A: The B-school, selected text sample.
Original Danish version

TRT1: Ritual becomes 'Friday prayer': Jette and Sulayman
Jette: Ja
Sulayman: Hvad betyder ritual?
Jette: ritual det er at T hver gang du er i T moskeen med nogen om fredagen P så gør I faktisk de samme ting
Sulayman: Ja
Jette: det er lidt forskelligt hvad imamen si- imamen siger men du starter med som en god muslim så starter du med at vaske dine hænder op til albuerne du vasker dit ansigt og du vasker dine fødder du stiller dine sko udenfor og du går ind P så har du måske mere eller mindre et nogenlunde bestemt sted du sætter dig hen hvor det er du gerne- godt kan lide at sidde når du beder du har måske også sådan en T lille fidus på hovedet
Sulayman: det har jeg ikke
Jette: nej men det er der mange der har men det er så måske med til at være voksen det ved jeg ikke men T så foregår- det der foregår under fredagsbønnen der er det sådan noget med at du godt kan sige til mig først så gør vi det så gør vi det så gør vi det så siger imamen noget det er lidt forskelligt og så sker der det og så sker der det. Så der er nogen ting som er lidt forskellige men de ting der er lidt forskellige er alligevel ens fordi at de foregår på samme tidspunkt i løbet af P det der sker P når man så siger at der er noget der er meget ens som sker P ofte så kalder man det et ritual P det er for eksempel et ritual at - at T muslimer inden de beder skal vaske ansigt og hænder og fødder P for at vise respekt P så det starter man med P og T jeg vil tro at hvis du kigger på mange T af dem du kender P hvis du bare kigger på én af dem så vil du se at de har den samme måde at gøre det på P nogen vil måske starte med at vaske hænder og så vasker de måske først den venstre arm inden de vasker den højre og når man først begynder at få sådan nogle vaner med præcis hvilken måde man gør det på så gør man det næsten ens hver gang

TRT2: An order of things? Jette and Meriam (and Sulayman ...)
Meriam: jette det er noget man skal gøre hver gang man skal begynde med-
Jette: ja
Meriam: ..så gør man
Jette: ja P og //det er så et ritual//
Meriam: //Jette Jette det er altså //noget-
Jette: //men der// står jo ikke-der står jo ikke du skal vaske dine fødder først T begynde med storetåen og slutte med lilletåen eller at du skal vaske ansigtet først men mange mennesker hvis du-
Meriam: der er en rækkefølge man gør det i
Jette: der er en rækkefølge man gør det i
Meriam: ja
Jette: men så står der- står der at den ene hånd er før den anden eller noget?
Meriam: T man starter med højre altid
Jette: man starter altid med højre P så det er- det kan være det står der men ellers er der måske nogen der gør det lidt forskelligt ja Sulayman
Sulayman: hvad hedder det T man behøves ikke altid at vaske sig i en moske det kan godt

være man har gjort det der hjemme P
Jette: ja P men så stoler de jo også på at du har udført dét ritual inden du kommer P
Sulayman: jamen når jeg- når jeg kommer ind så har jeg allerede vasket mig…

Appendix B: The C-school, selected text samples, original Danish version

Text sample 1 (TRT1-6)

Tine: …det fjerde ritual som vi er kommet til i dag P det er jo det P der handler P om livets afslutning P om begravelsen P hvad sker der når man dør P //i ritualerne//
Elev: //UF//
(elevstemmer/UF)
Tine: før man begraves eller bisættes eller hvad der skal ske P så er der jo en der dør P og når der er en i familien der dør så er der en masse ting man skal ordne P man skal jo P simpelthen finde ud af hvordan skal begravelsen overhovedet foregå P T og den der er død har jo også boet et eller andet sted og hvad skal man gøre med alle tingene og alle de der ting P så der er rig- P skal jeg starte allerede nu hvor vi kun er kommet til billede et med at sige schh første gang
Gülsen: så har du kun to gange P
Tine: så er der kun to gange tilbage ja P
Elev: UF
Tine: nå P der er rigtigt mange ting der skal ordnes og i Danmark har vi lavet sådan et system med at der er nogle mennesker der arbejder med det som hedder bedemænd P det kan både være kvinder og mænd P og dem P går man hen til P man kan også ordne det hele selv P men de er eksperter P så går man hen til dem P og siger nu er T mine- som regel er det jo nogen hvis far eller mor er død hvis en- hvis nu at T nikolines T farmor er død så er det jo din fars mor P så ville det være din far der skulle ordne det ikke også P
Nikoline: ja P
Tine: T så går han hen til bedemanden og siger nu er T min mor død P og P det skal vi have ordnet så laver man en masse aftaler hvordan skal det foregå P hvad for en kirke skal det være i P T skal vi have den her slags kiste eller den- alle de der ting snakker man med //bede-//
Elev: //og gravsten//
Tine: og gravsten kan man også aftale med bedemanden P og blomster kan man aftale med bedemanden P
Elev: blomster
Tine: fordi der er mange der vælger at have blomster oven på kisten P det er alt sammen noget man kan aftale med bedemanden P og bedemanden s- P han kan også finde ud af hvad for en kirke hører den der er død til P fordi hvis man skal begraves fra en kirke P så skal man lave en aftale med præsten P så har jeg skrevet her det er en stor sorg at miste én P man er i familie med P et menneske man holder af P men et ritual kan nogen gange hjælpe en P på den måde at det er i hvert fald noget man så ikke behøver også at være meget i tvivl om hvad man skal gøre P fordi der kommer alle mulige tanker oppe i hovedet P men så har man sådan et ritual P som er //helt fast//
Elev://UF//
Tine: og sådan gør man P og det ved man så P hvis det en kristen P der dør P så kan man blive begravet i en kirke P eller et kapel P eller et krematorium P en kirke det har vi snakket om det ved I hvad er P et kapel det er et sted som også kan være kristent men det kan også være at det ikke hører til nogen bestemt religion P som er et rum P og ofte er det

P et hus der ligger P på en kirkegård P sådan P at i stedet for at holde det i en kirke der ligger langt fra kirkegården så kan man holde det i et hus der simpelthen ligger på kirkegården P

Text sample 2 (TRT1-6)

<u>TRT1 Teacher presentation (Tine): The Muslim tradition and Muslims</u>
nu skal vi snakke om hvordan det er i den muslimske tradition hvis man er muslim P og- og ligesom jeg skrev i starten så er det jo en- en sorg for alle mennesker at miste en de kender T og det er det også for muslimer P så kan man sige i den muslimske tradition P har man måske en større respekt for gamle mennesker T fordi P det er T en måde at sige dem tak for at de har passet P én da man var lille P og der er også en tradition for P at børn passer deres forældre når de bliver gamle P i danmark er det jo
efterhånden sådan at langt de fleste gamle P kommer på //plejehjem//
Elev://plejehjem//
Tine: og de har hjemmehjælper fordi vi har alle sammen så travlt P

<u>TRT2 Hazem's contribution – dismissed as non-relevant</u>
Tine: … Hazem ville du lige sige noget P
Hazem: UF (lavt) hvad var det nu jeg ville sige P nogen muslimer UF mohammad altså den der reklame som ham P altså ikke ham mohammed
Tine: altså mohammad mohammad
Hazem: ikke ham der
Tine: nej P
Hazem: profeten
Tine: profeten mohammad P ja
Hazem: ja hvor de bare havde sat en sådan stjerne på hans hånd og sagde han var dum og skrev han var død
Tine: men det har ikke lige noget med det her at gøre nu

<u>TRT3 Teacher presentation: "When a Christian dies" vs. "The Muslim tradition"</u>
Tine: nå P når en kristen dør så varer det ofte op til fire dage op til at man har fået arrangeret begravelse og det hele så der går nogle dage før man T bliver begravet P i den muslimske tradition P der skal man helst blive begravet den samme dag som man dør P
Elevstemmer: åhr ja wuuh
Tine: og det er en tradition at det er sådan P det er også en tradition at man vasker den døde det gør man også med kristne men her P i den muslimske tradition der vasker man ligesom når man vasker før //bøn//

<u>TRT4 Lamine's contribution – dismissed as non-valid</u>
Lamine: //man// vasker sit hjerte P
Tine: man vasker nemlig hænderne P og fødderne og ansigtet først P
Elev: //og røvhullet//
Lamine://og hjertet//

Tine: og så vasker man bagefter kroppen P
Lamine: også hjertet P også hjertet
Tine: gør man det P
Lamine: ja //UF//
Tine: //det står// der ikke i den bog jeg læste T og så bliver man svøbt i et hvidt klæde og bliver lagt i en kiste
Gülsen: ja
Jens: sami (iret.)

TRT5 Teacher presentation: Funeral and Muslims
Tine: til selve begravelsen P så læser imamen en bøn P begravelsesbønnen- det er præsten kan man sige P den der står for ceremonien P i moskeen P han læser en bøn P og holder en tale til de efterladte P og det er jo også ligesom præsten holder en tale til de efterladte P så har jeg læst P at P i den brø- bøn P eller den tale som imamen holder P så husker han familien på de tre store ting som T den døde har givet dem P et godt liv erindringen om hvad der sker P og det er jo dejligt P og så er det meget vigtigt at muslimer-
Lubna: tine
Tine: muslimer bliver ikke brændt de bliver alle sammen begravet P

TRT6 Gülsen's contribution – incorporated
Gülsen: men de bliver begravet ind i de- deres hjemland nogen af dem-
Tine: nogen- Gülsen har en information
Gülsen: nogen de bliver begravet i deres hjemland og nogen begraver de i kirkegården
Tine: nogen bliver begravet her og nogen fløjet hjem til hvor de kommer fra- og bliver begravet der og så er der en meget vigtig ting P at man skal begraves så ansigtet vender mod mekka ligesom når man beder P så har man også hovedet mod mekka

Text sample 3

Tine: Så kan jeg fortælle at dét har jeg også læst og jeg kan huske at T så forstod jeg det lige pludselig- Lubna jeg kan huske T at du sidste år s-så tog I til en T en- T sådan en sammenkomst P fyrre dage efter der var en der var død
Hazem: det var mig
Tine: og det var du ogs- det var dig der var i sverige P
Hazem: ja
Tine: ja P hvem var det der var død
Hazem: T min farmor eller morfar det kan jeg ikke huske P
Tine: ja P og så tog i til sverige for det var en der var blevet begravet i sverige P og så to-
Hazem: nej P hun blev begravet i iran P
Tine: iran men i samledes i sverige så
Hazem: //ja//
Tine: //ja// P fordi det var en der boede i sverige P
Hazem: nej
Tine: nej hvorfor tog i så til sverige
Hazem: det er fordi T

Lamine: det var dér hun var
Hazem: T (lang Pause) min moster
Tine: din moster var derovre P men man-
Hazem: og hun skulle-
Tine: jeg har læst at de tre første dage efter der er en i familien der er død P så laver man ikke mad der hjemme men så kommer venner og familie med mad til én P

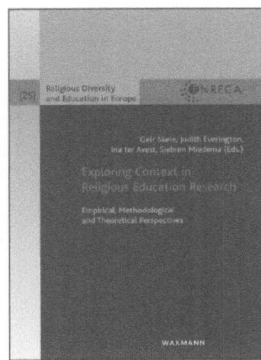

Geir Skeie, Judith Everington,
Ina ter Avest, Siebren Miedema (Ed.)

Exploring Context in Religious Education Research

Empirical, Methodological
and Theoretical Perspectives

Religious Diversity and Education in Europe, vol. 25
2013, 274 pages, pb, € 32,90
ISBN 978-3-8309-2902-4
E-Book: € 29,99; ISBN 978-3-8309-7902-9

The relevance of contextual perspectives in religious education has been growing for the last decade. It has been central to the European Network for Religious Education through Contextual Approaches (ENRECA) – the research network that has produced the present book. Several members of the network have contributed to the theoretical and empirical development of contextual approaches in different publications, but for the first time this has been the focus of an entire collectively produced volume.

The chapters are presenting both empirical research and scholarly investigation into methodological and theoretical dimensions. Taken together this book wants to contribute to the further development of contextual thinking in religious education research.

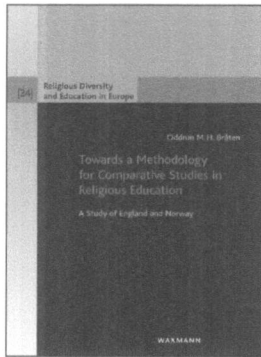

Oddrun M.H. Bråten

Towards a Methodology for Comparative Studies in Religious Education
A Study of England and Norway

Religious Diversity and Education in Europe, vol. 24
2013, 234 pages, pb, € 32,90
ISBN 978-3-8309-2887-4
E-Book: € 29,99; ISBN 978-3-8309-7887-9

In this groundbreaking study in the methodology of comparative religious education Oddrun Bråten set out to utilise and test her methodology for comparative religious education. This synthesises three sets of ideas. The first includes supranational, national and subnational processes. The second set of ideas concerns the societal, institutional, instructional and experiential levels of curriculum. They are affected by supranational, national and subnational processes. The third set of ideas includes Bråten's use of Schiffauer and collaborators' concepts of social/national imaginary and civil enculturation.